The Blackfeet

RAIDERS ON THE NORTHWESTERN PLAINS

THE CIVILIZATION OF THE AMERICAN INDIAN SERIES

RAIDERS ON

The Blackfeet

THE NORTHWESTERN PLAINS

by John C. Ewers

NORMAN : UNIVERSITY OF OKLAHOMA PRESS

By JOHN C. EWERS

Plains Indian Painting (Stanford, 1939)
Gustavus Sohon's Portraits of Flathead and Pend d'Oreille Indians (Washington, 1948)
The Horse in Blackfoot Indian Culture (Washington, 1955)
The Blackfeet: Raiders on the Northwestern Plains (Norman, 1958)
(Editor) *Adventures of Zenas Leonard, Fur Trader* (Norman, 1959)
(Editor) *Five Indian Tribes of the Upper Missouri* (Norman, 1961)
Artists of the Old West (Garden City, 1965)
(Editor) *George Catlin's O-kee-pa* (New Haven, 1967)
Indian Life on the Upper Missouri (Norman, 1968)
(Editor) *Indians of Texas in Eighteen Thirty* (Washington, 1969)
Plains Indian Sculpture (Washington, 1986)
Plains Indian History and Culture (Norman, 1997)

LIBRARY OF CONGRESS CATALOG CARD NUMBER: 58-7778
ISBN: 0-8061-1836-9 (paperback)

The Blackfeet: Raiders on the Northwestern Plains is Volume 49 in The Civilization of the American Indian Series.

14   15   16   17   18   19   20   21   22   23   24   25   26   27   28

TO MARGE

*In memory of our happy years together
on the Blackfeet Reservation*

Preface

FIFTEEN YEARS AGO Richard Sanderville, who for many years was the official interpreter on the Blackfeet Reservation in Montana, said to me, "When I was a boy, very few members of my tribe could read or write. But now all our young people are in school. They learn a lot about the Pilgrims, George Washington, and Abraham Lincoln. That's fine. But they learn nothing about the history of their own people and their great chiefs. That is American history too."

It is indeed. The drama of Blackfoot history covers a period of fully two centuries. It is replete with action and conflict, with some comedy and much tragedy. In the early years of the eighteenth century the Blackfeet were an independent, stone-age people. For more than a century thereafter they were the dominant military power on the northwestern plains, feared by all neighboring tribes, the inveterate enemies of white trappers. Only seventy-five years ago the extermination of the buffalo, their basic resource, quickly reduced these bold, proud people to a condition of dire poverty, making them dependent upon government rations for their daily bread. For many of them it has been a long, hard road back toward economic independence under radically changed conditions of life.

Long before the buffalo disappeared from their country the culture of the Blackfeet was enriched through selective borrowing from other Indian tribes. White traders, missionaries, treaty makers, soldiers, teachers, Indian agents, and other government officials encouraged the Blackfeet to adopt white men's ways. Eagerly these Indians accepted those items of the alien culture which they found immediately useful to them. But they stubbornly resisted pressures to get them to accept strange beliefs, customs, and economic programs which they thought were unsuited to their way of life. So Blackfoot history must be more than an account of the conditions and events which altered the habits and customs of a primitive people. It must describe the traditional culture and point out the changes that took place in their proper chronological settings. It must also portray the Indians' struggle to preserve those portions of their cultural heritage which were most dear to them.

My interest in the Blackfoot Indians was first aroused in the stimulating classes of the late Clark Wissler at the Yale University Graduate School in the years 1933–34. Professor Wissler's thorough field studies among the Blackfeet in the first decade of this century provided the bases for many class discussions. His published works on the ethnology of the Blackfeet should be familiar to every serious student of the history of these Indians.

Early in 1941 I became the first curator of the Museum of the Plains Indian on the Blackfeet Reservation west of the town of Browning, Montana. Even before this museum was completed, some of the older Indians brought their family heirlooms to be added to the collections, saying that they wanted these precious things to be preserved where their descendants could see them. Many Blackfoot Indians from Canada began to take a great interest and pride in this museum after it was formally opened to the public in June, 1941. As a museum man and as a year-round member of the local community I first came to know most of the elderly Indians who later served as my informants. During the three and one-half years I served as curator of that museum the Office of Indian Affairs encouraged me to devote a considerable portion of the winter months to research. I am grateful to Willard R. Beatty, then director of Indian education in Washington, and to René d'Harnoncourt, at that time manager of the Indian Arts and Crafts Board of the Department of the Interior, for their sympathetic encouragement.

In the summer of 1947 I returned to the West to conduct additional field work on the Blackfeet Reservation in Montana and the Blood Reserve in Alberta in connection with my studies of the horse in Blackfoot culture. The Smithsonian Institution, where I was employed as associate curator of ethnology in the U. S. National Museum, sponsored this investigation. In the summer of 1951 I was able to make further studies of traditional crafts and sacred objects among the Blood Indians as a recipient of a Neosha Grant from the late Frederic H. Douglas of the Denver Art Museum.

My principal Indian informants on the Blackfeet Reservation were the Blood Indian, Weasel Tail; the Piegan men, Lazy Boy, Green-Grass-Bull, Weasel Head, Rides-at-the-Door, Makes-Cold-Weather, Richard Sanderville (Chief Bull), Three Calf, Chewing-Black-Bones, Short Face, Mike-Day-Rider, and Wallace Night Gun; and the Piegan women, Deathly-Woman-Cree-Medicine and Elk-Hollering-in-the-Water-Bear-Chief. Reuben and Cecile Black Boy were my able and faithful interpreters in interviewing the elderly nonliterate Indians on that reservation.

On the Blood Reserve, Chief Percy Creighton served as both informant and interpreter. Other principal informants were Iron, Scraping White, Heavy Head, and Frank Red Crow (men), and Double-Victory-Calf-Robe (a woman).

All of my elderly informants who were born in the 1850's and 1860's have departed for the sand hills. Their lively accounts of Blackfoot life in buffalo days, based upon their personal recollections and experiences, are preserved in my field notes. Men of that generation had hunted buffalo and raided enemy camps for horses. Women had acquired skill in traditional crafts and performed household duties in the days before the buffalo disappeared. I remember these kindly old people as good friends who were sincerely interested in describing tribal life in their youth as completely and accurately as their memories would permit.

Their testimony made a substantial contribution to this volume. In several instances material told me by these Indians is indicated by French quotes.

So many Indians have provided information on Blackfoot life in more recent times that it is not possible to mention them all. Of this group I am especially grateful to Henry Magee (formerly chairman of the Blackfeet Tribal Council), George Bull Child, Adam White Man, John Old Chief, Jim Walters, Mrs. Nora Spanish, and Mrs. Mae Williamson, all Piegans.

Many knowledgeable white men have given me the benefit of their close observation of Blackfoot life in the present century. I have learned much from conversations with the late Walter McClintock, student and photographer of the Blackfeet; the late Frank C. Campbell, energetic superintendent of the Blackfeet Reservation in the early 1920's; Archdeacon Samuel K. Middleton of Fort Macleod, Alberta, for many years principal of St. Paul's Residential School on the Blood Reserve; and Frank Sherburne, practical philosopher and Browning merchant for more than half a century. Former Superintendent Roy Nash allowed me the privilege of participating in Blackfeet Agency staff conferences on contemporary administrative problems in 1942, and his successor, the late Freal McBride, gave me the opportunity to edit his Ten-year Program for the Blackfeet Indian Agency in 1943–44.

In pursuit of my Blackfoot studies I have examined sizable museum collections of dated and documented ethnological specimens and have read widely in the published literature and manuscript collections on the history of the Blackfeet and their neighbors. Museum colleagues in this country have assisted me by providing facilities for studying the collections of more than a dozen museums. Colleagues abroad have provided photographs of early documented pieces.

Both Mrs. Anne McDonnell and Miss Virginia Walton, librarians, have helped me to locate and use rare publications and valuable manuscripts pertaining to Blackfoot history in the outstanding collections of the Montana Historical Society in Helena.

My successors as curator of the Museum of the Plains Indian, Claude Schaeffer and Thomas Kehoe, have kindly made available to me the historical records of the Blackfeet Agency now preserved in the Blackfoot Archives in that museum. For nearly a decade Hugh Dempsey, now of the Glenbow Foundation, Calgary, Alberta, has been most generous in providing me with information on the Canadian Blackfoot tribes through correspondence.

The richest source of unpublished documents on the history of the Blackfeet undoubtedly is the National Archives in Washington, which contains the voluminous and enlightening correspondence of successive Blackfoot agents with the Washington office, in addition to the proceedings and reports of treaty councils and land negotiations and other official documents pertaining to government relations with the Blackfeet. I am grateful to Oliver W. Holmes and to the members of his efficient staff in the Indian Office Records Section for the opportunity to study these important papers.

Members of the staffs of the Library of Congress, the Interior Department Library, and the library of the Smithsonian Institution have been most painstaking and helpful in my search for published descriptions of and reports on the Blackfoot Indians.

This book would never have been written were it not for the encouragement of my wife, Margaret, and our two daughters. They have lived among the friendly Blackfeet. They have fallen in love with the Blackfoot country. And they look forward to the time when they can go back.

JOHN C. EWERS

Arlington, Virginia.

Eagle Ribs, a Blood warrior who claimed to have killed eight white trappers. From a painting by George Catlin in 1832 (*Courtesy Smithsonian Institution*).

Contents

Buffalo Bull's Back Fat, head chief of the Blood Indians. From a painting by George Catlin in 1832 (*Courtesy Smithsonian Institution*).

Illustrations

MAPS

The Blackfeet

RAIDERS ON THE NORTHWESTERN PLAINS

Crystal Stone, wife of Buffalo Bull's Back Fat. From a painting
by George Catlin in 1832 (*Courtesy Smithsonian Institution*).

1: Dog Days

ELDERLY BLACKFOOT men and women who grew to adulthood in buffalo days had no doubts about the origin of their people. They knew, because their grandparents had told them, that Napi, the Old Man, was the creator of the world and every living thing in it.

In the beginning all the world was water. One day Old Man, either by design or because he was just curious, decided to find out what might lie beneath the water. He sent animals to dive below the surface. First duck, then otter, then badger dived in vain. Then Old Man sent muskrat diving into the depths. Muskrat remained under water so long Old Man began to fear that he had drowned. At last muskrat rose slowly to the surface, holding between his paws a little ball of mud. Old Man took this small lump of mud and blew upon it. The mud began to swell. It continued to grow larger and larger until it became the whole earth.

Then Napi traveled about over the earth piling up rocks to make mountains, gouging out beds of rivers and lakes and filling them with water. He covered the plains with grass. He made roots and berries grow on the grasslands and timber in the mountains and river valleys. He made all the animals and the birds. And then, from a lump of clay, he made himself a wife.

Together Old Man and Old Woman designed the people and determined how they should live. Old Man insisted that he should have the first say in everything. Old Woman agreed, provided she might have the second say.

Old Man said, "Let the people have eyes and mouths in their faces, and let them be straight up and down." But Old Woman added, "Yes, let them have eyes and mouths; but they shall be set crosswise in their faces."

Old Man said, "Let the people have ten fingers on each hand." "No," declared Old Woman, "ten fingers are too many. They will be in the way. Let them have four fingers and a thumb on each hand." So the people were made.

But Old Man and Old Woman could not agree on one important point. Should the people live forever, or should they die? Finally Old Man said, "I will throw a buffalo chip into the water. If it floats, the people will die for four days and live again; but, if it sinks, they will die forever." He threw the buffalo chip into the water, and it floated. "No," said Old Woman, "I will throw this rock. If it floats, the people will die for four days. If it sinks, they will die forever." She threw the rock into the water, and it sank to the bottom. Then they agreed that it was better that way. If people lived forever they would never feel sorry for one another.

At first the people were hungry and cold. Then Old Man showed them how to collect edible roots and berries, how to make wooden bows and stone-headed arrows, how to use weapons, traps, and deadfalls to kill buffalo and the smaller animals for food, and how to dress animal skins for warm clothing.

His work of creation completed, Old Man climbed a high mountain and disappeared.[1]

Some say that Napi's home was in the mountains at the head of the stream that still bears his name, Oldman River, in the province of Alberta. Blackfoot Indians can still point out Old Man's gambling place west of Fort Macleod, where Napi played the hoop-and-pole game long, long ago. However, the fact that Old Man, the creator, also appears in the mythology of the Arapaho, Gros Ventre, and Cree tribes suggests that he may have been

[1] Alexander Henry and David Thompson, *New Light on the Early History of the Greater Northwest*, II, 528. Many versions of this story have been recorded since Henry first mentioned the Old Man legend in his journal in 1810.

known to the Blackfeet in prehistoric times. Their old men probably were telling their grandchildren of Napi's wonder-workings long before the three Blackfoot tribes moved westward to their historic homeland in Alberta and Montana.

For nearly two centuries the three Blackfoot tribes have been known to white men by their separate names. They are the Pikuni or Piegan (pronounced Pay-gan′), the Kainah or Blood, and the Siksika or Blackfoot proper, often referred to as the Northern Blackfoot to distinguish it from the other two tribes. The three tribes were politically independent. But they spoke the same language, shared the same customs (with the exception of a few ceremonial rituals), intermarried, and made war upon common enemies. So it has been customary to speak of these three tribes as one people, under the general name of Blackfoot or Blackfeet. The former is the more literal translation of the native name, Siksikauwᵃ (black-footed people). Together these three tribes comprised the strongest military power on the northwestern plains in historic buffalo days.

The Blackfoot tribes consider themselves to be of common descent. Long ago they probably were one tribe. But the three tribes were separate units at the beginning of the historic period.

Whether these Indians at one time dyed their footgear black or whether the moccasins of some of them happened to be coated with black earth or the ashes from prairie fires when the neighboring Cree Indians bestowed the name of Blackfoot upon them cannot be determined at this late date. Needless to say, the curious tourist who in recent years asked one of these Indians to remove his moccasins so she could see for herself was disappointed.

The name Piegan refers to a people who possessed poorly dressed or torn robes. The Blood tribe may have received its name from the Cree because its members were accustomed to paint their faces and robes with red earth, which is still the sacred paint among all the Blackfoot tribes. However, a century and a quarter ago the German scientist-explorer, Prince Maximilian zu Wied, was told that this tribe was named after some

5

of its members who returned with bloodstained hands and faces from the massacre of a small camp of Kutenai Indians.[2] In any case, this was not their name for themselves. The people of that tribe prefer to call themselves by the native name Kainah, meaning Many Chiefs.

Language certainly furnishes a much more valuable clue to the origin of the Blackfoot tribes than does their mythology. The fact that they speak an Algonkian dialect allies them with the host of other Algonkian-speaking tribes of North America. While it is true that Algonkian was more widely spoken than any other Indian language, it is significant that the great majority of the Algonkian tribes lived in the forests east of the Great Plains. Of the six Algonkian-speaking tribes who were living on the plains before 1830, the Cheyennes, Plains Crees, and Plains Ojibwas are known to have migrated westward within the historic period. The Arapahoes, Gros Ventres, and Blackfeet were older residents of the grasslands. However, persistent Arapaho traditions point to their migration from a region farther east, probably the Red River Valley of Minnesota, and to Gros Ventre separation from that tribe.[3] This leaves the Blackfeet as probably the earliest Algonkian residents of the plains.

Linguists tell us that of all Algonkian dialects Blackfoot differs most markedly in its word formation from the presumed parent tongue spoken by tribes living in the western Great Lakes region. Relative isolation from other Algonkian-speaking peoples, on the one hand, and prolonged contacts with tribes speaking alien tongues, on the other, may help to explain the considerable differences between Blackfoot and all other Algonkian dialects.[4]

The Blackfeet may have occupied the western frontier of Algonkian-speaking peoples for some time before they left the woodlands for the plains. After they reached the plains they be-

[2] Alexander Philip Maximilian, *Travels in the Interior of North America*, (Vol. XXIII in Thwaites' *Early Western Travels*), II, 95.

[3] F. W. Hodge (ed.), *Handbook of American Indians North of Mexico*, I, 72.

[4] Carl F. and E. W. Voegelin, "Linguistic Considerations of Northeastern North America," in Frederick Johnson (ed.), *Man in Northeastern North America*, 181, 189–90.

came more isolated from the great majority of forest-dwelling Algonkian tribes of the Middle West. At the same time they met Athapascan-, Shoshonean-, and Siouan-speaking Indians. The Blackfeet appear to have been the adventurous pioneers in the migration of a number of Algonkian tribes out of the timber onto the open grasslands, a movement which began in prehistoric times and ended only with the removal of some of the eastern Indians to lands west of the Mississippi to make room for white settlement in the nineteenth century.

Whether the Blackfeet moved west because they were attracted by opportunities for big-game hunting in the open country, or whether they were driven westward by other Algonkian tribes whose growing populations forced them to expand their own hunting territories, we do not know. Possibly both factors encouraged Blackfoot migration. At any rate, it is certain that the Blackfeet entered the plains on foot. It is just as certain that they were accustomed to plains life when the first white trader-explorers discovered them. The late Clark Wissler, for many years a thorough student of the Blackfeet, expressed the opinion that they "were on the plains a long time before the discovery of America."[5] But they may have tarried for an extended period, perhaps for centuries, in the transition zone between the short-grass plains and forests before they pushed on westward to lands watered by the upper tributaries of the Saskatchewan and Missouri rivers in the eighteenth century.

The Blackfeet had not yet reached their historic homeland near the eastern base of the Rockies when their aboriginal culture began to be modified, indeed revolutionized, by indirect influences from the white man's civilization—influences which rapidly transformed them from plodding, stone age pedestrians into mobile horsemen possessing some of the advantages of an age of metals. It will be easier to understand the changes in Blackfoot life wrought by these innovations if we try to picture their existence in the years immediately preceding their acquisition of horses, metal tools, and weapons, and their initial par-

[5] *Indians of the United States,* 85.

ticipation in the white man's fur trade. When elderly Blackfoot Indians refer to this pre-horse period they commonly identify it by the expression, "When we had only dogs for moving camp." Let us simply refer to that time as "dog days."

No white man visited the Blackfeet in dog days, so we have no contemporary descriptions of their life in those times. Nevertheless, we need not rely entirely upon Blackfoot traditions to gain a general impression of their life in dog days.

David Thompson, an intelligent, inquisitive fur trader, spent the winter of 1787–88 in a Piegan village in present southern Alberta. There were aged men in that Indian camp who recalled from personal experience tribal life in dog days. When Thompson sought to determine the origin of these Indians, they "always pointed out the North West as the place they came from, and their progress has always been to the southwest. Since the Traders came to the Saskatchewan River, this has been their course and progress for the distance of four hundred miles from the Eagle Hills to the Mountains near the Missouri but this rapid advance may be mostly attributed to their being armed with guns and iron weapons." Thompson's elderly informants made it clear that in their youth the Blackfeet possessed no firearms and neither horses nor canoes.[6] They were nomads who hunted game and fought enemy tribesmen with primitive weapons of their own manufacture. They traveled overland on foot. Their only domesticated animal was the dog.

So we may picture those aboriginal Blackfoot Indians living in the valley of the North Saskatchewan near the Eagle Hills in the early years of the eighteenth century, just before the dawn of history in that region. North of that great eastward-flowing river was the coniferous forest. The Blackfoot homeland lay south of that thickly wooded area in a country of grassy prairies broken by forested hills, timbered river valleys, and lakes of different sizes. Here the primitive Blackfeet found the necessities of life—wild game, wild plant foods, water, and firewood.

[6] David Thompson, *David Thompson's Narrative of his Explorations in Western America, 1784–1812*, 328–34, 348.

Long, cold winters and short summers were typical of that old Blackfoot country. It was too far north to permit the raising of Indian corn and other food crops. But it was fine country for the nomadic hunter. Here he found many small mammals— wolves, foxes, muskrats, beavers, badgers, minks, martens, rabbits, skunks, and porcupines. Here were the larger bear, deer, elk, and moose. But best of all, this was buffalo country.

The Plains Crees and Assiniboins who occupied this region in the nineteenth century hunted or trapped all of these animals. But they depended primarily upon buffalo for their subsistence. Both tribes were poor in horses and, save for their possession of firearms, metal traps, and tools, lived very much as the Blackfeet must have lived in the same region in earlier times. Our considerable knowledge of Cree and Assiniboin methods of exploiting the natural resources of this area in later years furnishes valuable clues to Blackfoot life in dog days.

Indians who preyed upon the buffalo had to adjust their way of life to the habits and movements of their prey. In spring, summer, and fall, buffalo grazed on the rich grasslands in open country. But in winter, the harsh season of sub-zero temperatures, deep snows, and strong winds, these animals sought food and shelter in wooded valleys and broken country where hills offered protection from the wind. So the Indians' buffalo-hunting techniques varied with the seasons.

The buffalo in its wild state was a gregarious animal. Throughout the greater part of the year buffalo could be killed most effectively through the co-operative efforts of groups of Indians working together in planned operations. So the tribes were divided into separate hunting bands. Each band probably comprised about twenty to thirty families, totaling some one hundred to two hundred men, women, and children. These bands were large enough to enable their members to encircle a small herd of buffalo on the prairie and large enough to offer a stiff defense against human enemies; yet they were small enough to permit survival during periods of game scarcity and limited rations. Probably each band was composed primarily of blood relatives, led by the most respected able-bodied man in the group.

9

Throughout most of the year these hunting bands moved from one temporary encampment to another, following the buffalo over the open grasslands. Each family was responsible for the movement of its own baggage. Its largest and heaviest possession was the tipi, a conical lodge with a foundation of stout poles over which was stretched a cover of buffalo hides. The size of this Indian home was limited by the weight its owners' wolflike dogs could haul. A strong dog could drag a load of about seventy-five pounds on the A-shaped, wooden travois. A lodge cover made from six or eight buffalo cowskins was a good load for one of these dogs. Larger covers could have been transported if they were made in two or more pieces so that they could be carried on two or more travois. But the necessity for dragging the lodgepoles, which increased in length and weight with the number of hides in the cover, must have encouraged the use of small lodges in dog days. The family's lodge furnishings and household utensils, also designed for ready transportation, were tied into compact bundles or fitted into skin sacks which could be hauled on dog travois or carried on the backs of dogs or women.

A Blackfoot camp on the march in dog days must have been a picturesque sight. Scouts led the way, walking a considerable distance in advance of the main party, constantly on the lookout for signs of game or enemies. The other able-bodied men of the band fell in on the flanks and in the rear of the main body to provide further protection. Men traveled light and carried only their weapons. In the center of the moving camp walked the women and children and the dogs with the baggage. Mothers carried their infants on their backs. Not infrequently women shouldered part of the baggage also.[7] The dogs, hitched to their loaded travois by hide straps, were not the most willing of burden bearers. Women had to keep them some distance apart to prevent dog fights. Occasionally a dog took off after a bitch or

---

[7] Pierre G. V. La Verendrye, *Journals and Letters of Pierre Gualtier de Varennes de la Verendrye and His Sons*, 317. The early French explorer observed this marching order among the pedestrian Assiniboins in 1738.

a rabbit, or merely to get a drink of cool water from a near-by lake or stream. Under these conditions long marches were out of the question. There were frequent stops. Five or six miles was a good day's march.

The great bulk of the baggage carried by the dogs and women must have consisted of articles essential to day-to-day living. Elaborate lodge furnishings, many changes of clothing, complex medicine bundles and ceremonial regalia, surpluses of fresh or dried meat, and wild fruits or vegetables would have been excess baggage in dog days.

Blackfoot traditions refer to the surround as the favorite method of hunting buffalo in the summer season in dog days. Probably they employed the same method as that observed among the Assiniboins or Crees by Henry Kelsey, the first white man known to have met Indians on the Northern Plains, in the year 1691:

> Now ye manner of their hunting these Beasts on ye barren ground is when they seek a great parcel of them together they surround them with men which done they gather themselves into a smaller Compass Keeping ye Beasts still in ye middle and so shooting ym till they break out at some place or other and so get away from ym.[8]

Weasel Tail, an aged Blood Indian, described to me a variant of the surround which he had been told was employed by his ancestors in dog days.

« « « After swift-running men located a herd of buffalo, the chief told all the women to get their dog travois. Men and women went out together, approaching the herd from down wind so the animals wouldn't get their scent and run off. The women were told to place their travois upright in the earth, small [front] end up. The travois were so spaced that they could be tied together to form a semicircular fence. Women and dogs hid behind them while two fast-running men circled the buffalo herd, approached the animals from up wind, and

[8] *The Kelsey Papers,* 13.

drove them toward the travois fence. Other men took positions along the sides of the route and closed in as the buffalo neared the travois barrier. Barking dogs and shouting women kept the buffalo back. The men rushed in and killed the buffalo with arrows and lances.

After the buffalo were killed the chief went into the center of the enclosure, counted the dead animals, and divided the meat equally among the participating families. He also distributed the hides to the families for making lodge covers. The women hauled the meat and hides to camp on their dog travois. This was called surround of the buffalo.[9] » » »

As the days grew shorter and colder in late fall, the hunting camp moved to the edge of a wooded area in anticipation of the buffalo migration to winter shelter. There they felled timber and built a rude corral into which they enticed the buffalo. Their method of corraling buffalo must have been very similar to one that survived among some Blood Indians until the early 1870's. Old Weasel Tail recalled how these corrals were made and used:

« « « Near the edge of timber and toward the bottom of a downhill slope the Indians built a corral of wooden posts set upright in the ground to a height of about seven feet. They connected the posts by crosspoles tied in place with rawhide ropes. Around three sides of the corral they laid stakes over the lowest crosspoles. Their butt ends were firmly braced in the ground outside the corral. These stakes projected about three feet or more inside the corral at an angle, so that their sharpened ends were about the height of a buffalo's body. If the buffalo tried to break through the corral, after they had been driven into it, they would be impaled on these stakes. From the open side of the corral the fence of poles extended in two wings outward and up the hill. These lines were further extended by piles of cut willows in the shape of conical lodges about half the height of a man, tied together at their tops. These brush piles were spaced at intervals of several feet. On the hill just above the corral opening a number of poles were placed on the ground crosswise of the slope and parallel

[9] George Bird Grinnell, *Blackfoot Lodge Tales*, 234, cites a tradition of a Piegan corral formed of tipis which served the same function as this dog travois fence.

to each other. The buffalo had to cross these poles to enter the corral. The poles were covered with manure and water, which froze and became slippery so that once the buffalo were in the corral they couldn't escape by climbing back up the hill.

Before the drive began a beaver bundle owner removed the sacred buffalo stones from his bundle and prayed. He sang a song, "Give me one buffalo or more. Help me to fall the buffalo."

Then men of the camp [probably swift-footed, long-winded young fellows] were sent out to get behind a herd of buffalo and drive it toward the corral. Another man stood at the top of the hill and gave a signal to the women and children, who were hiding behind the brush piles, that the buffalo were coming. As the animals passed them on their way down the slope the women and children ran out of their hiding places.

Once inside the corral the buffalo were killed by men and boys stationed around the outside of the stout fence. Then the camp chief went into the corral to take charge of the butchering and the division of the meat. While butchering, the people ate buffalo liver, kidneys, and slices of brisket raw. Two young men took choice pieces of liver, kidneys, liver, brisket, tripe, and manifold to the beaver bundle owner who had remained in his lodge during the slaughter, but whose power had brought success in the hunt. Each man who killed a buffalo was given its hide and ribs. The slaughtered animals were cut into quarters which were divided among the families in the camp. Each family, whether it was large or small, received an equal share.[10]))))))

Driving buffalo into a corral was no easy task. Sometimes these animals were not to be found within miles of the clever trap. At other times shifting winds brought the scent of people ahead, or some unusual sound or movement frightened the buffalo away from the funnel-like chute and left the corral empty. Blackfoot legends and early descriptions of buffalo pounding by neighboring tribes tell of repeated failures to get the big beasts into the trap. Yet the success or failure of their early winter corraling of buffalo was of vital importance to the Blackfeet in dog days. If many buffalo were taken it meant both a plentiful supply of

[10] John C. Ewers, "The Last Bison Drives of the Blackfoot Indians," *Journal Washington Academy of Sciences*, Vol. XXXIX, No. 11 (1949), 359–60.

fresh meat and a surplus that could be preserved for consumption through the hard winter months when intense cold and heavy snows might make hunting impossible. If corraling proved a failure it meant short rations. Should exhaustion of food reserves coincide with winter storms the band went hungry. If there was no break in the weather they starved.

Through the dead of winter the Blackfoot bands pitched their lodges among the trees in sheltered valleys offering maximum protection from winds and snow. It would have been suicidal for them to have remained in the open country for extended periods at that treacherous season. In stormy weather they huddled close to their campfires, which they fed with wood from near-by trees. But when the skies cleared they scoured the wooded areas for buffalo or smaller game, or they ventured out into the open country to kill buffalo that had bogged down in snowdrifts or fallen into ravines. On these short hunting trips they probably traveled on snowshoes. In late winter and early spring, when the supply of fresh meat was low, the Blackfoot hunters, alone or in small groups, stalked the buffalo. By approaching under a wolfskin or buffalo robe disguise while cleverly mimicking the actions of the animal they represented, they could get near enough to the wary buffalo to rise and make their kill with bow and arrow at close range.

When the snows melted and the ice in the rivers began to break up, the period of the winter camp came to an end. Joyfully, the Indians took down their lodges, packed their belongings, and once again journeyed over the grasslands on their co-operative, warm-weather hunts.

So long as there was buffalo available, these Indians needed no other meat. Buffalo flesh, with its rich, gamy taste, was both delicious and nourishing. This big-game animal furnished a host of other useful materials. Dressed cowskins sewn together with sinew of the same animal served for lodge covers. The heavy winter hides, covered with thick, shaggy hair, were wrapped around the body, hair side in, to make warm, snug overcoats. They also served for bedding. From winter hides they also made mittens, caps, and moccasins to protect their extremities from the freezing cold. They made shields from the thick hide of the buffalo's neck and used green rawhide for securely binding stone clubs, knives, mauls, and berry mashers to wooden handles. From soft-dressed buffalo skins they fashioned bags to hold their household goods when they moved camp. They made serviceable spoons and drinking cups from buffalo horns. The paunch of this animal made a tight water bucket. Buffalo sinew supplied thread, bow strings, and cord for binding both stone heads and feathers to wooden arrow shafts.

Important as the buffalo was in the life of the Blackfeet in dog days, they did not neglect the other natural resources of their country. Deer, moose, elk, and the smaller mammals provided a secondary food resource especially welcomed when buffalo were scarce. The lighter skins of deer were preferable to those of the buffalo for warm-weather clothing. Porcupine quills, delicately colored with vegetable dyes, probably were folded and sewn to their favorite garments to make them more handsome. Wild plants, especially roots in early summer and berries in fall, supplied vegetal foods which brought some variety to their heavy meat diet. The roots and leaves of many plants were prepared as medicines.

Persistent Blackfoot traditions tell of the crude clay cooking pots made and used by their ancestors.[11] Earth pigments served for face and body paints and for decorating clothing, tipis, and other skin articles. From stone they fashioned tobacco pipes and painstakingly chipped their sharp cutting tools and weapons— butchering knives, skin-scraping blades, arrow points, and lance heads. Each man either made his weapons for war and hunting or he employed a more skillful elderly man to make them for him.

Aged Indians told David Thompson of Blackfoot warfare in dog days. In the early years of the eighteenth century their bitterest enemies were the Snake or Shoshoni dwelling on the plains southwest of the Piegan, who were the frontier tribe of the

[11] John C. Ewers, "The Case for Blackfoot Pottery," *American Anthropologist*, Vol. XLVII, No. 2 (1945), 289–98.

Blackfoot Indians. Occasionally both sides mustered large forces of several hundred warriors drawn from a number of hunting bands. They gathered in summer when the food supply was sufficiently plentiful to feed a large encampment and leave a surplus to care for the women, children, and older men while the warriors were away from home. Under a war chief, the Piegan marched toward enemy country. If a sizable enemy war party was encountered, the opposing forces formed long lines facing one another, barely within arrow range. They knelt behind large rawhide shields some three feet in diameter while shooting their arrows at the enemy from their long bows, which came up to their chins. The fighting sometimes continued until darkness brought it to an end. Although warriors carried lances, knives, and clubs, they apparently made no use of these shock weapons unless one side outnumbered the other sufficiently to encourage it to close with the enemy. If the opposing forces were nearly equal, they appeared to be satisfied to fight a defensive action from behind the protection of their shields; in such a battle, casualties were few, and the fighting usually ended in an indecisive stalemate at day's end.[12]

More destructive and probably more typical of warfare in dog days was the surprise attack on a small hunting camp by a superior enemy force. In these actions casualties were heavy as the defenders fought desperately for their lives. Sometimes the men were wiped out, their scalps taken as trophies of war, and their children and women led into captivity by the victorious attackers. Captive women and children helped to replace previous losses on the side of the victors. Probably the women were taken as wives by enemy men, and they continued to perform much the same duties they had performed in their own camps, while the children were adopted into the alien tribe.

There is no denying it—a Blackfoot woman's life was hard in dog days. Not only did she bear and rear her children, prepare and cook the family meals, dress the hides of buffalo and other animals, make the tipi, the family clothing, and her domestic

[12] Thompson, *Narrative,* 328–32.

tools and utensils, but she was also responsible for the movement of the camp equipment. She dismantled the tipi, caught the reluctant dogs and tackled them to the travois, loaded the travois, and kept the lively dogs in line on the march. Often she carried heavy loads on her own back. At the end of a hard day's journey she could not rest until she had pitched the tipi and fed the family. Furthermore, as indicated above, women rendered active assistance in the co-operative buffalo hunt. In this toilsome life youthful beauty was short lived, and there was little comfort in old age. When they became bent with age and too feeble to follow the moving camp on foot, they were abandoned to face death alone.

Men were hunters, warriors, and craftsmen who made their weapons and their ceremonial and religious equipment. In dog days, when swiftness of foot and physical stamina were decided assets, young men must have been proud to have had the reputation of being good runners who could overtake a buffalo or an enemy on foot. Individuals who achieved outstanding war records, or who possessed powers to call the buffalo or heal the sick, must have enjoyed a distinction among their fellows denied the average man.

Probably many religious beliefs widely held by the forest Algonkian tribes survived among the Blackfeet in dog days. Undoubtedly they shared with the forest tribes a basic belief in the ability of supernatural birds or animals to communicate some of their sacred power to young men who actively sought it through prayers and fasting. This power, they believed, would aid and protect its human beneficiary throughout his life. Men who received power from the same animal, such as the bear, beaver, or buffalo, formed cults and performed ceremonies they believed were sacred to that animal. Perhaps the most important of these animal cults in dog days was that of the beaver, for it was the beaver medicine men whose rituals charmed the buffalo into the corral and brought food to their people in time of need.[13]

[13] Clark Wissler, "Ceremonial Bundles of the Blackfoot Indians," American Museum of Natural History *Anthropological Papers*, Vol. VII, Part 2 (1912), 282. Wissler considered the beaver ceremonies the oldest of the many Blackfoot bundle rituals.

Magic also played an important part in Blackfoot religion. One impressive magical performance known to many Algonkian tribes of the woodlands in historic times was seen among the Piegans by a white trader prior to 1795. Doubtless it was observed among the Blackfeet in dog days. It is the ritual most commonly known as the shaking tent rite.[14] A small tent was erected in the center of a lodge. The medicine man permitted himself to be bound tightly hand and foot with rawhide ropes and tossed into the tent. Soon the tent began to shake, and sounds of struggle came from within it, followed by the singing of strange songs. Then this primitive Houdini emerged from his confinement with his hands and feet free and made one or more predictions of future events. He told where buffalo would be found in great numbers, or foretold some sickness or good fortune which was to come to someone in the camp.

Probably lacking in Blackfoot religion in dog days was the great tribal ceremony of the sun dance, which was held each summer in more recent times. It also is unlikely that the hunting bands recognized a tribal chief. Certainly the hunting band must have been the primary political unit.

These, then, were the primitive Blackfoot Indians in dog days. They were a hardy, nomadic hunting people. When buffalo were plentiful, they shared their kill among all the families of the band. All feasted on choice cuts of meat. When game was scarce, they all tightened their belts. There were neither rich nor poor among them. Their limited transportation facilities made the accumulation of wealth, even in foodstuffs, impossible. They enjoyed few luxuries. But they were a self-reliant people who wrested a living from the resources of their own country and depended upon no alien folk for any of life's necessities.

[14] James Mackay, Indian Notes, Note 5. Manuscript in the Missouri Historical Society, St. Louis. This early fur trader gives his eye-witness account of this Piegan magical rite.

2: The Wonders of Napikwan

Gradually, during the eighteenth century, the stone-age Blackfeet became acquainted with an alien people whose miracles rivaled those of their traditional creator, Napi. They were pale-faced, bearded men who paddled their bark canoes westward up the Saskatchewan River and continued overland to the Indian camps, bringing with them an assortment of useful weapons, tools, and utensils and a variety of attractive luxuries to exchange for the Indians' furs and foods. Appropriately, the Blackfeet named this strange, white-skinned wonder worker "Napikwan," meaning Old Man Person. This is still the Blackfoot name for the white man.

Living as they did in the very heart of the North American continent, the primitive Blackfeet did not meet Napikwan until long after the Algonkian tribes of the eastern forests and the Indian tribes on the Southern Plains came to know him well. Not for two and one-half centuries after the landing of Columbus did they see the face of Napikwan. Meanwhile, intrepid Spanish horsemen explored the forested southeast, the southwestern deserts, and the grassy plains far to the south of the Blackfeet. The French planted colonies on the St. Lawrence. English settlements spread westward from the Atlantic seaboard to the Alleghenies. In advance of the settlers, French and English traders penetrated farther and farther westward in quest of beaver pelts, much in demand in the markets of Europe. These stouthearted backwoods businessmen were ever on the alert for areas rich in

19

beaver and inhabited by unsophisticated Indians willing to procure and exchange fine furs for inexpensive European-made articles at a handsome profit to the traders.

Daring French trader-explorers pushed westward from Montreal through the Great Lakes and into the Mississippi Valley during the seventeenth century. While Frenchmen were busy extending their operations among the Central Algonkians and the warlike Sioux in the western lakes region, their English rivals were gaining a foothold on Hudson Bay. In the year 1670, King Charles II granted a charter to "The Governor and Company of Adventurers of England" trading around Hudson Bay, giving that company title to all lands drained by waters flowing into Hudson Bay, a huge area of unexplored north country. This Hudson's Bay Company, as it became generally known, proceeded to build trading posts on the bay, to open trade with neighboring Cree Indians, and to encourage them to bring in their furs and those of more distant tribes. The company built no posts in the interior, nor did it explore the hinterlands extensively for many decades after its posts were established on the bay. Nevertheless, it was a runaway servant from its post of York Factory, young Henry Kelsey, who became the first white man to reach the Canadian plains and to see the great buffalo herds south of the Saskatchewan River. Kelsey spent some time among the Cree and Assiniboin Indians in 1791. They told him of a warlike people, the "Naywattamee Poets," dwelling to the west. We cannot be sure, but those distant westerners known only by this strange name may have been the Blackfeet.[1]

The primitive Indians' moccasin telegraph carried news widely if not rapidly. Probably some word of white traders, in the form of exaggerated tales of their strange appearance and magical feats, reached the Blackfeet during the first quarter of the eighteenth century. Yet by the close of that period no white man had come within hundreds of miles of the Blackfoot country. The Blackfeet themselves may have discounted stories of white-

[1] Charles N. Bell, "The Journal of Henry Kelsey (1691–1692)," Historical and Scientific Society of Manitoba *Transactions,* No. 4, 27–28.

skinned newcomers farther east. At any rate, they were too busy making a living and fighting off the intrusions of neighboring tribes upon their own hunting grounds to go see for themselves.

The Shoshonis on their southwestern flank were giving them a particularly bad time. About the year 1730, as nearly as can be determined from the recollections of an aged Indian who confided to David Thompson nearly six decades later, the Shoshonis surprised their traditional Piegan enemies with a strange new weapon—big, four-footed animals "on which they rode swift as a deer." They "dashed at the Peeagans, and with their stone Pukamoggan (war clubs) knocked them on the head." In this unequal conflict the Piegans "lost several of their best men."[2]

Never before had the Blackfoot Indians seen horses. Unable to cope with their enemies' new mobility alone, the Piegans sent messengers to friendly Cree and Assiniboin camps asking for help. These neighbors not only sent warriors but brought with them a new and equally strange secret weapon—a curious hollow rod of iron which made a terrifying noise and hurled a tiny missile so swiftly that the human eye could not follow its flight, and with such force that it could kill or cripple an animal or a man at a distance. The allies brought ten of these newfangled contraptions, with about thirty rounds of ammunition for each. The Piegans and their allies marched forth to do battle with the Shoshonis, carrying the new weapons concealed in long leather cases. Scouts reported a large enemy war party ahead. It outnumbered their own force. But, fortunately, the Shoshonis were all afoot.

As was their traditional tactic, the opposing forces formed long lines facing each other a strong arrow flight apart, hid behind their large shields, and made ready for battle. Eager to see the effect of the new weapons, the Piegan war chief ordered his line to advance within about sixty yards of the enemy. The ten Cree and Assiniboin gunmen unsheathed their weapons. Each held two balls in his mouth and powder in his left hand ready to reload. Then, lying flat on the ground and waiting for

2 Thompson, *Narrative*, 300.

the enemy to expose their bodies while shooting their arrows, the gunners fired with deadly aim, killing or wounding a Shoshoni with every shot. The Shoshonis, terrified by the report and the fatal magic of the new weapons, were thrown into a panic. Many of them broke and ran. The few stouthearted warriors who dared to stand their ground were overwhelmed in the Piegan charge. In their excitement over the success of this new weapon and their eagerness to take the scalps of some fifty fallen Shoshonis and to capture enemy weapons and war clothes abandoned on the field, the Piegans failed to follow up their advantage.[3]

Soon thereafter, while hunting buffalo on the frontier of the Shoshoni country, the Piegans encountered a lone mounted enemy. Although the rider got away, they managed to kill his horse with an arrow shot into its belly. The Piegans and their allies crowded around the fallen animal in admiration and wonder. It reminded them of a stag that had lost its horns. But as it was a slave to man, like the dog which carried their belongings, they named it "Big Dog."[4] Later the Blackfeet renamed this animal "ponokamita," meaning "elk dog," in recognition of its size and its usefulness.[5]

Fearful of their enemies' new weapons the Shoshonis retreated southwestward, and the Piegans took over the Red Deer Valley. The experience gained in their recent battles with the Shoshonis taught the Blackfoot tribes two important lessons. To gain the mobility of the Shoshonis, they needed horses too. To obtain the deadly firepower of the Crees and Assiniboins, they needed guns. Shortly thereafter they must have begun to acquire both.

The source of the first horses acquired by the Blackfeet is still something of a mystery. Of course, they might have captured them from the Shoshonis, but it seems very improbable that a people unfamiliar with the riding or handling of these

---

[3] *Ibid.*, 330–32.

[4] *Ibid.*, 334.

[5] Edward Umfreville, *Present State of Hudson's Bay*, 202. He gives the name for horses as "Pin-ne-cho-me-tar," indicating that the change in the native name for this animal took place prior to Umfreville's time (1790).

lively animals would have gained their first experience with them in this way. It is much more likely that their first mounts were obtained in peaceful trade with one of the other tribes to the west who possessed horses before the Blackfeet had any—the Flatheads, the Kutenais, or even the Nez Percés. Once they gained some familiarity with horses, they could have secured more of them by raiding their Shoshoni enemies.

The tribes to the south and west possessed no firearms. Guns could be obtained through trade with Cree or Assiniboin middlemen who were doing business with the English on Hudson Bay or with French traders from Montreal, who were steadily moving westward out of the forests and on to the plains. In the 1730's the French established posts on the Assiniboine River, west of Red River. In the forties they built the first trading posts on the Saskatchewan. Perhaps this indirect trade in firearms and a few other European-made goods began with a trickle of articles from Hudson Bay in the 1730's. It was expanded by similar items from the French posts nearer the Blackfoot country during the next decade.

In addition to the few guns, Indian middlemen began to supply the Blackfeet with such other useful items as iron arrowheads, metal knives, and axes. A Blackfoot tradition claims that the first axeheads their ancestors received were a puzzle to them. Some men proudly strung them on skin cords and wore them around their necks as ornaments. If they ever did that the more sophisticated Cree and Assiniboin traders must have laughed heartily at their naïveté before showing them the error of their ways.

By 1748 the French had established posts on the lower Saskatchewan. The westernmost of these forts was Fort à la Corne, some fifteen miles east of the forks and only a few days' journey from the Blackfoot country. Three years later a small party of Frenchmen was sent westward to build an outlying post, possibly in the Blackfoot country itself. The location of this Fort La Jonquière is in doubt. There is even some doubt whether it existed. If this fort was established it must have been short-lived.[6]

Whether the Blackfeet first saw them at their downriver posts on the Saskatchewan or in their own country, Frenchmen must have been the first whites these Indians met. A strong indication of this survives in the Blackfoot name for Frenchmen, "Real (or original) Old Man People."

Hudson's Bay Company officials, sitting in their posts on the bay, viewed with increasing alarm the steady progress of their French rivals in pushing trading operations up the Saskatchewan toward the country of the Indians their Cree friends called "ayatchiyiniw," meaning "foreigner or stranger." As early as 1743 they had learned something of these strangers from a young woman of their number whom the Crees had brought to the bay as a slave. The lands of the strangers were described to them as ones blessed with "great plenty of the best and finest furs."[7]

Not until 1754 did the Hudson's Bay Company send one of its men southwestward to try to persuade the strangers to bring their furs to trade with the company at the bay. In June of that year a lone white man, Anthony Hendry, guided by a small group of Cree Indians, left York Factory. They traveled southwestward to the Saskatchewan and then westward over the plains on foot, in search of the fabulous strangers. Hendry's record of distances traveled overland was largely guesswork, and both the directions and distances of his movements west of a point south of present Battleford, Saskatchewan (which he reached early in September), have been differently interpreted by scholars.

We know that Hendry received a friendly reception in a great camp of 200 lodges of "Archithinue Natives" (his name for the "strangers") in mid-October. Other bands soon joined this camp, and its size grew to 322 lodges. The most recent thorough student of Hendry's travels locates this camp about eighteen miles southeast of the present town of Red Deer, Alberta.[8]

[6] Charles M. MacInnes, *In the Shadow of the Rockies*, 27–28.
[7] James Isham, *James Isham's Observations on Hudson's Bay: 1743*, 113.
[8] James G. MacGregor, *Behold the Shining Mountains*, 147.

To this trader, who had known Indians as travelers on foot or by canoe, nothing in the life of the strangers was quite as fascinating as their use of horses. He called their mounts "fine tractable animals, lively and clean made, about 14 hands high." The Indians picketed their horses with buffalo-skin lines to stakes driven in the ground near their lodges and hobbled them when turned out to graze. Their riding gear consisted of "hair halters, Buffalo skin pads, & stirrups of the same." Hendry welcomed an opportunity to accompany a small party on a buffalo hunt. He observed, "They are so expert that with one or two arrows they will drop a buffalo. As for me I had sufficient employ to manage my horse."[9]

Hendry did not identify these people by any name other than "Archithinue Natives," his rendering of the Cree term for the strangers. Possibly in his time the Crees may have used this general term in speaking not only of the Blackfoot tribes and their Sarsi and Gros Ventre allies, but of the hostile Shoshoni as well, for Hendry said they comprised several tribes at war with one another. He saw enemy scalps displayed on long poles near the Indians' lodges and met boys, girls, and women taken captive from other "Archithinue" tribes.

The white trader wintered on the plains. In spring he started on his long trip back to the bay. On his way down the Saskatchewan he met and visited four camps of "Archithinue" totalling 327 lodges. These may have been the same Indians whom he had visited the previous fall in the great camp of 322 lodges. At each camp he urged the leaders to send young men with their furs to trade at the bay. He had made the same plea at the big encampment in the fall. But the strangers always showed little interest in his proposal. They explained that they lived very well by hunting buffalo in their own country. They might starve on that long trip to the bay, for, they pointed out, they were unacquainted with canoes and would not eat fish.[10]

[9] Anthony Hendry, *York Factory to the Blackfeet Country. The Journal of Anthony Hendry, 1754–55,* 338, 350.

[10] *Ibid.,* 338–39, 350–51.

Meanwhile, Hendry noticed that the Assiniboin middlemen, the advance agents of the French on the Saskatchewan, were doing a land office business among the strangers. When he joined a flotilla of sixty canoes for the trip downstream in May, he noted, "There are scarce a Gun, Kettle, Hatchet, or Knife amongst us, having traded them with the Archithinue Natives."[11] Undoubtedly, the shrewd Assiniboin traders had encouraged the strangers to resist Hendry's efforts to lure them to the far-off posts on Hudson Bay. It would have ruined their lucrative business.

Interesting as was Hendry's experience among the "Archithinue Natives," his long and courageous journey brought no profit to his company. His failure to give any tribal name or names for the Indians he met in the west leaves their identification in doubt. He may have encountered one of the Blackfoot tribes. It is more probable the Indians were the Gros Ventres, easternmost of the tribes known to the Crees as "strangers," and the first of them likely to have been met by a visitor from farther east.[12] Even so, this earliest white man's account of Indian life on the plains of the upper Saskatchewan is important to our understanding of Indian customs in that region at that time. The daily life of the Blackfeet and Gros Ventres must have been very similar in the middle of the eighteenth century. Hendry's brief descriptions of their use of horses and their hunting, war, and trading activities probably typified either or both peoples' way of life at that time.

France relinquished her possessions in Canada to England by the Treaty of Paris in 1763. But the withdrawal of the French only served to stimulate competition for the trade of the Indians on the Saskatchewan. Independent traders from Montreal, whom the Hudson's Bay men termed "peddlers," began to move westward, taking with them English-made trade goods which were superior in quality to those previously offered by the French.

Again, in 1772, the Hudson's Bay Company sent a trader to

---

[11] *Ibid.*, 351.

[12] Clark Wissler, *Population Changes Among the Northern Plains Indians,* Yale University Publications in Anthropology, No. 1, 5. Wissler was convinced that these Indians were Gros Ventres rather than Blackfeet.

try to persuade the strangers to bring their furs to the bay. Mathew Cocking left York Factory in June for the Saskatchewan. Leaving that river below the forks, he traveled overland until, on the first day of December, he encountered a band of twenty-eight lodges of Indians west of the Eagle Hills. They met at a buffalo pound, which Cocking described:

> It is a circle fenced round with trees laid one upon another, at the foot of an Hill about 7 feet high & an hundred yards in Circumference: the entrance on the Hill-side where the Animals can easily go over; but when in, cannot return: From this entrance small sticks are laid on each side like a fence, in form of an angle extending from the pound; beyond these to about 1½ mile distant Buffalo dung or old roots are laid in Heaps, in the same direction as the fence: These are to frighten the Beasts from deviating from either side.[13]

For two weeks, while they tried to drive buffalo into the pound with little success, Cocking lived with these Indians and tried to persuade them to accompany him to York Factory to trade. They countered with the same arguments given Hendry two decades before, saying "that they would be starved & were unacquainted with Canoes & mentioned the long distance." Cocking was convinced that "they never can be prevailed upon to undertake such journeys."[14] Again the Hudson's Bay Company's drummer returned home without even a promise of trade.

But Cocking had been more observant than Hendry and named the tribes of "Archithinue Natives," stating, "This tribe is named Powestic-Athinuewuck (ie.) Water-fall Indians. There are four Tribes, or Nations more, which are all Equestrian Indians, viz. Mithco-Athinuwuck or Bloody Indians, Koskitow-Wathesitock or Blackfooted Indians, Pegonow or Muddy-Water Indians & Suxxewuck or Wood Country Indians." Thus, in the language of the Cree Indians who accompanied him, he iden-

[13] Mathew Cocking, *An Adventurer from Hudson Bay. Journal of Mathew Cocking from York Factory to the Blackfeet Country, 1772–1773*, 109.
[14] *Ibid.*, 92.

tified the five allied tribes of Gros Ventres, Bloods, Blackfeet, Pie-gans, and Sarsis. Cocking made it clear that the Indians he met at the buffalo pound were Gros Ventres.[15]

Cocking learned that these tribes were at war with the Snake (Shoshoni) Indians farther west. He was shown heavy, sleeve-less jackets of sixfold, quilted moosehide worn by men on both sides in their battles. He noted that the Gros Ventres cooked their victuals in earthen vessels "much the same in form as New-castle pots but without feet" and that they raised small plots of tobacco.[16]

Mathew Cocking's report of his fruitless negotiations with the Gros Ventres convinced Hudson's Bay Company officials that it was useless to try to get the tribes of the upper Saskatchewan to make the long journey to the bay. If they were to compete successfully with the "peddlers" from Montreal they must ex-pand their operations southwestward. In 1774 they took their first important step in this direction by establishing Cumber-land House on the lower Saskatchewan, which served as a base for upriver trade. Gradually, Napikwan, in the person of the agents of the great Hudson's Bay Company and competing in-dependent traders from Montreal, moved up the Saskatchewan. By the autumn of 1780 the Hudson's Bay Company had built Buckingham House, 550 miles up river from Cumberland House. Traders had reached the Blackfoot country at last. No doubt they were looking forward optimistically to an extended period of profitable trade—when a great catastrophe robbed them of a host of customers.

In the year 1781 the Piegans on Red Deer River sent a scouting party into the country of their traditional enemies, the Shoshonis. The scouts returned, bearing a strange report. They had located a large Shoshoni camp, had watched it carefully from a high knoll, but had seen no activity. Fearing their wily enemies might be luring them into a trap, the Piegan council instructed their scouts to go back and look for other Shoshoni camps in the vicin-

15 *Ibid.*, 110–11.
16 *Ibid.*, 103–11.

ity. Again the scouts returned, saying they had seen no other lodges. At dawn next morning the Piegans attacked the silent village, ripped open the lodge covers with their sharp knives and daggers, and made ready to fall upon their hated enemies. But there was no one to fight back. The occupants of the lodges were all dead or dying. Each was a mass of corruption.

Believing a bad spirit had destroyed their enemies, the Piegans collected the best of their lodges, camp equipment, and horses and returned home. Two days later the deadly smallpox broke out in their camp. It spread from lodge to lodge. The Indians were helpless in the face of this strange plague. They had no idea that one person could communicate a disease to another. Their medicine men had no cure for it. Frantic, infected men rushed into the river and died. More than half the people perished before the plague was spent. Those who remained to cry and mourn for the dead concluded that the Good Spirit had forsaken them. In their desperation they sacrificed feathers, branches of trees, and sweetgrass to the Bad Spirit, imploring it to leave them alone.

Humbled by the plague, the Piegans considered making peace with the Shoshonis, little knowing that their enemies had suffered even more severe losses in the epidemic. Indeed, the weakened Shoshonis withdrew southward, leaving the rich Bow River country to the Blackfeet.[17]

For two or three years the Blackfeet were at peace. Then the occupants of five lodges who had separated from a Piegan band to hunt mountain sheep on the upper Bow River failed to return. A searching party found their bodies and, near them—in the form of snake heads painted on sticks—the unmistakable evidence that they had been massacred by the Shoshonis. This deed rekindled Piegan hatred for their old enemy. Yet in their war council they decided to temper their revenge with practical action. They would kill Shoshoni warriors. But they would capture and adopt their women and children in order to regain their numbers lost in the great plague.[18]

17 Thompson, *Narrative*, 336–38.   18 *Ibid.*, 338–40.

Relentlessly, the Blackfeet turned upon the Shoshonis on the south and upon the latter's allies, the Flatheads and Kutenais, who stood between the Blackfoot tribes and the Rockies. These enemies, armed only with primitive bows and arrows and lances, were no match for the Blackfeet, whose guns now were fed with a ready supply of shot and powder obtained from white traders in their own country. By the end of the century the Blackfeet had become masters of the northwestern plains, from the North Saskatchewan River southward to the northern tributaries of the Missouri and from Battle River eastward to the Rockies. The haughty Piegans talked of their old Shoshoni enemies as miserable old women whom they could kill with sticks and stones.[19]

The Shoshonis must have suffered terrible losses in their losing fight with the Blackfeet. In 1805, a French trader, François Larocque, found twelve lodges of Shoshonis living with the Crow Indians on the Yellowstone. He identified them as the remnant of one of their "tribes" that had been destroyed.[20] But the greater number of the Shoshonis retreated westward, crossing the Rockies to avoid the relentless attacks of their old enemies.

The Flatheads and Kutenais also sought to avoid extermination by seeking safety west of the mountains. In 1811 empty Kutenai lodges were still standing near Rocky Mountain House, mute reminders of the tribe's former residence on the plains.[21] Twenty-two years later a middle-aged Flathead recalled the hectic days of his youth when his courageous people, unable to defend themselves against repeated attacks by the better-armed Blackfeet, decided to leave the plains to find peace behind the Rocky Mountain barrier.[22]

While the Blackfeet were aggressively expanding their territory to the south and west, white traders were actively contending for their friendship on the Saskatchewan. In 1779 a group of independent traders in Montreal organized the North West Company to enable them to compete more successfully with the

[19] Henry and Thompson, *New Light*, II, 726.
[20] *Journal of Larocque from the Assiniboine to the Yellowstone*, 73.
[21] Henry and Thompson, *New Light*, II, 707.
[22] W. A. Ferris, *Life in the Rocky Mountains*, 91–92.

powerful Hudson's Bay Company in the western trade. By 1784 they were offering stiff competition in the Blackfoot country. They more than held their own in attracting the Blood and Blackfoot tribes. But when their rivals sent David Thompson to winter among the Piegans on Bow River in 1787, the Hudson's Bay Company gained the favor of that largest of the Blackfoot tribes. Not until the Nor'Westers built Rocky Mountain House far up the Saskatchewan at the mouth of the Clearwater in 1799 did they begin to get a goodly share of the Piegan trade.

For their mutual protection against the host of warlike Indians on and near the Saskatchewan the rival companies commonly built their trading posts within sight of each other in strong defensive positions on the river bluffs. These posts were in truth forts. Each fort comprised a cluster of buildings constructed of heavy logs in the traditional post-in-sill style long favored by the French in Eastern Canada. These buildings were surrounded by a stout stockade, and the fort was defended with cannon. In the winter of 1809 the North West Company's Fort Vermilion, one of the most important posts on the Saskatchewan at that time, housed the factor in charge, 35 employees, most of them French-Canadians, and their Indian wives and mixed-blood children. They totaled 130 persons, living in ten houses and two tents within the stockade.[23] At that time there probably were fewer than 200 white men in all of the traders' forts in the Blackfoot country. These forts were the first white men's homes the Blackfoot Indians had ever seen. Naturally they called them "Old Man Person's Lodges."

Trading with Napikwan involved a long and tedious ritual each time a hunting band approached one of the forts. First the band chief sent several of his young men ahead to announce the arrival of his party and to obtain a few small presents—some powder, tobacco, and face paint. When they returned and all had dressed in their best clothes and painted their faces to their own satisfaction, the chief led his men to the fort. Within a few yards of the gate the Indians discharged their guns in the air

[23] Henry and Thompson, *New Light*, II, 553–55.

as a token of friendship. The traders replied by raising a flag and firing a few guns. On entering the trading house, the Indians were disarmed, formally seated on the floor in order of rank, and served a few drams of rum and some tobacco. Pipes were lighted and slowly passed around while the news was told at great length. When the women had erected the Indians' lodges near the fort, the traders gave out enough rum to permit the whole camp to enjoy a prolonged drinking spree. Not until the Indians sobered up, perhaps the next morning, perhaps a full day later, did they bring their goods into the fort to begin the trade.[24]

If the traders anticipated a rich harvest of beaver in the Blackfoot trade, they were soon disillusioned. There were plenty of beaver in the creeks and rivers. A good hunter could have killed a hundred of them a month with his bow and arrows. But, with the exception of one small band of Piegans who lived near the mountains and may not have owned many horses with which to hunt buffalo on the plains, the Blackfeet were generally not beaver hunters. To some the beaver was a sacred animal. Others found alibis for not hunting beaver, such as "the ground was too hard for their hands to work in."[25] Their trade in small-animal pelts consisted primarily of wolves and foxes, which they caught in snares or deep pits. The animals jumped into the pits to get the buffalo meat bait left by the Indians and could not get out again.

On the other hand, the Blackfeet loved to hunt buffalo on horseback, and could kill many more of these animals than they needed for their subsistence during their fall hunts. They offered quantities of fresh meat, dried meat, and pemmican to the traders. Consequently, the Blackfoot trade became primarily a source of provisions for the fur traders who could use this food while they were engaged in their more lucrative quest for beaver among the Indians north of the Saskatchewan.

The Blackfoot tribes also supplied horses to the traders cheap-

[24] This ritual was enacted at Fort George in 1794 and at Rocky Mountain House sixteen years later in much the same way. Duncan M'Gillivray, *The Journal of Duncan M'Gillivray of the Northwest Company at Fort George on the Saskatchewan, 1794–1795*, 30; Henry and Thompson, *New Light*, II, 728–31.

[25] Henry and Thompson, *New Light*, II, 724.

ly. At Fort Vermilion in 1809 the price of a common horse was "a gallon keg of Blackfoot rum, 2 fathoms of new twist tobacco, 20 balls and powder enough to fire them, 1 awl, 1 scalper, 1 fleshing knife, 1 gun worm, 1 P. C. glass, 1 fire steel and 1 flint."[26]

There were a few items in the traders' stock which the Blackfeet preferred above others—firearms and the ammunition to serve them, tobacco, and liquor. The desire for guns and ammunition was an obvious one. Firearms had enabled them to turn the tables on their Shoshoni enemies and to chase the Flatheads and Kutenais across the mountains. The trade musket, by modern standards, was a rather primitive instrument. Nor did it have either the range or accuracy of the contemporary Kentucky rifle. Yet to Indians, who knew no better weapon, it was a miracleworker—especially against tribes which had no firearms at all. It was deadly at close range, light in weight, sturdy, and not too expensive. This trade gun was a full-stocked, muzzle-loading, smoothbore flintlock with a five-eighths-inch bore. It was supplied in barrel lengths ranging from two and one-half to three and one-half feet. Blackfoot warriors commonly filed off several inches of the barrel to convert it into a light, makeshift carbine which they could use on foot or horseback. The gun was furnished with a large trigger guard, making it easy to use by a mitten-wearing Indian in winter. Its counter-lockplate was a handsome brass representation of a dragon or sea monster. Weapons of this kind were made to the same specifications by London and Birmingham gunsmiths for both the North West Company and the Hudson's Bay Company.[27] At Fort George on the Saskatchewan in 1794 the traders asked fourteen beaver pelts or their equivalent in value for a trade gun. Twenty rounds of shot cost an additional beaver skin, and powder was extra.[28]

Long before traders came among them the Blackfoot Indians had the tobacco habit. But the tobacco they grew in their small plots was strong and bitter compared with that offered by the

[26] *Ibid.*, II, 542.
[27] John C. Ewers, "The North West Trade Gun," *Alberta Historical Review,*. Vol. IV, No. 2 (1956), 3–9.
[28] M'Gillivray, *Journal*, 30–31.

traders. In 1754, Hendry had found the "Archithinue Natives" little interested in his tobacco, while he called theirs "dryed horse dung"—undoubtedly his frank appraisal of its quality rather than an identification of its substance.[29] Yet by 1800 the Piegans found the traders' tobacco so superior that they discontinued growing their own.[30]

The traders offered two kinds of tobacco. One type was twisted into a rope nearly an inch in diameter, wound into large rolls, and measured off by the inch for trade to the Indians. Six inches of this tobacco commonly was given to Indian leaders when they came into the forts to trade. Traders knew this as Brazil tobacco because it was grown in the valley of the Amazon, as well as in Trinidad. The Blackfeet called it "gut tobacco" after its appearance.

The other kind of trade tobacco came in the form of sausage-shaped plugs as much as eighteen inches or more in length. Each plug was tied with cord and marked in sections about every two inches of its length, so that it could be easily cut and sold in pieces. Traders called this "carrot tobacco." The Blackfeet gave a common horse for a carrot of tobacco weighing about three pounds and costing four shillings in Montreal.[31] The Blackfeet came to prefer this "big tobacco," as they called it, to the "gut" kind. They commonly mixed their trade tobacco with dried leaves of the bearberry, which grew wild in their country. Burning bearberry leaves have a pleasant odor. By mixing them with tobacco, of course, they made the tobacco go further.

Liquor proved a troublesome trump in the traders' pack of miracles. Before the whites came among them, the Blackfeet had no acquaintance with intoxicants. The whites well knew the fatal fascination of this article of commerce among the Indian tribes with whom they had dealt farther east. They offered it to the Blackfoot tribes in a weaker, watered-down form. Alexander Henry described the concoction of this Blackfoot rum:

[29] Hendry, *Journal*, 338.
[30] Thompson, *Narrative*, 365.
[31] Henry and Thompson, *New Light*, II, 526.

We do not mix our liquor so strong as we do for tribes who are more accustomed to its use. To make a nine gallon keg of liquor we generally put in four or five quarts of high wine [alcohol] and then fill up with water. For the Crees and Assiniboines we put in six quarts of high wine, and for the Saulteurs [Chippewa] eight or nine quarts.[32]

At Fort George in 1794, the traders asked thirty beaver pelts for a "large keg." They found it profitable, however, to make liberal presents of drinks before trading began. Duncan M'Gillivray, clerk at the fort, argued that liquor played a very important role in the Indian trade:

The love of rum is their first inducement to industry, they undergo every hardship and fatigue to procure a Skinfull of this delicious beverage, and when a Nation becomes addicted to drinking, it affords a strong presumption that they will soon become excellent hunters.[33]

This theory, however, backfired in the case of the Piegans. Sixteen years later, Alexander Henry, tough-minded, practical trader at Rocky Mountain House, wrote of that tribe:

That power for all evil, spiritous liquor, now seems to dominate them, and has taken such hold on them that they are no longer the quiet people they were. They appear fully as addicted to liquor as the Crees, though, unlike the latter, they will not purchase it. They cannot be made to comprehend that anything of value should be paid for what they term "water."[34]

A century and a half later the Blackfeet still call liquor "white men's water."

It was customary for the traders to give handsome scarlet coats to band chiefs when they came to the forts to trade for

32 *Ibid.*, II, 542.
33 Journal, 30, 47.
34 Henry and Thompson, *New Light*, II, 723.

the first time. These presents appealed to the chiefs' vanity and advertised coarse woolens for replacement of native clothing among the chiefs' followers. Point blankets, handkerchiefs, and other materials of cloth were also stocked by the traders.

To a stone age people the traders offered a variety of metal objects in addition to firearms. There were metal arrowheads, lance heads, knives for hand-to-hand fighting and for scalping, files for working pipestone, and steels for kindling fire. Women found equally useful metal articles among the traders' wares. There were knives for cutting tough rawhide, kettles for cooking, and axes for cutting firewood and tipi poles. At the close of the first decade of the nineteenth century both kettles and axes still were scarce among the Blackfeet. Most women collected firewood by breaking off dead branches rather than by felling trees and chopping them into convenient pieces with axes.[35]

Among the luxury items in the traders' stock that attracted Indian women were metal finger rings and large glass beads. They strung the beads on buckskin cords to make necklaces. Various colors of beads were available, but blue seems to have been the favorite.[36] Indians of both sexes obtained commercial colors for painting clothing, lodge covers, and their own faces. Chinese vermilion was particularly in demand for face painting.

We are indebted to some of these traders for the first certain contemporary descriptions of Blackfoot life. Most traders were men of action with little education, skill, or interest in recording their observations. But, fortunately, two of them, Alexander Henry and David Thompson, both men of keen intelligence who had had previous experience among Indian tribes, took the trouble to record their observations on the Blackfoot tribes during the period 1787 to 1811.

Tribal populations were of practical importance to fur traders interested in the numbers of their prospective customers and

[35] *Ibid.,* II, 724.
[36] Umfreville, *Present State of Hudson's Bay,* 202. The Blackfoot word for bead before 1790 was rendered "Com-on-e-cristo-man." This is literally "blue bead."

the relative strengths of the warlike tribes in whose country they lived and worked. Probably the most reliable early estimate of Blackfoot numbers was compiled by Henry in 1809. It is a round number estimate of lodges and warriors. I have added the last column, arrived at by allowing an average of eight persons per lodge:

Tribe	Lodges	Warriors	Persons
Piegan	350	700	2,800
Blackfoot	200	520	1,600
Blood	100	200	800
	——	——	——
	650	1,420	5,200

At that time the Blackfoot tribes were "increasing fast."[37] The Piegans were thought to have more than doubled their numbers in the three decades after the terrible smallpox epidemic. Male births outnumbered female ones, but adult women exceeded the number of men by a ratio of about five to three. Losses of men in warfare and hunting accidents created this disproportion between the sexes. The practice of polygamy helped to correct the situation. Husbands of more than one wife commonly married sisters. A widow could find a home as the wife of a friend of her deceased husband. Until a woman was nearly fifty years of age she was sure to find a husband. Some prominent chiefs had three to seven wives and many children. Kootenae Appe, the Piegan war chief, had twenty-two sons and four daughters by his five wives.[38]

Blackfoot men were described as tall, well proportioned, and muscular, with manly features and intelligent countenances. Their eyes were large, black, and piercing, their noses full and straight, their teeth white and regular, and their hair long, straight, and black. They plucked the hair from their faces to keep them smooth. The women were known for their good fea-

[37] Henry and Thompson, *New Light,* II, 530.
[38] Thompson, *Narrative,* 347–52.

tures, which were somewhat hardened by constant exposure to the weather. Traders thought the skin color of the Blackfeet was rather swarthy, but not unlike that of Europeans from the south of France or Spain. Already there must have been some mixed-blood children among the Blackfoot tribes, for the men were liberal in offering their wives to the traders when they visited the forts, and were satisfied with "a mere trifle" in payment for this service.[39]

Blackfoot men generally wore their hair loose around their necks, with a long, narrow lock falling over the bridge of the nose and cut square at the lower end. Young dandies painted their faces in stripes, circles, dots, and other designs in several colors. After they married and settled down, men were content to use a single color of face paint. Red was the preferred color, but the warriors also employed yellow ochre and a glossy lead color obtained from west of the Rockies.

Men did not wear breechclouts. However, their long skin leggings, which were tied to the belt, may have crossed in front, affording concealment of the privates while leaving the buttocks bare. Skin moccasins, which were lined with buffalo hair in winter, and a buffalo robe completed the man's everyday costume. On dress occasions men wore skin shirts trimmed with locks of their enemies' hair and cut skin fringes, and decorated with porcupine quill embroidery. Some men wore feathers in their hair and necklaces of grizzly bear claws.

Women wore their hair long and loose. Their principal garment was a sleeveless, skin dress in the form of a slip. Its length fell to the wearer's ankles. This slip was supported by straps over the shoulders. Probably women wore separate skin sleeves in cold weather, held up by skin cords tied at the back of the neck. Cut fringes and porcupine quillwork decorated these dresses. Women's ornaments included bracelets of deer or elk teeth, necklaces of sweet-smelling roots, and finger rings and pendants of metal bells or thimbles obtained from the traders.

In spite of the traders' efforts to induce the Indians to purchase

[39] *Ibid.*, 347–49; Henry and Thompson, *New Light*, II, 524–26, 660.

woolens for winter wear, the buffalo robe remained their common cold-weather outer garment. Their finest shirts, leggings, and dresses were of antelope or mountain sheep skins. Deer and elk skins were more serviceable for daily wear. Many garments were painted with earth pigments, in solid colors or in simple designs.[40]

In summer the Blackfeet lived in large tribal camps to defend themselves better against their enemies. They hunted buffalo on horseback with bow and arrow. As winter approached, they separated into bands of ten to twenty lodges, to make buffalo pounds and to take wolves and foxes for the trade. The Piegans living in the broken country near the mountains lured buffalo herds over high precipices along river valleys instead of bothering to make traditional pounds with fenced corrals. If the animals were not killed or entirely disabled by their fall, they were so badly bruised and shaken up that they were easily dispatched by hunters waiting with bows and arrows at the cliff base. It was not necessary to expend valuable powder and ball in this operation. So successful were Blackfoot buffalo hunters that they could furnish supplies of meat and pemmican to the traders and still accumulate surpluses to provide the Indians with food during the lean winter months.[41]

Blackfoot Indian homes were clean tipis covered with dressed buffalo skins. Some of the covers were painted with rude representations of buffalo, bear, and other animals and birds.[42]

The Piegans—if not the other tribes also—then had a civil chief and a war chief. The former was renowned for his eloquence, the latter for his success in leading large war parties. Both held limited authority. They, as well as the chiefs of hunting bands, were leaders only by the consent and will of their people. They "had no power beyond their influence, which would immediately cease by any act of authority and they are all very careful not to arrogate any superiority over others."[43]

[40] Thompson, *Narrative*, 349–51; Henry and Thompson, *New Light*, 525–26, 725–26.
[41] Henry and Thompson, *New Light*, II, 530, 723–25.
[42] *Ibid.*, II, 527.
[43] Thompson, *Narrative*, 346–47, 364–65.

War was the principal occupation of the young men. The Piegans, who continued to be the frontier tribe—living farther south and west than the others—were the most active aggressors in the successful wars against the Shoshonis. The Blackfeet, living farthest northeast, bore the brunt of Cree and Assiniboin pressures from the east. The Blood tribe in the center warred in both directions. Many older men among the Blackfoot tribes bragged of killing fifteen or twenty of the enemy. He was but a modest warrior who could claim less than ten scalps. The successful ones delighted in recounting their battle records.

In their wars with the Shoshonis and Flatheads, the Piegans sent out large parties of several hundred men to do battle. However, much of their warlike activity took the form of raiding for horses by small groups of young men. By raiding and raising horses some Indians managed to build up large herds. In 1809 one Piegan was said to own three hundred, while some Northern Blackfeet owned thirty or forty horses. Two kinds of saddles were used, a buffalo-hide pad stuffed with moose or elk hair, employed by active young men, and a rawhide-covered, wooden-framed saddle with high pommel and cantle, ridden by women.[44]

The traders' accounts of Indian religious beliefs are of less value than their observations of everyday life and customs. They depended to a great extent on the Cree language in their conversations with the Blackfeet. They saw little of the Indians during the summer months when furs were not prime and the natives were hunting far from the trading posts. That was also the traditional ceremonial season. Although Henry learned that the Blackfeet then recognized the sun as their supreme being, he did not mention the tribal sun dance. If that important religious observance of later years was performed at that time it would have been held in the summer far away from the trading posts.

Traders were intrigued by the painstaking attention given by the Blackfoot tribes to ceremonial smoking. Yet the medicine

[44] Henry and Thompson, *New Light*, II, 526–27, 726–27.

pipe is the only recognizable ritual to which they referred. Thompson remarked upon the great length of these pipestems, some three or four feet long, and noted that they were carried on the backs of their owners with care when camp was moved. Henry learned of the Blackfoot tradition that the medicine pipe was given to the people by Thunder.

Alexander Henry was told that when a Blackfoot Indian died, his spirit traveled to a great hummock between Red Deer River and the South Saskatchewan. There it ascended into the air and proceeded southward "to a delightful country, well stocked with horses, buffalo, and women and there lives happy to all eternity, making pounds, chasing buffalo, and enjoying handsome women."[45]

Henry regarded the Blackfoot tribes as "the most independent and happy people of all the tribes E. of the Rocky mountains. War, women, horses and buffalo are their delights, and all these they have at command."[46]

Strong and warlike as the Blackfoot tribes were, the traders had little to fear from them as long as they gave fair return for furs, horses, and provisions in such coveted wonders as guns and "white man's water." The Indians knew the traders were too few in number to offer a threat to their security. During the 1780's the Blackfoot tribes were uniformly friendly to the white businessmen in their country. In the early nineties, however, their Gros Ventre allies, living on the plains between the South Saskatchewan and the Missouri, twice destroyed Hudson's Bay Company posts. In 1811, believing the traders were discriminating against them, the Gros Ventres proposed an attack upon Rocky Mountain House. When the Piegans learned of this plan they nipped it in the bud by warning the Gros Ventres in no uncertain terms that if they carried out their threat against the traders, they would have to fight them too. The traders themselves had roused the resentment of the Piegans by sending arms

[45] *Ibid.*, II, 527–29; Thompson, *Narrative*, 366.
[46] Henry and Thompson, *New Light*, II, 737.

Assiniboin-Cree attack on small Piegan camp outside Fort
McKensie, August 28, 1833. From a drawing by Karl Bodmer.

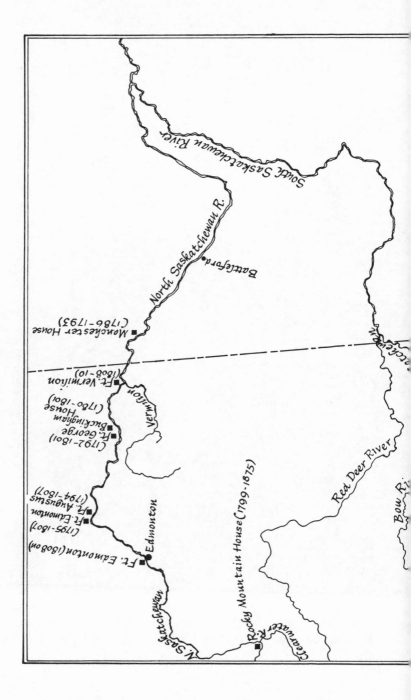

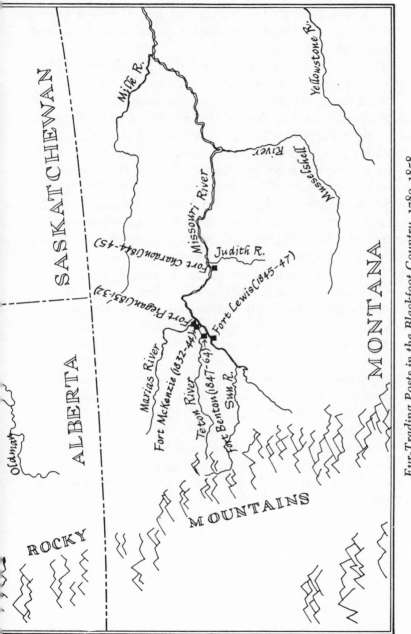

Fur-Trading Posts in the Blackfoot Country, 1780–1858

over the Rockies to the old enemies of the Blackfoot tribes. But the Piegans still could boast that they had never murdered a Canadian trader.[47]

The Piegans must have realized how they had prospered since the traders came among them. Their lives had become infinitely richer than those of their stone-age great-grandfathers. Part of their prosperity resulted from their acquisition of swift horses from neighboring tribes. Horses greatly eased their daily tasks of obtaining food and skins and of moving camps, and enabled them to accumulate more possessions. Part of their prosperity was due to the improved weapons, tools, and utensils obtained from the traders. Some of the traders' wares replaced items the Indians formerly made for themselves with time-consuming care. Metal knives, files, and awls enabled them to fashion articles of rawhide, soft skin, stone, and wood quicker than they could have made them with stone and bone tools. The Indians gained more leisure. They could devote more time to warfare, to accumulating wealth in horses through raids on enemy camps, to prolonged religious ceremonies, to social gatherings, and to feasting. They grew strong and confident as they extended their conquests and expanded their territory. Neighboring Indians and whites alike recognized them as the dominant military power on the northwestern plains. Woe to those who incited their hostility!

At the same time Napikwan had gained a precarious foothold in the Blackfoot country. His wonders were subtly undermining the Indians' vaunted independence, even as the Blackfeet boasted of their power and prowess. The Indians were becoming more and more dependent upon him as they came to regard as necessities those traders' wares which they could not make themselves.

[47] *Ibid.*, II, 719–23.

3: Big Knives on the Missouri

THE BLACKFOOT tribes' friendly relations with British and Canadian traders on the Saskatchewan in the early years of their acquaintance were in sharp contrast to their aggressive hostility toward American explorers and traders whom they met in the valley of the Missouri River during the first three decades of the nineteenth century. These Indians soon learned to distinguish between their old friends, "the Northern White Men," and their new enemies, the Americans, whom they called "Big Knives." The latter name may refer to the sharp, dangerous hunting knives carried by the Americans.

Blackfoot hostility toward the Americans began with their very first meeting, three summers after formal ceremonies were held in St. Louis transferring Upper Louisiana, a huge unexplored area including the drainage basin of the Missouri River, to the United States on March 10, 1804. Two months later Captains Meriwether Lewis and William Clark started up the Missouri on their epoch-making journey of discovery. Their party wintered near the Mandan villages in present North Dakota. The following spring they continued westward, following the Missouri across the plains of present Montana to the Rocky Mountains. On this portion of their trek to the Pacific the leaders were apprehensive of meeting the warlike Gros Ventres, whom they knew as the Minnetarees of the Plains. Their worries were solidly grounded. The Gros Ventres had a reputation for treachery among Canadian traders, and they made long journeys southward, crossing and recrossing the Missouri on their raids against the Crow Indians on the Yellowstone. We know that in the fall of 1805 Gros Ventre warriors were far south of the Missouri, attempting to make an expedient peace with their Crow enemies in order to obtain some fine horses in trade.[1]

From the mouth of the Musselshell River westward to beyond the mouth of Sun River the Lewis and Clark party frequently sighted and occasionally spent the night in rude lodges of poles and bark, built as temporary shelters by passing Indian war parties among the trees bordering the Missouri. The explorers thought some of these war lodges did not "seem to have been long evacuated."[2] Between the Musselshell and the Marias they passed "the remains of a vast many mangled carcasses of Buffalo which had been driven over a precipice of 120 feet by the Indians & perished; the water appeared to have washed away a part of this immence pile of slaughter and still there remained the fragments of at least a hundred carcasses. They created a horrid stench."[3] Indian signs were plentiful, and the party proceeded cautiously. Nevertheless, they crossed the Montana plains without meeting a single Indian, either friendly or hostile.

On the return eastward from the Pacific in 1806 the party divided into two groups for further exploration of the Montana plains. While Clark led one group down the Yellowstone, Lewis, with nine men, followed a more northerly course down the Missouri. In mid-July Captain Lewis, accompanied by three enlisted men, left the rest of his small party on the Missouri and headed northward to try to determine the sources of the Marias River, which he believed marked the northwestern boundary of the Louisiana Purchase and hence the northwestern limit of the United States. They traveled on horseback as far north as Cutbank Creek on the present Blackfeet Reservation. There Lewis attempted to make observations, with but limited success on account of cloudy and rainy weather.

[1] Larocque, *Journal*, 44.
[2] Meriwether Lewis and William Clark, *Original Journals of the Lewis and Clark Expedition, 1804–1806*, II, 80–249.
[3] *Ibid.*, II, 94.

On July 25, Lewis was convinced that the sources of the Marias were to the west rather than farther north. Fearing further delay would unnecessarily slow the eastward progress of his party, he turned south. Besides, two of his men returned with the disturbing news that they had seen a great number of Indian campsites near the forks of the Marias which appeared to have been occupied scarcely six weeks before. Lewis frankly recorded in his journal: "We consider ourselves extremely fortunate not having met with these people."[4]

Their luck was too good to last. Next afternoon Lewis ascended a hill at a point some four miles below the junction of Two Medicine River and Badger Creek to view the country. Instead he saw a party of Indians. To Lewis "this was a very unpleasant site," but since the Indians had seen him too, he "resolved to make the best of our situation and to approach them in a friendly manner."[5]

Cautiously, eight Indians came forward and shook the hands of the equally cautious whites. Although his party was outnumbered two to one, Lewis had little choice but to camp with the Indians in the river valley that night. During the evening he smoked with the Indians and conversed with them through his accomplished sign talker, George Drouillard. Solemnly, with tongue in cheek, Lewis proclaimed that he had "come in surch of them in order to prevail upon them to be at peace with their neighbors . . . and to engage them to come and trade with me when the establishment is made at the entrance of this river." Not to be outdone by Lewis' diplomacy, these Piegan Indians readily assented to his apparent insistence that they were Gros Ventres. They claimed there were three chiefs in their party and declared their desire for peace with the Flatheads.

Fearful that the Indians might try to steal his horses during the night, Lewis posted a guard before he went to sleep. Shortly after daylight he was roused by the sharp voice of Drouillard, shouting, "Damn you. Let go my gun." George was struggling

4 *Ibid.*, V, 216.
5 *Ibid.*, V, 219.

with one of the red men for possession of his weapon. J. Fields had carelessly laid his gun behind him while on guard, and one of the watchful Indians had seized the opportunity to take it and the gun of his sleeping brother. The Fields brothers ran after the Indian, overtook him, and Reuben Fields stabbed him in the heart. The Indian ran about fifteen yards and fell dead.

Foiled in their attempt to disarm the whites, the Indians then tried to run off their horses. In the ensuing melee Lewis wounded one of the red men with a shot through the belly before the Indians rode away, leaving behind some of their own horses and weapons as well as their dead comrade. Lewis placed a medal such as he had been accustomed to give friendly Indian leaders upon the body of the dead Piegan. Then, fearing their late adversaries might soon return with reinforcements, the four whites beat a hasty retreat southward to rendezvous with the rest of their party at the mouth of the Marias next day. There they lost little time abandoning their horses, taking to their canoes, and paddling rapidly downstream toward civilization.[6]

In spite of Lewis' identification of the Indians in this scrap as Gros Ventres, there need no longer be any doubt that they were Piegans. The knowledgeable contemporary Canadian trader, David Thompson, so identified them, and years later the Piegans recalled both the fight and the name of their tribesman killed in the action, He-that-looks-at-the-Calf.[7]

If this unfortunate run-in with Lewis and his men hardened the hearts of Blackfeet toward Americans, subsequent events greatly aggravated that attitude. Even before Lewis and Clark returned to St. Louis, the rich, unexploited beaver country west of the Missouri-Yellowstone junction began to prove a magnetic attraction to adventurous white men. At the Mandan villages in mid-August, John Colter, one of the ablest hunters of the Lewis and Clark party, asked and received permission of the captains to join two young men from Illinois on a hunting and trapping

[6] *Ibid.*, V, 218–28.

[7] Thompson, *Narrative*, 375; James H. Bradley, "The Bradley Manuscript," Montana Historical Society *Contributions*, Vol. VIII (1917), 135. (Hereafter referred to as Bradley, "Manuscript," *MHSC*.)

expedition to the Yellowstone Valley. The following spring, while paddling his fur down river to market, Colter met a party of forty men en route to the Yellowstone under the leadership of Manuel Lisa, the most daring St. Louis trader of his day. George Drouillard, veteran of the Lewis and Clark expedition, was among them. Probably he helped Lisa persuade his old comrade-in-arms to join the party.

Guided by the experienced Colter, they followed the Yellow-stone to the country of the Crow Indians, enemies of the Black-feet and Gros Ventres. At the mouth of the Bighorn they built a small post, Fort Remon, and opened peaceful trade with the Crows. Lisa sent the experienced Colter with two Crow guides to explore westward. On Shoshone River this little party was attacked by "Blackfeet." Colter's companions deserted him. Alone and in the dead of winter he traversed the wonderland that is now Yellowstone National Park and returned downriver to Lisa's fort.

The next spring Colter, in company with John Potts, another veteran of the Lewis and Clark expedition, boldly set out for the Missouri headwaters to trap beaver. Fearing the Blackfeet, they worked by night and hid during the day. Early one morning they were surprised by several hundred of the dread "Black-feet." The Indians killed Potts and captured Colter. For this old enemy they devised a special torture. They stripped him naked and gave him a short start in a race for life. Colter's chances were probably less than one in a hundred. Yet, running like a scared antelope, he outdistanced the pursuing red men, jumped into a near-by stream, swam a short distance, and concealed himself so well in the underbrush that the Indians could not find him. Almost miraculously, this naked, unarmed man found his way back to the fort at the mouth of the Bighorn.[8]

Colter escaped with his own skin, but he left behind all his valuable beaver pelts. This rich booty helped salve the Indians' keen disappointment at his escape. It provided them with a

[8] Hiram M. Chittenden, *The American Fur Trade of the Far West* (2nd ed.), II, 708–709.

supply of fine furs for which their trader friends on the Sas-katchewan would give them more ammunition and plenty of that wonderful "white man's water."[9]

Lisa's early success on the Yellowstone and the rosy prospect of exploiting the still richer fur resources of the Missouri head-waters farther west encouraged the formation of a large fur-trading company in St. Louis. This Missouri Fur Company was backed by such prominent citizens as the Chouteaus and William Clark. In the spring of 1810 Lisa was again trading with the friendly Crow Indians on the Yellowstone, while two of his part-ners in the new firm, Andrew Henry and Pierre Menard, led a party westward to the Three Forks of the Missouri. There, on a tongue of land between the Jefferson and Madison rivers, they built a fort. They had high hopes of obtaining three hundred packs of beaver that year from the small streams in the vicinity, but they reckoned without the aggressive opposition of the Black-feet. So constant were the Indian attacks that little trapping could be done. That spring the Indians killed more than twenty trappers. Many of the remaining whites were ready to call it quits, so Menard returned to the fort at the mouth of the Bighorn, accompanied by the faint-hearted majority, and sent the paltry twenty to thirty packs of beaver taken from the Missouri head-waters downstream to St. Louis. By autumn Lisa and Menard decided to take most of the equipment from the Bighorn post and go back to St. Louis.

Henry, with a few brave followers, stayed on at the little fort until fall. Then, convinced of the impossibility of successful beaver trapping in the face of relentless Blackfoot opposition, he led his little party over the Rockies and built Fort Henry on the North Fork of Snake River. That winter, by trapping and trading with peaceful Shoshoni Indians, Henry collected barely forty packs of beaver. The new location proved a disappointment. The following spring Henry decided to give up and return to St. Louis. En route down the Yellowstone he passed the deserted post at the mouth of the Bighorn and dismantled it.[10]

[9] Henry and Thompson, *New Light*, II, 539-40.

So the Missouri Fur Company, after a year of discouragement in fine beaver country, abandoned the Montana region. The furs were there, all right, but the Blackfeet were too much for them. Thus the Blackfeet won their first round with the American fur traders. Perhaps the trappers had underestimated the courage and determination of their Blackfoot adversaries. If so they paid for their miscalculation with the blood of their men. On the other hand, the Blackfeet purchased their victory at a heavy price. Many good men had fallen victim to the trappers' guns. But the Blackfeet remained in possession of the field.

The American trappers had never become well enough acquainted with their opponents to identify them by tribe. To them the Indian raiders were all "Blackfeet." So there is doubt as to which or how many of these tribes were involved in these incessant attacks. At Rocky Mountain House on the Saskatchewan in the winter of 1810–11, Alexander Henry learned of both Blood and Gros Ventre depredations against the Americans in preceding months. The booty they brought to the post furnished ample proof of their attacks on whites. From one raid the Blood Indians brought beaver traps, knives, dirks, clothing, and even some bank notes signed by the New Jersey and Trenton Banking Company. Henry understood that the Indians had murdered and probably butchered and eaten an American officer or trader to avenge the death of several red men at his hands.

On another raid the Gros Ventres murdered members of a party of free traders and robbed them of their beaver pelts, utensils, and a big black dog which Henry purchased from them for a fathom of tobacco and a scalping knife.[11]

The Northern Blackfeet and Piegans may have been too absorbed in combating their Indian enemies to take much part in the raids on the Americans. The Northern Blackfeet bore the brunt of increasing hostile pressures from both Crees and Assiniboins moving westward up the Saskatchewan. The over-moun-

[10] Chittenden, *American Fur Trade of the Far West*, I, 127–44; Bradley, "Manuscript," *MHSC*, Vol. VIII, 188–90.

[11] Henry and Thompson, *New Light*, II, 735–36.

tain tribes were making trouble for the Piegans. For years those tribes had sought firearms with which to defend themselves against the Blackfeet while they journeyed to the plains on seasonal buffalo hunts. As early as 1795 the Kutenais tried to bribe the Blackfeet with payments of horses to let them visit Fort George on the Saskatchewan to trade. But their old enemies recognized this Kutenai plan to obtain firearms for use against them and would not fall for the scheme.[12]

In the first decade of the nineteenth century the Blackfoot barrier to the arming of the tribes west of the Rockies began to lose its effectiveness. Crow Indian intermediaries obtained large numbers of guns at the Mandan and Hidatsa villages on the Missouri and traded some of them to the Shoshonis and Flatheads farther west. Lewis and Clark found a few guns in the possession of the Shoshonis in 1805. That year the Nez Percés sent a small delegation to the distant Mandan villages and procured six of the precious firearms.[13] Trade guns began to reach the Kutenais and Flatheads through direct exchange with Canadian traders after David Thompson and Finan McDonald built posts among them in 1808 and 1809.

By the summer of 1810 the Flatheads owned some twenty guns. In mid-July they boldly crossed the Rockies to hunt buffalo on the plains. Near the eastern base of the Rockies they were attacked by a superior Piegan force. In the ensuing battle the Flatheads made good use of their new weapons. Not only did they defend themselves successfully, but they killed some sixteen Piegan aggressors. This first defeat at the hands of their formerly helpless Flathead opponents was bitter medicine to the proud Piegans. They attributed it to the perversity of their old friends the Canadian traders, who supplied guns and ammunition to their enemies. That fall they tried to prevent the passage of firearms over the mountains by patrolling the approaches to the Rockies west of Rocky Mountain House. Their vigilance forced

[12] M'Gillivray, *Journal*, 56.

[13] John C. Ewers, "The Indian Trade of the Upper Missouri before Lewis and Clark: An Interpretation," Missouri Historical Society *Bulletin*, Vol. X, No. 4 (1954), 445.

David Thompson to make a roundabout crossing of the Rockies at the head of Athabaska River, far to the north of the Blackfoot country. But the Flatheads continued to receive supplies of the coveted weapons.[14]

Withdrawal of the American traders in 1811 left Blackfoot warriors free to concentrate upon their Indian enemies for a full decade. The western tribes were banding together to form large-scale hunting expeditions to the plains. The Crees and Assiniboins were moving in from the east; the Crows on the Yellowstone sent war parties northward. Surrounded by enemies, the Blackfoot tribes and their Gros Ventre allies were fully occupied during this period in defending themselves, their horses, and their hunting grounds from hostile Indians. Fortunately, they did not have to fight large numbers of trappers too.

So great was American respect for the power of the Blackfoot warriors that overland parties of traders were willing to detour to the south on their way to or from the Pacific slope, rather than risk combat with these rough-and-ready redskins. In 1811, Wilson Price Hunt, outward bound from St. Louis to the Pacific Northwest, left the Missouri at the Arikara villages rather than chance the old Lewis and Clark route up the Missouri. The following year Robert Stuart's party, traveling eastward from Astoria, carefully picked a route which was "out of the walks of the Blackfoot Indians, who are very numerous and inimical to whites." In so doing they discovered that most famous of overland migration routes, the Oregon Trail.[15]

Not until 1821 did a reorganized Missouri Fur Company extend its operations into the country of the dread Blackfeet. Again its leaders chose to establish an operating base among the friendly Crow Indians on the Yellowstone, building a new fort on the site of Lisa's post at the mouth of the Bighorn. Again they sent an expedition farther west. Robert Jones and Michael Immell led a party of trappers up the Yellowstone in the early spring.

[14] Thompson, *Narrative*, 423–25; Henry and Thompson, *New Light*, II, 643–52, 715.
[15] Robert Stuart, *On the Oregon Trail: Robert Stuart's Journey of Discovery* (*1812–1813*), 94.

In the streams at the head of that river they obtained a fine collection of beaver pelts. On their return downstream in mid-May they encountered some thirty-eight "Blackfeet" who professed to be friendly. It appeared that Immell's long experience in dealing with Indians and his impressive size, physical strength, and courage might be winning the friendship of the American traders' old foes. Then, fifteen days later, while the trappers were riding single file through a narrow pass, some three hundred to four hundred warriors descended upon them. Powerful Immell was cut to pieces. Jones' breast was pierced with arrows. Five other whites were killed and four were wounded. The Indians carried off at least $15,000 worth of property.

News of this disaster caused Joshua Pilcher, new head of the Missouri Fur Company, to lament, "The flower of my business is gone." Again that company abandoned operations in present-day Montana.[16]

Next, the newly formed Rocky Mountain Fur Company entered the field. Andrew Henry built a temporary post at the mouth of the Yellowstone in 1822. The following spring he led a party of trappers up the Missouri. He should have known better. Near the Great Falls they were attacked by the ubiquitous "Blackfeet," and four men were killed before the trappers retreated back downstream. By fall the "Blackfeet" and Assiniboins had stolen so many horses from the little post at the mouth of the Yellowstone that the location was abandoned. Again the traders sought the greater security of the Crow country and built a post at the mouth of the Bighorn.[17]

On the western side of the Rockies, in present-day Wyoming, the Rocky Mountain Fur Company adopted a different system of collecting furs. Instead of building trading posts, they began in 1825 to hold an annual spring rendezvous to which itinerant white trappers and friendly Indians brought the furs they had collected in widely scattered operations during the previous win-

16 Bradley, "Manuscript," *MHSC*, Vol. II, 226–27, Vol. IX, 129; Chittenden, *American Fur Trade of the Far West*, I, 148–51.
17 Chittenden, *American Fur Trade of the Far West*, I, 261–71.

ter, exchanging them for supplies and trade goods transported from St. Louis up the Platte and over the Rockies. These great annual fairs, held in Shoshoni country, also attracted the Crows, Flatheads, Nez Percés, and other over-mountain tribes—all long-time enemies of the Blackfeet. Blackfoot warriors knew this trade strengthened their Indian foes. They came to regard the white trappers of that mountainous region with a special hatred. Not only were they robbing Indian lands of their fur resources, but they were giving aid and comfort to the enemy.

Through the remaining years of the twenties and in the thirties war parties of Blackfeet and Gros Ventres ranged far and wide on both sides of the Rockies south of the Three Forks. Repeatedly, they attacked the mountain men in their isolated camps or on the trail. The hardy trappers stood their ground. In numerous small-scale actions, many lives were lost on both sides. In 1837, Alfred Jacob Miller reckoned the beaver trappers' losses averaged forty or fifty men a season.[18] Blackfoot losses may have been even greater.

West of the Rockies, in the valley of the Missouri and southward, the Blackfeet made no distinctions among beaver trappers. Hudson's Bay Company men who moved eastward from the upper Columbia, American company men, or free trappers—they were all enemies. In 1832, George Catlin met a free trapper at Fort Union who had made seven expeditions westward. Five times the Blackfeet had robbed him of his furs, horses, and equipment. He considered himself lucky to have escaped with his life, and he was ready to call it quits.[19]

In those days American trappers blamed the British traders for inciting "Blackfeet" raids upon their Big Knife rivals. Whether the "Northern White Men" on the Saskatchewan actively encouraged this guerrilla warfare against their business rivals south of the border may be open to question; that they profited by it is certain. Valuable beaver pelts were carried northward as booty by the Blackfoot raiders, and the Canadian trading forts were

[18] *The West of Alfred Jacob Miller,* 148.
[19] George Catlin, *Letters and Notes on the Manners, Customs and Condition of the North American Indians,* I, 74.

also the armories from which Blackfoot warriors obtained their firearms and ammunition. They were also the dispensers of that marvelous stimulant to trade, "white men's water."

For a quarter of a century after Captain Lewis' initial meeting with the Piegans the Americans failed to make peace with the Blackfeet. When peace did come it was negotiated by two former "Northern White Men" who had become "Big Knives." Kenneth McKenzie was a canny Scot who participated for many years in the Canadian fur trade before entering the service of the American Fur Company. In 1828 he built a trading post on the Missouri at the mouth of the Yellowstone, in the country of the Assiniboins, enemies of the Blackfeet. McKenzie began at once to lure the border tribes away from Hudson's Bay Company traders. He was successful in bringing the southern bands of Assiniboins and Plains Crees and the Plains Ojibwas to his post. But he well knew that the real prize was the Blackfoot trade. The Blackfoot country was richer in valuable furs than that of the other tribes. McKenzie was determined that his company should gain a share of the Blackfoot trade. But how?

Among the men at Fort Union there was a seasoned old trader who had served some twenty-one years in the Canadian fur trade, a goodly part of it with the Hudson's Bay Company in the Blackfoot country. This man, Jacob Berger, spoke the Blackfoot language. He had known many of their important chiefs. McKenzie persuaded him to try to bring a party of Blackfeet to Fort Union. At the head of a small party of other courageous men, and carrying an American flag, Berger left the fort in the fall or early winter of 1830. So little faith did many of the men at Fort Union have in this expedition that they dubbed it "the forlorn hope."

Accounts of this journey differ in detail. According to the fullest one, the party proceeded up the Missouri to the mouth of the Marias, followed the Marias to Badger Creek, and went up Badger Creek to its head, without finding the Blackfeet. There, within a few miles of the site where Captain Lewis had fought the small group of Piegans a quarter-century before, Berger encamped and raised the Stars and Stripes. At daybreak the next morning a passing Piegan party discovered the camp. Some of its members wanted to attack and destroy the white intruders. But an old warrior, Pretty Woman, pointed to the flag as a symbol of the white man's peaceful intentions. He prevailed upon his comrades to receive these strangers as friends.

Berger calmly explained his mission to the Indian warriors in their own tongue and induced them to guide him to their village. At the winter encampment he persuaded about one hundred Piegans to accompany him to Fort Union to meet his great chief. Upon their arrival McKenzie welcomed the Indians with liberal presents and promised to build a trading post in their country the following fall.[20]

McKenzie succeeded in establishing peaceful relations with the warlike Piegans because he offered them a real Indian trade. The Indians themselves would collect the furs and barter them at the posts of his company. This adoption of the Canadian system by the Big Knives won the approval of the Indians. The Blackfoot chiefs told Major Sanford, Indian agent for the Upper Missouri tribes, "If you will send Traders into our Country we will protect them & treat them well; but for Trappers—Never."[21]

In the fall of 1831, Kenneth McKenzie sent James Kipp with forty-four men and a large keelboat loaded with trade goods up the Missouri. On the north bank of that river, at the mouth of the Marias, they set to work building the first American post in the Blackfoot country. The day after work began several hundred lodges of Piegans arrived, eager to open trade. With some difficulty Kipp persuaded them to withdraw, promising that the fort would be finished and ready for trade in seventy-five days. Promptly on the seventy-fifth day the Indians were back. They were astonished to find a completed fort—three large log buildings for quarters, stockhouses, and a trading room, surrounded

---

[20] Bradley, "Manuscript," *MHSC*, Vol. III, 202–203; Charles Larpenteur, *Forty Years a Fur Trader on the Upper Missouri*, I, 109–15; James Stuart, "Adventures on the Upper Missouri," Montana Historical Society *Contributions*, I, 84–85.

[21] François Chardon, *Chardon's Journal at Fort Clark, 1834–1839*, 253.

by a stockade twenty-five feet high, with loopholes for cannon and small arms. Kipp named it Fort Piegan, in honor of the first Blackfoot tribe to make peace with the Americans.

Kipp realized that if he was to win the trade of these Indians away from the Hudson's Bay Company, he had to demonstrate clearly his greater liberality. From a barrel of whisky he made two hundred gallons of Blackfoot rum and distributed it among the Indians. Never before had they seen "white men's water" flow so freely. For three days the entire Indian camp enjoyed a beautiful binge. When they sobered up, they beseiged the fort with their peltries. They were overjoyed to find that Kipp offered them considerably more goods in return for their furs than did their old friends, the "Northern White Men." In a few days Kipp obtained 6,450 pounds of beaver from which his company realized $46,000 the next spring.

During the winter a large force of Blood Indians besieged the fort, intent on destroying it and taking the furs that had been traded by the Piegans. For eleven days Kipp held his fire, hoping to conciliate the attackers and secure their trade. Then, with his supply of water nearly exhausted, Kipp charged a four-pound cannon heavily with grape-shot and fired it at a huge cottonwood tree growing near the fort. The thunder of this discharge and the shower of broken limbs and splintered wood that rained down from the tree frightened the Indians so that they fled in every direction.

Shortly thereafter two Blood chiefs came to the fort. They blamed Hudson's Bay Company agents for talking them into attacking Kipp's post. Clever Kipp reminded them that he had withheld his fire and convinced them of his good intentions. Then the Blood Indians brought him some three thousand buffalo robes which the Canadian traders would not take because they were too heavy for them to transport with profit.

When spring arrived and Kipp prepared to take the first winter's returns downriver, only two or three of his men (who had taken Indian wives) were willing to remain at the isolated post among the dread Blackfeet. Those men were too few to man the fort during the summer, so Kipp dismantled it before setting out for Fort Union in his loaded keelboat. Soon after the traders' departure, Blood or Assiniboin Indians burned Fort Piegan.[22]

In the fall of 1831 McKenzie negotiated a formal peace between the Blackfeet and the Assiniboins. The following summer Bull's Back Fat, head chief of the Blood Indians, and other prominent Blackfeet visited Fort Union. It was a memorable season, marked by the arrival of the first steamboat to make the long journey upriver from St. Louis. One of its passengers was the self-taught artist and Indian enthusiast, George Catlin. Catlin painted the earliest known portraits of Blackfoot Indians at Fort Union that summer. Thirteen in number, these portraits include likenesses of old Bull's Back Fat and his wife and grandchild. Catlin was greatly impressed by Eagle Ribs, a war leader who "stands here in the fort and deliberately boasts of eight scalps, which he says he has taken from the heads of trappers and traders with his own hand." Eagle Ribs was no idle boaster. That very fall he was sent westward from Fort Union with letters for Henry Vandenburgh, a principal clerk of the American Fur Company. While approaching the whites near Jefferson River, just east of the Rockies, Eagle Ribs' party was mistaken for hostile Indians and was fired upon. In the ensuing battle Vandenburgh was killed, his body stripped of flesh, and his bones thrown in the river. Eagle Ribs, the efficient killer, brought Vandenburgh's pistols back to Fort Union.[23]

Catlin's portraits reveal that some basic changes had taken place in Blackfoot dress since the days of Alexander Henry twenty years earlier. Men were wearing breechclouts. Women were wearing skin dresses with full, elbow-length sleeves. These dresses were tastefully embroidered with narrow bands of blue trade beads.

George Catlin's comments on the Blackfeet undoubtedly reflect the opinions of his trader informants at Fort Union in the

[22] Bradley, "Manuscript," *MHSC*, Vol. VIII, 244–50.
[23] Catlin, *Letters and Notes*, I, 39; James Carnegie (Earl of Southesk), *Saskatchewan and the Rocky Mountains*, 160–61.

summer of 1832. He called the Blackfeet "perhaps, the most powerful tribe of Indians on the Continent," who, "having been less traded with, and less seen by white men than most other tribes, are more imperfectly understood." Catlin estimated the Northern Blackfeet at 450 lodges, the Bloods at 450 lodges, the Piegans at 500 lodges, and the Small Robes (who were actually a large Piegan band) at 250 lodges, giving a total of 1,650 lodges, or (averaging 10 persons to a lodge) 16,500 persons. This figure is lower than Prince Maximilian's estimate of 18,000 to 20,000 persons made the following year.[24]

While Catlin was at Fort Union, McKenzie sent David Mitchell, a clerk of the American Fur Company, upriver to re-establish a trading post among the Blackfeet. Six miles above the mouth of the Marias, Mitchell's men built a new quadrangular fort some forty-seven paces on a side. It was defended by two blockhouses and several pieces of cannon. In honor of his superior, Mitchell named the new post Fort McKenzie.[25]

When Mitchell returned upriver in the summer of 1833, he was accompanied by the famous German scientist, Prince Maximilian zu Wied, and the latter's artist companion, Carl Bodmer. The keelboat trip from Fort Union to Fort McKenzie required thirty-four days. En route they passed the mouth of Milk River, then considered the western boundary of the Assiniboin tribe and the eastern boundary of the allied Blackfoot and Gros Ventre tribes. At the mouth of Arrow River they found some 260 lodges, housing practically the entire Gros Ventre tribe which, two years before had destroyed a Canadian trading post, killing nineteen persons, and which had fought a bitter battle with American traders in Pierre's Hole (present Wyoming) in July, 1832. As Mitchell's keelboat approached, the crew could see the American flag flying on a high pole near the principal chief's lodge. Yet so treacherous were the Gros Ventres considered that the traders were relieved when they got by their village without trouble.[26]

[24] Catlin, *Letters and Notes*, I, 59–60; Maximilian, *Travels*, II, 95.
[25] Maximilian, *Travels*, II, 91–92; Bradley, "Manuscript," *MHSC*, III, 204–206.

Maximilian and Bodmer spent more than a month at Fort McKenzie, in the heart of the Blackfoot country. During this period (August 9–September 14, 1833) all three Blackfoot tribes came in to trade. While Bodmer was busy making excellent water color portraits of many of the most influential chiefs and drawing a panoramic view of the great camp of the Piegans, the Prince recorded his observations of Blackfoot customs and of the conduct of the trade at Fort McKenzie.

Mitchell was making definite progress wooing the Blackfoot trade away from the Hudson's Bay Company. At the conclusion of a feast given by the Northern Blackfoot chief Iron Shirt, that leader gave Mitchell the scarlet uniform with blue facings and yellow lace which he had received from the "Northern White Men." Later Mitchell gave the Piegan leader, Bear Chief, a handsome uniform, a red felt hat ornamented with feathers, and a new double-barreled percussion gun, to let the other chiefs see "how the American Fur Company distinguished its faithful friends."

Prince Maximilian was the first white observer to describe the Blackfoot men's societies. He named seven of these fraternities and noted that they were age-graded. That is, young men purchased membership in the Mosquito Society and gradually progressed through the other societies to the Bull Society of elderly men. Each society had its peculiar regalia, songs, and dances. All societies except the Mosquitos and Bulls assumed responsibilities for keeping order in the camp. He also witnessed and briefly described the dramatic reinactment of the driving of buffalo into a pound by the colorfully garbed members of the Women's Society.

Maximilian was disappointed in the information he obtained about Blackfoot religion, explaining, "Mr. Berger the interpreter, who was otherwise well acquainted with the Blackfoot Indians, could not give me any information respecting their religious ideas, further than that they worship the sun."[27]

26 Maximilian, *Travels*, II, 46, 71–76.
27 *Ibid.*, 112–17, 122.

During their visit to Fort McKenzie the two Europeans had the exciting experience of witnessing an intertribal battle from an elevated position atop one of the buildings in the fort, which afforded them a bird's-eye view over the palisade at the lively action just outside the post.

At daybreak on the morning of August 28 the occupants of Fort McKenzie were awakened by sounds of gunfire. Ascending the rooftops they saw the whole prairie covered with Indians on foot and horseback. At first they feared the fort was being attacked. But soon they realized that the attackers, some six hundred Assiniboin and Cree Indians, were intent upon wiping out some eighteen or twenty lodges of Piegans camped just outside the fort. It was a little trading party whose members had been drinking and singing most of the night and had fallen into a deep sleep toward morning. Before the luckless Piegans could retreat to safety inside the fort, their surprise attackers ripped open their lodges with knives, discharged their guns and arrows, and killed or wounded a number of men, women, and children.

At the outset of this action the Piegans sent a messenger to their main camp about eight or ten miles distant. Soon reinforcements came "galloping in groups, from three to twenty together, their horses covered with foam, and they themselves in their finest apparel, with all kinds of ornaments and arms, bows and quivers on their backs, guns in their hands, furnished with their medicines, with feathers on their heads; some had splendid crowns of black and white eagles' feathers, and a large hood of feathers hanging down behind . . . the upper part of their bodies partly naked . . . and carrying shields adorned with feathers and pieces of coloured cloth." Soon the little force of Piegan defenders grew to five hundred or more. Then, ably assisted by Mitchell and some of the white hunters from the fort, they pushed the enemy back to the Marias. A fire fight continued until, as evening approached, the Assiniboins and Crees withdrew toward the Bearpaws.

Maximilian watched the Piegans wreak their vengeance upon the body of an enemy killed near the fort. "The men fired their guns at it; the women and children beat it with clubs, and pelted it with stones, the furey of the latter was particularly directed against the privy parts." The Prince wanted to obtain the dead man's skull for his collection, but "before I could obtain my wish, not a trace of the head was to be seen."

After the battle, the Piegans returned to the fort seeking treatment for their wounded. They took Mitchell by the hand and "welcomed him as their friend and ally." Old Bear Chief bragged that "no ball had touched him; doubtless because Mr. Bodmer had taken his portrait a few days before."[28]

On the basis of his own eyewitness recollections of this battle, Carl Bodmer made a very realistic drawing of the attack on the small Piegan camp outside Fort McKenzie on that morning of August 28, 1833. It depicts vividly the ferocity of the action and the variety of weapons employed—bows and arrows, trade guns, and several types of knives and war clubs.

This battle brought to an end the Piegan-Assiniboin peace Mc-Kenzie had negotiated at Fort Union less than two years before. But the assistance Mitchell and his men gave to the Piegans in the fight further cemented their friendship with the Big Knife traders. Fearing the defection of the Piegans, the Hudson's Bay Company had built Piegan Post on Bow River that very summer. They hoped its more southerly location would attract the Piegans and prevent the more northerly Blackfoot tribes from carrying their furs south to trade with the Americans on the Missouri. But the Canadians abandoned this post after five months' trial because of the restlessness of the Indians and the necessity for hauling goods overland from the Bow to the North Saskatchewan. So the Hudson's Bay Company traders returned to old Rocky Mountain House.[29]

Although the Hudson's Bay Company had absorbed its rival North West Company in 1821 and held a monopoly of the Indian trade on the Canadian plains, geography favored its American rivals. The "Northern White Men" relied upon canoes to carry

---

[28] *Ibid.*, II, 146–53.
[29] MacInnes, *In the Shadow of the Rockies*, 41.

Great camp of 400 Piegan lodges near Fort McKensie, August 31, 1833. From a drawing by Karl Bodmer.

their furs eastward. They confined their trade primarily to the finer furs. It did not pay for them to take heavy buffalo robes of little value on their long canoe trips. The Americans, on the other hand, found the broad Missouri River an open highway down which they could transport large boatloads of bulky buffalo robes as well as the more precious furs. They knew the Blackfeet were indifferent beaver hunters but would provide large numbers of buffalo robes. As the demand for beaver declined markedly after the invention of the silk hat in the early thirties, trade in buffalo robes increased, and the buffalo robe became the standard of value in the Blackfoot trade with the Big Knives. In 1834–35 the winter's trade at Fort McKenzie amounted to 9,000 buffalo robes and only 1,020 beaver pelts, together with 40 of otter, 2,800 muskrat, 180 wolves, 200 red foxes, 1,500 prairie dogs, 19 bears, and 390 buffalo tongues.[30]

For fourteen years the American Fur Company traded with the Northern Blackfeet and Blood Indians as well as with their old friends, the Piegans, at Fort McKenzie. During this period only four of their men were killed by the Indians, and they may have deserved their fate because of their own misconduct.[31]

Establishment of regular trading relationships with the Big Knives on the Missouri encouraged a southward shift of the Blackfoot tribes, especially the Piegans. According to Alexander Culbertson, a trader who knew them well, the Piegans usually summered near the Three Forks of the Missouri and wintered on Sun River. They ranged over the intervening country, frequently visiting the Prickly Pear Valley east of present-day Helena. They numbered 550 lodges. At that time the Blood Indians (some 500 lodges) and the Northern Blackfeet (500 lodges) usually wintered north of the international line on Belly River and summered on the Saskatchewan.[32]

In the year 1833 a brilliant display of falling stars and a total

[30] Larpenteur, *Forty Years a Fur Trader*, I, 79.
[31] Anne McDonnell (ed.), "The Fort Benton Journal, 1854–1855 and Fort Sarpy Journal, 1855–1856," Montana Historical Society *Contributions*, Vol. X, 300. (Hereafter referred to as McDonnell, "Fort Benton Journal," *MHSC*.)
[32] Bradley, "Manuscript," *MHSC*, Vol. VIII, 153.

eclipse of the sun were observed at Fort McKenzie. The Indians viewed these strange phenomena as forerunners of some great catastrophe.[33] Four years later this dire prophecy seemed to come true when the Blackfoot tribes were again humbled by a devastating smallpox plague. The epidemic originated in infected clothing carelessly placed aboard the American Fur Company's steamer in St. Louis. It spread to some of the passengers and eventually to all of the Upper Missouri tribes north of the Sioux. At the mouth of the Little Missouri a Blackfoot Indian en route home boarded the steamboat. At Fort Union he changed to the company's keelboat bound for Fort McKenzie with supplies and goods for the Blackfoot trade. On the way upriver this man and two other passengers broke out with smallpox. Informed of the approach of this disease-ridden boat, Alexander Culbertson, then in charge at Fort McKenzie, thought it prudent to halt its progress at the mouth of the Judith until the disease abated and cold weather set in. But the large camp of some five hundred lodges of Piegans and Blood Indians awaiting the arrival of the trade goods refused to listen to Culbertson's warning about the fatal disease. They threatened to bring the boat to the fort themselves if he wouldn't do so. So Culbertson ordered the keelboat to proceed to Fort McKenzie, where two of its infected passengers died shortly thereafter.

The Indians insisted on opening trade as usual. When they finished trading, they departed. Disease swept the fort, killing twenty-six Indian women and a white man. Ten days after they left the fort, smallpox began to break out among the Piegans and Blood Indians. Terrified at the sight of their healthy kinsmen wasting away with corruption, some of them committed suicide at the first symptoms of the disease by stabbing themselves or throwing themselves into streams. That fall Culbertson visited a Piegan camp of about sixty lodges in which two old women, too feeble to travel, were the sole survivors. At the junction of the Belly and St. Mary rivers the mortality was so high among the Bloods and Northern Blackfeet that they named the place

[33] *Ibid.*, Vol. VIII, 134.

"The Grave Yard." Before the plague abated some six thousand persons, or nearly two-thirds of the entire Blackfoot population, succumbed. Old people who had survived the smallpox epidemic of 1781 generally weathered this one. Many of the strong, impatient young men who would not heed Culbertson's warnings were victims. Nevertheless, unlike the Mandans farther down the Missouri, who were the hardest hit of all the Northern Plains tribes, Blackfoot survivors did not blame the whites for their misfortune.[34]

Culbertson claimed that following this epidemic and the dispersal of the Indians into different bands, knowledge of relationships sometimes was lost to the young, so that marriages took place between first cousins and even brothers and sisters. Yet so rapidly did the Blackfeet recover population-wise that seventeen years after the terrific loss Edwin T. Denig, an intelligent and experienced trader, estimated their numbers were only one-third less than they had been before the smallpox epidemic.[35]

The volume of Indian trade at Fort McKenzie continued to increase. In the winter after the smallpox epidemic ten thousand buffalo robes were traded. Robes belonging to victims of the plague may have been included in this number. The trade steadily increased to about twenty-one thousand robes by 1841. Stimulated by desire for the white man's attractive trade goods, Indian hunters were killing more buffalo and their womenfolk were dressing more robes for market.[36]

Blackfoot relations with American traders remained friendly until 1844. That January a passing war party requested and was refused admittance to Fort McKenzie. Incensed by this treatment, the red warriors killed a pig belonging to the fort. When men from the fort pursued the Indians, the Blackfeet ambushed and killed one of their number. Vowing vengeance, François Chardon and Alexander Harvey loaded the fort cannon with

[34] *Ibid.*, Vol. III, 221–26; Chardon, *Journal*, 394–95.

[35] Bradley, "Manuscript," *MHSC*, Vol. III, 232–33; Denig, "Indian Tribes of the Upper Missouri," Bureau of American Ethnology, *Forty-sixth Annual Report*, 625.

[36] Bradley, "Manuscript," *MHSC*, Vol. III, 226, 233.

about 150 lead bullets, aimed it at the approach to the main gate, and waited for the next Indian trading party. In mid-February a large band of Piegans brought robes to trade. When they assembled in front of the gate to await admittance, Harvey fired the cannon, killing ten or more of the Indians and wounding many others, among them women and children. The fort gates were opened and some members of the garrison rushed out upon the panic-stricken Piegans. Several of the wounded were overtaken and killed. After the remaining Indians dispersed, the whites scalped the fallen, some thirty victims, and celebrated with a scalp dance in the fort that night.[37]

This unwarranted cruelty on the part of the vengeful traders made Fort McKenzie untenable. Chardon secretly built a small new post downstream at the mouth of the Judith, burned Fort McKenzie, and moved to the new location, which was named after him. But Chardon's revenge virtually killed the Blackfoot trade. Instead of peaceful trading parties, hostile Indian groups stalked the neighborhood, killing horses and cattle belonging to the fort and occasionally murdering a member of the garrison who dared to expose himself to the Indians' fire. Not only was Fort Chardon virtually in a state of siege, but Blackfoot hostility was extended to Fort Union, where two men were killed and horses driven off.[38]

The following summer the American Fur Company sent one of its most able leaders upriver to try to recover their Blackfoot trade. Alexander Culbertson had had more than a decade of successful experience in fair dealing with these Indians. He was married to a woman from one of the most prominent Blood Indian families. Culbertson abandoned Fort Chardon and built a new post on the south side of the Missouri, about three miles upriver from the present Fort Benton. He named it Fort Lewis in honor of Captain Meriwether Lewis, leader of the first Americans to meet Blackfoot Indians four decades before. Culbertson

[37] *Ibid.*, Vol. III, 235–37; Paul Kane, *Wanderings of an Artist Among the Indians of North America*, 296–98.
[38] Bradley, "Manuscript," *MHSC*, Vol. III, 237–38.

diplomatically sent presents and tobacco, at the same time inviting the chiefs of the Blackfoot tribes to come to Fort Lewis to
trade. His efforts bore fruit, and a brisk trade resulted. In 1846
the Indians brought to Fort Lewis some twenty-one thousand
buffalo robes, in addition to beaver, wolf, and fox skins.[39]

At the request of the Indians, who wished to camp in the
well-timbered valley of the Teton while trading at the fort and
who sometimes found crossing the ice-filled Missouri impossible
in the spring, Culbertson in the spring of 1847 moved Fort Lewis
to a site three miles downriver on the north bank. There, 6 miles
above the mouth of the Teton and 2,415 miles up the Missouri
from St. Louis, was located Fort Clay, soon to be renamed Fort
Benton and destined to become the most important trading center in Montana. It was a quadrangular structure with bastions at
the alternate angles. Inside the fort were the chief factor's house,
the homes of his crew, the storage and warehouses, and a corral.
When Governor Isaac I. Stevens visited Fort Benton in the summer of 1853, he described it as "smaller than Fort Union. Its
front is made of wood, and the other sides of adobe or unburned
brick. It usually contains about a dozen men and the families of
several of them."[40]

In the forties the American Fur Company had competition
from other companies for the Blackfoot trade. Fort Cotton, operated by Fox Livingstone and Company, opened for business on
the site of old Fort Lewis in 1842, but its life was short. Fort
Campbell was built by Harvey, Primeau and Company a short
distance above Fort Benton in 1846. In the winter of 1856 trade
was so good that Fort Benton obtained more than fifteen hundred
packs of buffalo robes and disposed of most of its desirable trade
goods before the end of February. That year the opposition post
also did a good business, and the rival traders were on friendly
terms.[41]

[39] *Ibid.*, Vol. III, 242–44.
[40] *Ibid.*, Vol. III, 151–52, 243–44; Stevens, "Isaac I. Stevens' Narrative of
1853–1855," in *Pacific Railroad Report of Exploration*, XII, 102 (Hereafter referred to as Stevens, "Narrative," *PRR*.)
[41] McDonnell, "Fort Benton Journal," *MHSC*, Vol. X, 64–70.

Competition for their furs benefited the Indians. They could obtain more in return for their buffalo robes. In the 1840's a robe brought twenty-five loads of ammunition, a gallon kettle, three knives, or one and one-half yards of calico. A two-and-one-half-point blanket cost the Indian three robes, a trade gun, ten robes.[42] The Blackfeet brought their prime robes to the posts in winter and early spring. Company employees baled them in crude presses into packs of about one hundred pounds or ten robes each. Traders shipped them by keelboat or flatboat to Fort Union and by flatboat or steamboat from there to St. Louis. In the east buffalo robes were used for heavy overcoats and for sleigh and carriage robes.

To encourage the Indians to bring in more and more buffalo robes, the traders offered a greater variety of wares. The great manufacturing centers of Europe and eastern America supplied the growing wants of the Indians. There were bells and mirrors from Leipzig, clay pipes from Cologne, beads from Venice, calico and other cloths from France, woolen goods and firearms from England, clothing and knives from New York and vicinity, shell ornaments from the Bahamas and the West Coast, guns from Pennsylvania, and powder and shot from St. Louis. An inventory of goods remaining after the spring trade at Fort Benton in 1851 shows the great variety of goods offered the discriminating Indian in the drygoods and hardware fields. Among the items listed were twenty-two kinds of yard goods (some in several colors), fourteen types or colors of blankets, three kinds of shawls, four kinds of handkerchiefs, four types of men's headgear, twenty-one kinds of men's or boys' coats or overcoats, and at least eight varieties of beads (some in several colors). There were also four sizes of tin kettles, six kinds of knives, four kinds of axes (including one termed "battle axes"), four varieties of guns and all the parts needed to keep them in repair, ready-made ammunition, and both molds and lead for making one's own shot. There were also the old favorites, carrot and twist tobacco.[43]

[42] Bradley, "Manuscript," *MHSC*, Vol. II, 203–204.
[43] McDonnell, "Fort Benton Journal," *MHSC*, Vol. X, 199–205.

Although the United States prohibited the use of liquor in the Indian trade in 1834, authorities made little effort to prevent its being transported into the Indian country. In the remote Blackfoot country there was no real obstacle to its sale. American traders justified liquor as a necessity if they were to compete successfully with the Hudson's Bay Company. In 1845 a disgruntled employee, Alexander Harvey, reported to the government the American Fur Company's use of liquor in the Indian trade. The company was fined $12,000. For a number of years thereafter it introduced no liquor into the Indian country.[44]

During the late thirties and the forties the Big Knives on the Missouri gained the lion's share of the Blackfoot trade, nearly monopolizing the trade of some of the southernmost Piegan bands. The Northern Blackfeet and Blood Indians came south to trade their buffalo robes and traveled north to Edmonton to dispose of many of their small furs to the Hudson's Bay Company.

By the 1850's the Blackfoot tribes had been trading directly with whites for three-quarters of a century. They had become completely dependent upon the traders for many articles which they now considered necessities, such as guns and ammunition, metal tools, and utensils. Undoubtedly, these new articles saved the Indians much labor. The iron arrowpoint provides a good example. The inventory value of an iron arrowpoint at Fort Benton was one and one-half cents. A single dressed buffalo robe brought the Indian dozens of them. They were cheap compared with the time and patience required to chip arrowpoints from stone. Is it any wonder that elderly Indians born in the 1850's could not remember the use of stone arrowheads by their tribe? Indeed they did not know how they were made. The metal kettle offers another example. Why should Indians continue to fashion breakable cooking pots of clay when a trade kettle that could be banged about over the plains for years without damage could be obtained from the trader in exchange for a single buffalo robe?

[44] Bradley, "Manuscript," *MHSC*, Vol. III, 246.

By 1850 white men were still few in the Blackfoot country. All were employed in the fur trade. There were no white women. The traders commonly found wives among the Indians. Indian girls looked upon the traders as good catches because they treated their wives well. Most of the leading traders had no desire to make permanent homes in the Indian country. After an active business life in the wilderness they retired to the white settlements in the Middle West to spend their remaining years. Some of them took their Indian wives and mixed-blood children with them. Many of the lesser employees remained in the country of their Indian wives.

Fur traders were businessmen intent on exploiting the rich resources of animal life. Many of them were able, courageous, and honorable men. Some were wild, adventurous fellows, stifled by the routine of civilized life, who preferred the greater freedom and excitement of life in the Indian country. In any case, the fur traders were not in any real sense missionaries of civilization to the Indians. Few of them had any serious interest in the future welfare of the Indians. By encouraging the Indians to slaughter many more buffalo than they needed for their own subsistence, the traders helped to hasten the extermination of the Indian's primary resource. Some wise whites could foresee the eventual disappearance of the buffalo from the plains as early as the 1830's, but it was not in the interest of the traders to discourage Indian slaughter of these animals nor to propose any conservation program.

Decades of association with white traders had taught the Blackfeet little of the real nature of that larger white man's civilization of which the fur traders were but a small part. The presence of fur traders among them did little to prepare the Indians for the full impact of white civilization which was to come when the land-hungry settlers began to arrive a few years later.

4: The Staff of Life

IN THE MIDDLE of the nineteenth century Blackfoot life was a remarkable blend of traditional Indian customs modified by white influences. It was a way of life that would have been impossible without the European horse and the white man's trade goods. Nevertheless, Blackfoot economy was still based primarily upon buffalo hunting, as it had been in prehistoric times. Indeed, after American traders began to accept buffalo robes in trade, Blackfoot hunters had a greater incentive for killing buffalo than ever before. Then the buffalo not only furnished the Indians' subsistence but indirectly enabled them to obtain luxuries they never dreamed of before the coming of Napikwan.

Fortunately, buffalo were still very plentiful in the Blackfoot country. Governor Isaac I. Stevens, who explored westward up the Missouri Valley in 1853, noted that the "quantity of buffalo" between Fort Union and the Rocky Mountains was "almost unbelievable." In September of that year Lieutenant Mullen found "innumerable herds of buffalo" feeding in the Judith Basin south of the Missouri, while John Mix Stanley saw "numerous herds" of them grazing in the vicinity of the Sweetgrass Hills on Milk River. At that time Alexander Culbertson regarded "the entire country of the Blackfoot" as "perhaps the best Buffalo Country in the N.W."[1]

[1] Stevens, "Narrative," *PRR*, 123, 239; Stevens, "Report on Mr. J. M. Stanley's Visit to the Piegan Camp at the Cypress Mountains," in *Pacific Railroad Report of Explorations*, I, 447 Alexander Culbertson to Isaac I. Stevens, *ca.* 1853, Indian Office Records.

A century ago Alfred Vaughan aptly termed the buffalo the Blackfoot Indians' "staff of life."[2] Surely the great number and variety of uses for that animal justified that characterization.

Buffalo supplied a tasty, easily digested, nourishing, year-round food for Indians of all ages. Blackfoot mothers gave their infants choice pieces of meat to suck. Toothless old people sucked the juices in the same way. Many Indians preferred the tongue and ribs. A soup made from buffalo fat and berries mixed with buffalo blood was a favorite dessert at Blackfoot feasts. Several parts of the animal were devoured during butchering, without benefit of cookery. On a buffalo hunt near Fort Union in the summer of 1843 the famous naturalist John James Audubon was appalled when the handsome, refined Blood Indian wife of Alexander Culbertson requested that the skull of a fallen beast be broken open so that she could eat its brains.[3] She was just following the custom of her people, who also enjoyed raw buffalo liver, kidneys, soft nose gristle, and marrow from the leg bones. Older men ate the raw testicles with relish, claiming this food made them healthy and virile. The cheeselike contents of the intestines of newborn calves killed in the spring was a delicacy to the aged of both sexes.

Fresh buffalo meat was cooked by roasting or boiling. Ribs usually were roasted on coals or on wooden spits. A dish known as Crow-guts was prepared by cleaning a section of the small intestine, turning it fat side in and stuffing it with a long, thin strip of meat, then roasting it. The intestine of a large buffalo cow or bull was cleaned, one end tied, filled with blood, and the other end tied. After it was boiled in water, pieces were cut off like sausage. Marrow fat was boiled. When the water cooled and the fat rose to the surface, it was skimmed off and stored in buffalo-skin sacks.

When meat was plentiful, large quantities of the lean flesh were cut into long, thin strips and dried in the sun on racks of poles. The dried meat was packed in buffalo rawhide envelopes

[2] Reports of the Commissioner of Indian Affairs, 1858, 435.
[3] Maria Audubon (ed.), *Audubon and his Journals*, II, 111.

known as parfleches. Layers of the dried meat were separated by layers of uncooked back fat, wild peppermint, and berries. After a successful fall hunt dried meat was made into pemmican. It was cooked, pounded into small bits with a stone hammer, and mixed with boiled marrow grease. Sometimes mashed pits and pulp of dried sarvis berries or chokecherries were added to make a berry pemmican. The pemmican was stored in bags made from the skins of unborn buffalo calves.

In hard winters when supplies of dried meat and pemmican were exhausted and other food was not available, even the grease-soaked pemmican sacks were eaten. The white under-scrapings of buffalo hides also were softened in boiled water into a pasty food which tasted something like boiled potatoes.

The Blackfoot Indians in the middle of the nineteenth century found more varied uses for buffalo rawhide than had their ancestors in prehistoric times. In earlier times they had made many of their containers of soft skin. The acquisition of sharp, steel trade knives enabled women to cut tough rawhide with greater ease than could their forebears with their stone knives. The long-wearing, waterproof qualities of buffalo rawhide made it the preferred material for containers in which to transport and store food, clothing, and camp equipment. The flexibility and durability of rawhide made it useful for men's and women's belts and for repairing and reinforcing the bottoms of worn, soft-soled moccasins. Most horsegear was also of rawhide—hobbles, picket lines, bridles, hackamores, martingales, cruppers, whip lashes, saddle and travois rigging straps, shoes for sore-footed horses, and portable watering troughs. Indians took advantage of the fact that green rawhide shrinks as it dries by using it to bind articles made of two or more pieces securely together. The wet rawhide was used to secure the heads and handles of mauls, berry mashers, and war clubs. After the rawhide dried, the parts were held together as firmly as if they had been nailed or screwed in place. The same principle was employed in covering wooden frame saddles with wet rawhide. Thick shields were made from the hide of the bull's neck.

Women who dressed thousands of robes for the fur trade each year also prepared hairy buffalo robes for the winter overclothing and bedding of their own families. Robes were cut up to make hair-lined mittens, winter caps with ear flaps, winter moccasins, and ceremonial headdresses.

Soft-dressed buffalo skins without the hair were used for lodge covers and linings, for pad saddles, and for winding sheets for the dead. The smoke-softened upper portions of old, worn lodge covers were salvaged, cut up, and reused for breechclouts and items of winter clothing—men's and boys' shirts, women's and girls' dresses, and leggings for both sexes. The thinner skins of buffalo calves were made into tobacco pouches and winter underpants worn by girls and women.

Buffalo horns made practical powder flasks for Blackfoot warriors. Horns were also fashioned into spoons, cups, and ladles. The long, shaggy hair of the head, beard, and shoulders was braided into rope halters and bridles. Hair supplied the soft stuffing for pad saddles and balls used in games. Hair ornaments hung from lodges, headdresses, and war clubs. The buffalo's tail also was used for tipi ornaments. Mounted on a stick, the tail served as a fly brush. Buffalo hoofs strung on rawhide cords made noisy rattles. The scrotum of a bull provided a durable stirrup cover. The Blackfoot Indians derived their best glue from a bull's phallus, cut into small pieces and boiled.

No less useful were many of the internal parts of this animal. Buffalo sinew supplied thread for sewing and a strong, flat cord for binding heads and feathers to arrowshafts. Bow strings and bow backings were both of twisted bull sinew. The brains, liver, and fat were rubbed into hides to soften them during the skin-dressing process. Buffalo fat also was used to polish stone tobacco pipes and to mix with earth pigments to provide an oily base for paints. A yellow paint could be obtained from the buffalo's gallstone. Water buckets were made from the paunch, and the bladder was used as a bag for marrow grease.

The boss rib of a buffalo made a serviceable tool for straightening arrowshafts. A series of curved rib bones furnished the runners for a boy's sled. Pieces of ribbone were fashioned into gambling dice. Wedge-shaped pieces of the porous hipbone or shoulder blade made useful paint brushes. A buffalo skull was placed on the altar in the tribal sun dance. Some women dehaired rawhide rope by pulling the rope back and forth through the eye sockets of a buffalo skull.

Many buffalo cows killed in early spring contained the almost fully developed embryos of calves. Indian women cut off the heads of these unborn calves and used the entire body skin for berry, pemmican, and tobacco sacks. Finally, dried buffalo dung provided a practical substitute for firewood when Indians were camped on the open plains at a distance from firewood.

Most of these articles were by-products of the buffalo chase. Blackfoot Indians hunted buffalo for food and hides. The great number of animals killed provided ample supplies of the materials required to make the many other items listed above. Although buffalo were hunted throughout the year, the Indians recognized seasonal differences in the quality of the meat and the utility of the hides. Throughout most of the year the meat of bulls was tough and unpalatable compared with that of cows. So the Blackfeet preferred to kill cows for food except during the early summer months when bulls were prime. They recognized the approach of the bull-hunting season when they saw the yellow flowers of "tooth grass." During the warm summer months, when buffalo hair was short, skins were taken for tipi covers and the numerous other articles made from soft-dressed skins or rawhide. Cows were at their best in the fall. This was the period of intensive hunting to secure winter meat supplies. It was only during the cold months, from November through February, that buffalo hair was long. That was the season for killing buffalo to obtain robes for the American traders and for Indian use in making bedding and winter clothing. Calves, generally born in May, were hunted soon thereafter.

Although their pedestrian ancestors surrounded buffalo on the open plains in the warmer months, Blackfoot horsemen rarely employed the mounted surround. They preferred the chase, a straightaway rush by mounted men. Each hunter singled out an animal in the herd, rode along side it, and killed it at close range, then sped on to another buffalo and killed it in the same way. The chase took full advantage of the ability of a well-trained, long-winded buffalo horse to run faster than the buffalo and to bring its rider close to his prey for a shot or series of shots at point-blank range.

Because it was difficult to reload a muzzle-loading trade gun while riding a fast-moving horse, the great majority of Blackfoot hunters continued to employ the primitive bow and arrow in the buffalo chase. Another factor also favored the retention of the bow and arrow. After the chase a man could go over the field and claim the animals he had killed by identifying his arrows. How could anyone determine which hunter had killed a buffalo with a bullet? The bows of these mounted hunters were much shorter than those of their pedestrian ancestors. A bow not much over three feet long could be much more easily managed by a mounted hunter than the prehistoric bow which was nearly two feet longer. The quiver, slung at the rider's back, generally contained twenty or more sharp, iron-headed arrows. Flint arrowheads, those relics of the stone age, became obsolete several generations earlier. A few men preferred to hunt buffalo with short-poled, iron-headed lances.

The key to success in the chase was the hunter's carefully selected and thoroughly trained buffalo horse. A good buffalo horse possessed a rare combination of qualities not required of an ordinary riding horse or pack animal. It had to be fast and long-winded—able to retain speed over a distance of several miles. It had to be alert—able to respond instantly to the rider's commands or to act properly on its own initiative. It had to possess courage and agility—a willingness to move in close to the buffalo and the ability to avoid contact with the larger animal and to keep clear of its horns. It had to be sure of foot to be able to run swiftly over uneven ground without stumbling. Usually the hunter chose the horse he wished to train for buffalo hunting on the basis of its proven swiftness and alertness. Its courage

77

could only be determined through experience in chasing buffalo. Some horses never overcame their fear of buffalo and so were useless in the chase. In any case, it required patient practice and use of the whip to train a horse to run close beside a buffalo. But eventually a courageous horse learned to follow the buffalo, move alongside, and do its work with little urging from its rider, leaving the latter free to concentrate upon making his kill. A well-trained buffalo horse would turn as the rider shifted his weight to one side or pressed one knee against his ribs. Most men selected horses three or four years old to train for buffalo hunting. A few of these animals were mares. Only wealthy Indians who owned several buffalo horses could afford to trade or give one of them away. A buffalo runner of known ability was worth several common riding horses or pack animals.

Hunters treated their buffalo runners with great care. They warned boys not to ride or molest them. Before a hunt the owner's wife prepared his horse for him. Unless he preferred to ride bareback, she placed a light, hair-stuffed pad saddle on its back and carefully adjusted its girth. Many hunters preferred to use a pad saddle because it added little weight, yet provided a firm seat and bracing for their feet in the stirrups, permitting a steadier aim than was possible from a barebacked horse. The hunter usually left camp riding a common horse and leading his buffalo runner in order to save its strength for the chase. He never packed butchered buffalo home on his prized buffalo runner. When he returned from the chase, his wife took his horse to a near-by stream, threw water on it, and rubbed it down. Some men dashed water on their buffalo horses every morning and evening to toughen them and prepare them for hard winters.

The bloody business of killing and butchering buffalo was an old-clothes function. Generally hunters wore leggings, a breechclout, moccasins, and a shirt with short sleeves which would not get in the way or become bloodied in the process of butchering. Whether of buckskin or trade cloth, these garments were undecorated.

The hunting party moved cautiously toward the herd of buffalo their scouts had located. They approached from downwind to prevent their prey from catching human scent and taking alarm. If the terrain permitted, they liked to approach from behind a hill or from the mouth of a coulee where the hunters could be concealed from the sight of the buffalo until they were nearly upon them. When they were as close to the buffalo as they could get without the game's being aware of their presence, the hunters dismounted from their common horses and left them in the hands of the women or boys, who remained in concealment with the pack animals. Quickly they mounted their buffalo runners. Their leader lined the hunters up to give them an equal chance. At a signal from him they whipped their horses into a run. Each hunter was eager to be the first to make a kill. Sometimes they approached the game in two groups. The righthanded bowmen rode along the right side of the herd and the lefthanded bowmen and the lancers rode on the left.

No time was lost once the buffalo became aware of the approaching hunters and started to run in the opposite direction. Healthy cows could run faster than bulls. In a small running herd the cows generally took the lead, followed by the bulls, which, in turn, were trailed by the calves. Except in the early summer when the bulls were prime, Blackfoot hunters who were confident of the speed of their mounts by-passed the running bulls to get to the choice cows. The righthanded bowman approached the buffalo he had singled out for slaughter from its right side, brought his horse close, fitted an arrow to his bow, and aimed at the vital spot immediately behind the foreleg. He shot his arrow without sighting, generally with his bow held a little off vertical, the top tilted to his right. However, each hunter used the bow position and arrow release easiest for him.

As the arrow left the bow the trained buffalo horse swerved away from its quarry, running in close again to allow the rider another shot if it was needed to bring down the buffalo. Then the hunter quickly drew another arrow from the quiver opening behind his left shoulder, fitted it to his bow, and shot again. Usually more than one arrow was needed to fell a buffalo.

On the run the hunter carried the long end of his bridle rope coiled and tucked closely under his belt. If he should be thrown but not badly hurt or shaken up, he could grab the free end of this long line as it paid out on the ground and retrieve his horse, perhaps in time to remount and continue the chase.

Usually the chase lasted until the running herd outdistanced the pursuing hunters. Four or five buffalo cows was about the greatest number a good bowman riding a fine horse could dispatch on a single chase. Most hunters rarely killed more than two buffalo. A man riding an inferior horse had to be satisfied with killing the slower-running bulls.

Boys of ten years or older, mounted on frisky colts, rode after the calves left in the wake of a running herd. They imitated the hunting techniques of their elders, riding in close and shooting the calves with bow and arrow. In this way they gained experience in buffalo hunting, so that by the time they reached their middle teens they had sufficient confidence and skill to chase adult buffalo with the men.

The chase was not without its dangers. Sometimes horses stumbled on uneven ground, stepped into badger holes, or were gored by wounded bulls. Riders were thrown and severely injured or killed. Generally, the less well trained his buffalo horse, the greater was the rider's chance of accident.

When the men finished their killing, their leader waved to the women to bring the pack animals. Meanwhile, the hunters located the buffalo they had killed by identifying their arrows in the fallen beasts. Using common butcher knives obtained from the traders, a man and wife could cut up a buffalo in about an hour. Surely butchering must have been more of a task for their prehistoric ancestors, who had to saw away at the carcass with knife blades of stone.

If the chase was made far from camp or if meat was very plentiful only the best parts of the buffalo were taken. This was known as "light butchering." But when food was scarce or winter approaching and large quantities of meat were needed, "heavy butchering" of the entire animal was more common.

Sometimes the number of buffalo killed and the number of pack animals available determined the method of butchering. A single horse could carry the fleshy parts obtained by "light butchering." The bones were left behind. However, it required two horses to carry the more than four hundred pounds of meat products obtained from a "heavily butchered" buffalo cow. One pack horse carried only the four quarters of the animal. The tendons of the forequarters were tied together with a piece of rawhide and slung from the pack saddle so that one quarter fell at each side of the pack animal. The hindquarters were carried in the same way. The buffalo hide was thrown over the back of the second pack horse, the two slabs of backfat folded over this, and the ribs tied with rawhide cord and added to the load. Then the two flanks were tied together and placed on the horse. A hole was punched in the boss ribs, through which a cord was passed and tied to the pack. Next the hipbones were packed and the neck cut away from the head, split open from the bottom, and spread out on top of the load. Finally the edges of the robe (on the bottom of the pack) were raised and tied together to hold the load securely. The hunter's wife generally wrapped the entrails in a separate bundle and carried them herself.

Owners of few horses rarely possessed a good buffalo horse. They tried to borrow trained buffalo runners from wealthy relatives or band chiefs. Wolf Plume, a Blood Indian, owned several buffalo runners. If a poor man asked him for the loan of a buffalo horse, he would tell him, "Go get that pinto [pointing to a particular horse in his herd] and another horse to pack with if you need it." If the borrower was kind and appreciative, he gave Wolf Plume a lot of the best meat from the buffalo he killed. If the man was selfish and offered no meat, Wolf Plume would not lend him a horse again. If the buffalo runner met with an accident while hunting on loan, and the borrower was known to be a reliable, earnest fellow, Wolf Plume told him, "That was nothing to be ashamed of. It was an accident. Young man, your body is worth more than that horse. Let's have no hard feelings." But if the borrower was an irresponsible fellow, Wolf Plume made him replace the lost horse.

81

Poor families without an able-bodied hunter in their group or unable to borrow buffalo horses were forced to rely upon the charity of the wealthy for their buffalo meat. When the chase took place near camp, some poor people took their dogs or scrawny horses out where the buffalo were butchered. There they generally could find successful hunters who would give them meat.

Once an old couple went out from camp hoping to receive some meat from the hunters. They found a young man lying beside a partly butchered buffalo. The old people threw water in his face and he did not move. Thinking he was dead, they started back to camp to tell the people. When they had gone a short distance, they turned around and saw the young man standing up butchering the animal. When he returned to camp, the old people told him they had brought him back to life. Then he reluctantly gave them some of the best cuts of his meat. Other people claimed the young fellow had played dead to avoid giving any of his meat to the aged couple. He was nicknamed Playing-Dead-Beside-the-Buffalo. This trait of stinginess was detested by the Blackfeet.

In summer, when all the bands of the tribe gathered prior to the sun dance, the head chief, through his announcer, declared the hunting regulation in force. All the Indians fully understood that this meant that anyone who sought to kill buffalo on his own before the tribal hunt was organized would be severely punished by members of the men's societies chosen to police the camp. Anyone caught disturbing the buffalo herds upon which the whole camp relied for their subsistence had his meat taken from him, his weapons broken, his clothing torn, and perhaps his riding gear destroyed by the police.[4]

Among those bands well supplied with horses, the traditional winter method of hunting buffalo by driving them into pounds or over high cliffs was falling into disuse. The last Piegan buffalo drive took place in the 1850's. The peculiar circumstances of

[4] John C. Ewers, "The Horse in Blackfoot Indian Culture," B.A.E. *Bulletin 159*, 153-66.

that event were recalled by some of my elderly informants in the 1940's.

The Piegan band called Never Laughs was camped on the Teton River a few miles north of the present town of Choteau, Montana. Their chief announced, "Now we are going to make a buffalo fall." They built a corral below a cliff and piled rocks at intervals in a great V-shape on the slope above the fall. Then they chose a man to lead the buffalo to the fall. But each time he lured them between the lines of rocks, they broke away before they reached the cliff edge. After this had occurred three times, Many Tail Feathers, a young man of that band, became angry. That night he made a fire and burned the corral.

That same night a war party started from the camp. Many Tail Feathers followed it. When he caught up with the warriors, their leader told him, "You go back home. Everyone is against you because you burned the corral."

Many Tail Feathers returned to Harm Hill overlooking the Teton River. He slept on top of the hill that night, seeking a vision. But no dream came. A second night he slept there. In his dream he saw two young boys coming toward him.

They asked, "Are you the man who saved all the women and children?"

He answered, "Yes." As the two boys walked away he saw them turn into buffalo.

On the third night he saw in his dream a group of people—men, women, and children. They were dancing toward him. Their leader wore a handsome red war bonnet. When he came near the leader asked, "Are you the man who saved all the buffalo by burning down the corral?"

Many Tail Feathers replied, "Yes."

Then the leader said, "We are the buffalo. For saving all our men, women, and children we thank you. I give you my bonnet—the red war bonnet." The group turned away, but before they disappeared they turned into buffalo. Two old scabby bulls running behind the rest turned back and gave Many Tail Feathers their power too.

After Many Tail Feathers returned to camp, he set about collecting materials to make the bonnet given him in his dream. It was a straight-up bonnet of eagle tail feathers, decorated with white weasel-skin pendants, red flannel, and brass tacks. It looked so handsome all the men wanted it, but Many Tail Feathers kept it for his own. He wore it on many successful war parties.

Doubtless, Piegan interest in the origin of this sacred red war bonnet helped to preserve this story of the last buffalo drive of their tribe.[5] Northern Blackfoot bands, poorer in horses than the Piegans, continued to make some use of the traditional buffalo pound until the early 1870's.

After their abandonment of the drive the Piegans hunted buffalo on horseback in winter when the ground was relatively free of snow. Broad-backed, solidly-built, mature horses were preferred for running buffalo over hard-frozen ground. These winter hunting horses had to be animals that did not mind the strong, cold wintry blasts, because the hunter's approach was always into the wind. In the winter season small hunting parties composed of several men and one or more women to cook for them made short excursions on which they located and killed as many buffalo as they could pack back to their band camp.

When snows were deep and meat was scarce, Blackfoot hunters reverted to techniques of stalking buffalo on foot which must have been practiced by their prehistoric ancestors long before horses were acquired by these tribes. However, these hunters afoot used firearms as well as bows and arrows.

When buffalo were plentiful, the Blackfeet hunted other hoofed mammals primarily for their hides and horns. In the brush along stream valleys footmen patiently stalked deer, antelope, and elk. They preferred noiseless arrows to noisy guns which would frighten the game away should they miss their first shot. The bighorn, or mountain sheep, then ranged through the Sun River badlands east of the Rockies. Indian hunters surrounded them and drove them into narrow defiles where they

[5] Ewers, "The Last Bison Drives of the Blackfoot Indians," *Journal* Washington Academy of Sciences, Vol. XXXIX, No. 11 (1949), 358–60.

were shot with guns or arrows. Men would lie in wait for mountain goats to pass along their well-marked trails. The hides of bighorn and antelope were prized for making fine dress clothing. Both bighorn and mountain goat horns were made into spoons and ladles. Elkhorns were used for war clubs, whip handles, and bows and cantles of pack saddles.

Adventurous young men hunted the powerful grizzly bear for its claws, which they proudly displayed in the form of necklaces. However, most Blackfoot Indians feared and avoided this dangerous beast. They regarded it as a sacred animal of great supernatural as well as physical power.

The smaller fur-bearing animals were caught in traps and deadfalls during the winter months when their furs were prime. As early as 1833 the American Fur Company was lending steel beaver traps to the Piegans to encourage them to trap these animals.[6] Mink, muskrat, and otter also were trapped. Wolves and foxes were caught in baited pits or deadfalls. The clever weasel, whose white winter skin was in demand for decorating headdresses and men's dress suits, was taken in an ingenious series of sinew snares arranged inside a cylindrical wooden frame. One end of the cylinder was placed over the weasel hole. When the curious animal poked his head out of the hole to see what was there it was caught in the snares.

The most highly prized bird of the Blackfoot country was the golden eagle. The striking black-tipped feathers of this bird were used for making bonnets and for decorating shields. Eagle catching was a dangerous feat performed only by men who claimed to possess secret power. On the top of a hill a warrior dug a pit about four feet deep, large enough for him to hide in. He roofed the pit with poles, twigs, and grass. After he placed a large piece of meat or a dead rabbit or other small mammal on the roof for bait, he entered the pit and rearranged the cover to conceal himself from view. There he waited until an eagle swooped down to take the meat. Then he quickly reached through a crevice in the roof, grasped the eagle by both feet, pulled it into the pit, and wrung its neck.

[6] Maximilian, *Travels*, II, 162.

In the spring, summer, and fall women and children gathered wild plant foods. They used a birchwood digging stick for collecting roots. The sharp lower end was hardened in a fire and the upper end was rounded so that a woman could bear upon it with her stomach muscles in loosening roots from the ground. In late spring they dug bitterroot, steeped the root in water until it swelled to several times its size, then boiled it for eating. In June or July they dug quantities of starchy prairie turnips which the Indians ate raw, roasted, or boiled, or dried for winter food. Near the mountains women dug camass bulbs during the same season. They roasted these sweet-tasting bulbs in pits about three feet deep. The pits were lined with flat stones, grass, and leaves, filled with camass bulbs, then covered with earth. A fire was built on top, and the bulbs were thoroughly baked for about three days.

Women and children gathered sarvis berries in midsummer. They beat the bushes with sticks, causing the berries to fall on robes or blankets spread out on the ground. Sarvis berries were eaten raw or cooked in soups and stews. They also were dried and stored in sacks made from the skins of unborn buffalo calves. In September or October the women and children collected chokecherries, which were abundant in the stream valleys of the foothills. They were a favorite flavoring for soups. Large quantities of them were laid on hides, dried in the sun, pounded, and used as an ingredient in pemmican. After the first frost, buffalo berries (also known as bullberries) were gathered from their thorny, silver-leafed bushes. They were eaten fresh or were dried for winter consumption. When berries were ripe and juicy, the Blackfeet sometimes mashed them with a stick in a buffalo horn and drank the juice from the horn.

In summer or winter children loved to suck the sweet inner bark of the cottonwood trees, which were plentiful in the river valleys.

Some flesh foods were taboo to many, though not all, Blackfoot Indians. Prairie chickens, wild geese, ducks, and curlews were plentiful, and the mountain streams were full of trout, but most of these Indians would eat neither fish nor fowl. Although the majority of the Blackfeet regarded fish as unclean, the Fish Eaters band of the Blood Indians derived their name from their custom of eating them. Reptiles, amphibians, and grizzly bears were not considered proper food. These Indians also looked upon their dogs as friends and would eat them only to avoid starvation. They were too fond of horses to eat them save under very unusual circumstances. Sometimes a group of warriors returning from a horse raid west of the Rockies strangled and ate a captured colt rather than risk being overtaken by enemies while hunting game or giving away their position by the noise of gunfire.

Usually Blackfoot Indians ate but two cooked meals a day—breakfast and supper. When camp was on the move, they stopped at midday for a cold lunch of dried meat and berries or pemmican. In spite of the variety of other foods available, the Blackfeet called the buffalo their "real food." When they were scarce, the Indians were miserable. After a successful buffalo hunt they feasted far into the night, devouring almost unbelievable quantities of this favorite food. It was not unusual for a healthy man to eat five or more pounds of choice buffalo meat at one of these feasts.

5: Camp Life

IN THE MIDDLE of the nineteenth century, Blackfoot hunting bands roamed over a vast area nearly twice the size of New England, extending from the North Saskatchewan River southward to the headwaters of the Missouri and from the Bearpaw Mountains westward to the Rockies.

The Blackfoot Indians' year was divided into four seasons of unequal length. The longest period was the one spent in winter camp. Each band wintered separately. In late October or early November the band chief selected a winter campsite in a broad river valley sheltered from winds and snow by the high, natural walls of the valley itself. The valley floor afforded grass for the horses. The river itself offered clear, cold drinking water, and the cottonwood groves bordering the stream provided firewood. As colder weather arrived in late November or early December men and women cut out the underbrush and some of the trees and moved their lodges into the timber. The standing trees served as windbreak and snow fence. Unless food became scarce or the wild grass for the horses was exhausted they remained in this locality throughout the winter.

Blackfoot winter dress was designed for comfort rather than for beauty. It bore little resemblance to the elaborately decorated costume we usually have in mind when we think of Plains Indians. When out-of-doors, men and boys wore buffalo-hide caps with ear flaps, buffalo robes with the hair next to the body or Hudson's Bay blanket coats, and hair-lined mittens and moccasins. Women and girls wore the same kind of moccasins, mittens, and headgear. Trade blankets or buffalo robes covered their undecorated dresses.

The Indians obtained their drinking water from holes chopped in the river ice. At these water holes the horses were watered three times daily. The horses were left to rustle for their food by pawing away the snow to the grass below. Some men fed their best horses the inner bark of cottonwood, which the Indians considered "better than oats." Others employed this supplemental feed only when the snow was too deep for the horses to rustle their own food. In some winters deep snows combined with very cold weather killed off many horses. In spite of everything their owners could do for them, the animals froze to death.

Throughout the winter, beaver-bundle owners kept primitive calendars of notched sticks, one notch representing each day, by which they could predict the approach of spring. The band chief carefully examined the development of embryos taken from buffalo cows killed in late winter hunts. When he saw that the unborn calves were beginning to develop hair, he knew spring was near. Before the river ice broke up, the beaver men held their ceremonies. When geese were seen flying north, all knew it was time to leave their winter camp. This was usually in late March or early April. After five or more months in one location the people were restless. They were glad to roam the plains again.

March was a difficult month during which the buffalo began to drift away from the sheltered river valleys. Unless the bands packed and followed the buffalo, they would have to subsist on small game or go hungry. Each band went its separate way in pursuit of buffalo. Buffalo calves were born in spring, between the breakup of winter camp and the annual May storm, a sudden and in some years heavy fall of snow which melted and disappeared almost over night. The Indians killed calves for children's robes and soft skin sacks. The medicine pipe ceremony was performed after the first thunder was heard in spring, usually in April or May. Spring was also the season for making willow backrests to furnish tipis, constructing and repairing riding gear, and fashioning warm-weather clothing. Horses, thinned and weakened during the winter months, fattened and grew strong on the rich spring grasses. Toward the end of spring women dug bulbs, which provided a welcome change in diet after the long winter of eating meat and dried foods.

When buffalo bulls became prime in June, the scattered hunting bands began to gather for the tribal summer hunt. It required several weeks for these bands to assemble and for each to occupy its assigned segment of the tribal camp circle. Then began the organized summer hunt under the leadership of the tribal chief and the strict regulation of men's societies chosen to police the camp and hunt. This summer hunt provided cowhides for new tipi covers, meat, and most important of all, the sacrificial food for the sun dance—buffalo tongues. Only bull tongues were collected, and as many as three hundred might be needed. After the tongues were prepared and scouts had selected the site for the sun dance encampment, the entire tribe moved toward the site in four daily marches. These were dress parades on which the people wore their finest clothes, decorated their horses with their most elaborate trappings, and the men displayed their weapons and shields. Sarvis berries were ripe when the sun dance began, usually in August. Some eight or ten days were spent in the sun dance encampment. At the end of that period the tipis were taken down, the camp circle was dissolved, and the bands separated for their fall hunt. This summer season was the only time of year when all the bands of the tribe camped together in one great village. In this tribal encampment friendships between individuals of the different bands were formed, renewed, and strengthened, the men's societies held their ceremonies and competed against one another in games and races, young men courted girls of other bands, horses were bartered, painted lodges and sacred bundles were ceremonially transferred, successful warriors were honored, visitors from friendly tribes were feasted and showered with gifts, and the chiefs and headmen of the tribe met in council to discuss the economic, political, and military problems of the entire tribe and to make plans for the future. All these varied activities helped to strengthen feelings of tribal unity and solidarity among members of hunting bands who might not even see each other from one summer until the next.

Fall, when cows were prime, was the great buffalo-hunting season. Berries also were collected, dried, and mixed with meat to make pemmican. Each family tried to put up as much dried meat, berries, and pemmican as their winter needs required or their means of transportation would permit. The number of camp moves during this autumn season depended largely upon the availability of buffalo. The more plentiful the buffalo in the vicinity of a band camp, the less frequent were its movements. Even though this mobile period ended with the establishment of winter camp, men continued to hunt in the vicinity of the camp and women continued to prepare stores of food for winter and to dress buffalo robes for the trade until heavy snows and bitter cold weather restricted their activity.[1]

As the weather permitted, and when an accumulation of buffalo robes was available, the bands visited the trading posts. This trading season generally lasted from about the middle of November until the middle of April. In mid-April the traders began to press their winter's receipts in robes and furs into bales. By the end of the month they were ready to start loading their boats, and early in May their cargoes of robes and furs started on the long journey downriver to market.[2]

Thus the annual cycle of camp movements varied with the seasons. It was influenced not only by the availability of game and the ripening of wild plant foods, but also by the severity of the winter weather and the demands of the Indians' own ceremonial calendar. Through the cold months the bands were settled in their winter camps. At that season they were no more nomadic than many tribes of the eastern forests who did not rely upon wandering buffalo herds for their subsistence. In their

[1] Ewers, "Horse in Blackfoot Indian Culture," B.A.E. *Bull. 159*, 123–29.
[2] McDonnell, "Fort Benton Journal," *MHSC*, Vol. X, 7–30.

tribal sun dance encampment they obtained a brief rest between the most active hunting seasons in summer and fall.

Frequent camp movements during spring, summer, and fall required that Blackfoot Indian homes be portable and that their household furnishings and ceremonial equipment be easily and efficiently packaged. The head chief, with the advice of the band chiefs, determined the movements of the great tribal camp in summer. He sent his herald around the camp circle the night before a move was to be made to tell the people to be ready to get under way early the next morning. In the much smaller band camps during spring and fall the band chief consulted with other prominent men of his band before announcing a move.

On the morning camp movement was to get under way women were up and bustling around at dawn. They prepared the family breakfast, finished packing, and were on the move before eight o'clock. Most of the family belongings were packed the night before. They needed only to be tied in their assigned places on horses or travois. The principal task was that of taking down the lodge. Two or more experienced women could accomplish this in a few minutes. The buffalo-hide cover of an average-sized lodge weighed about one hundred pounds. It was carefully folded and tied in place between the horns of a pack saddle. The poles of such a lodge numbered nineteen. Each was about eighteen to twenty-two feet long and weighed a little less than twenty pounds. Women divided the lodge poles into bundles of about five poles each. They tied the poles of each bundle together by a rawhide cord threaded through a hole burned in each pole near its upper end and tied one bundle of poles on each side of a pack horse. Thus two horses were needed to drag the poles of an average-sized lodge.

Buffalo-robe bedding and willow backrests, the principal lodge furnishings, were packed on a horse travois. Dried meat, tallow, and pemmican were placed in rectangular, rawhide parfleches which were suspended over the horns of a saddle, one on each side of the pack horse. Berries and tobacco were packed in sacks made from the skins of unborn buffalo calves and placed in the side pockets of buffalo-hide saddlebags. Kettles were put into skin sacks and tied on top of the pack horses' loads. Tools and utensils were placed in rectangular rawhide cases, which usually were carried on the horse travois. Ceremonial equipment was carried in bundles on the travois or in fringed rawhide containers over the horns of the favorite wife's saddle.

Scouts rode well in advance of the moving caravan, on constant lookout for signs of game or enemies. The other active warriors rode on the flanks and in the rear of the moving camp, carrying their weapons. The medicine pipe owner and the chief or chiefs and their families led the main body. Other camp members fell in behind the chiefs in family groups with their travois, pack animals, riding horses, and loose horses. Older boys drove the loose horses. Babies rode on their mothers' backs in the folds of their mothers' buffalo robes. Toddlers often rode on the travois. When they tired of riding, they got off and ran for a while. Older children usually rode horseback, sometimes two or three of them on a horse.

At noon the chief halted the caravan for a short rest and lunch. This was a cold meal of prepared meat, pemmican, or dried plant foods, and water. Usually the day's march ended in the middle or late afternoon so there was ample time for the women to erect the lodges, unpack the horses, and prepare the evening meal before dark. The chief chose the campsite and selected the spot for his lodge. Only during tribal movements in summer was the camp circle formed. At the end of a day's march by a separate hunting band the families pitched their lodges around that of their chief in an uneven cluster. They did not scatter widely because of the danger of enemy attack.

Usually the Indians knew in advance if their night camp was to be made without wood or water. If wood was lacking, dried buffalo chips were collected. Dried grass was used for tinder. The grass was ignited by sparks made by striking a curved fire-steel against a piece of flint. Water was brought along in buffalo paunches to supply a dry camp. Horses and dogs were watered in basin-shaped troughs of rawhide. There was little difficulty in obtaining water in spring. At that season the water from melting snows collected in many depressions which dried out by summer time.

When the Indians had to cross deep streams or rivers on the march, they rolled up the sides of their lodge covers to form rude boats in which baggage and children were placed. Horse travois poles and tipi poles were lashed together to form crude rafts on which other baggage was ferried. Horses towed these improvised craft while men swam ahead with tow lines, guiding the way, and women pushed from behind. Horses whinnied, dogs yelped, and people shouted as the crossing was made. When the Indians reached the far side of the stream, they generally stopped for the day to dry their clothes and gear.

On a rainy morning the Indians usually did not try to move camp. If a heavy rain fell while the band was on the march, they generally stopped for the day. Other factors helped to determine both the speed of movement and the distance covered. Among them were the character of the terrain traversed (whether level or hilly, the number and sizes of the water courses to be crossed), the availability of game, fear of enemy raiding parties in the vicinity, and the desire to reach a trading post or a particular camping spot before nightfall.

A normal day's march was about ten to fifteen miles. This was fully twice the distance the prehistoric ancestors of the Blackfeet could have made on foot carrying their meager possessions on dog travois and the backs of their women. A horse packing two hundred pounds on its back or hauling three hundred pounds on the travois could move four times the load of a heavily burdened dog twice as far on a day's march. So, animal for animal, the horse was eight times more efficient than the dog as a burden bearer. The application of horse power to camp movement thus enabled the Blackfeet to accumulate more property and to move it faster and farther as well.

An average family of eight persons (including two grown males, three women, and three children) needed ten horses to move camp efficiently. They needed a horse to carry the lodge cover and its accessories; two horses to drag the lodge poles; two for packing meat, other food, and equipment; three horses to carry the women (at least two of which would drag travois); and two riding horses for the men. Each of the men would also need a buffalo horse. A young married couple with a baby or no children needed no more than five horses. However, a large family of more than five adults required fifteen to twenty or more horses.[3]

Nevertheless, there were many poor families among the Blackfeet who owned only one or two horses. Their poverty in horses caused their standard of living to be well below that of the average family in their tribe at the time. Their possessions more nearly resembled those of the pre-horse Indians in quantity. Their lodges were small, covered with no more than six or seven buffalo hides, with short, light foundation poles. Their clothing, household utensils, and weapons were few and poor in quality. They owned no fancy dress clothes, no handsome riding gear. Their guns, if they owned any, were worn, broken, and repaired with rawhide cord. They had few if any buffalo robes to offer the traders.

At the other end of the Blackfoot economic and social ladder were the relatively few wealthy families—the owners of large horse herds. The fur trader, Charles Larpenteur, writing in 1860, aptly characterized the rich Indian:

> It is a fine sight to see one of these big men among the Blackfeet, who has two or three lodges, five or six wives, twenty or thirty children, and fifty to a hundred horses; for his trade amounts to upward of $2,000 a year.[4]

The man of wealth and the members of his family dressed well. They owned several changes of clothing, including elaborately decorated garments to wear in dress parades, ceremonies, and feasts in honor of important visitors and on their own visits to

---

[3] Ewers, "Horse in Blackfoot Indian Culture," B.A.E. *Bull.* 159, 129–39.
[4] *Forty Years a Fur Trader*, II, 401.

Blackfoot women erecting a tipi
in the traditional manner.
From *Crowfoot, Chief of the
Blackfeet,* by Hugh A. Dempsey
(*Courtesy Western History
Collections, University of
Oklahoma Library*).

other Indian camps or to the trading posts. They obtained the most attractive ornaments and best weapons from the traders' stock. They owned important and costly medicine bundles and showy and well-made riding gear. Their tipis were both large and handsomely furnished. As Larpenteur stated, some of them owned more than one tipi.

Wealth brought both opportunity and responsibility to the man who possessed it. The stingy rich man was despised by his less fortunate fellows. The generous man of wealth was beloved by them. If he was liberal in feasting and in giving away food and horses to the needy, if he lent horses to the poor for their use in hunting and moving camp, his fellow band members would want him for their chief—provided he also possessed a fine war record. James Doty described the Blackfoot chieftaincy thus in 1854:

> Every man who can acquire a large herd of horses, keep a good Lodge and make a large trade in Buffalo Robes is a chief, and he will maintain a persuasive influence over his people just so long as he continues wealthy, and ministers to the popular voice in directing the movements of the camp, leading war parties etc. Whenever he opposes his wishes to those of his band, it will desert him and turn to some chief more pliable.[5]

The hunting band, which was still the basic political unit among the Blackfeet, was probably a much more fluid unit than it had been in prehistoric times. In early times, when everyone stood literally and figuratively on an equal footing, the chiefs had no property to dispense. But in the middle of the nineteenth century poor families looked to their chief for charity. They changed their band allegiance if they believed they might better their economic condition as followers of a more liberal chief. Some of the larger bands had more than one chief. New bands were created when a rising leader and his followers broke away from an existing band. An older band might dissolve after the

5 Doty to Isaac I. Stevens, December 20, 1854. Indian Office Records.

death of a prominent chief if there was no one who could take his place in the hearts of his followers. Even the names of bands were changed in honor of particular chiefs or in memory of some unusual happening to the band. As a result, contemporary and later estimates of the number of hunting bands in each of the three Blackfoot tribes in the middle of the nineteenth century vary widely. The tendency of later students was to list every band encountered as a separate one, whether or not they were all contemporaneous. It seems most probable that in mid-century the Piegans comprised about thirteen bands, averaging about twenty-five lodges and about two hundred souls per band. In the winter of 1869–70 General Sully listed fifteen Piegan bands and nine bands each in the Blood and North Blackfoot tribes. These bands ranged from ten to thirty-six lodges each. Their average size was twenty-four lodges.[6]

The most influential band chief became recognized as the head chief of his tribe. However, his rank was of little significance except during the period of the tribal encampment in summer. Even then his role was more that of chairman of the council of chiefs than of ruler of his people. Important decisions were reached by agreement in council after each chief had an opportunity to speak his mind.

The chiefs exercised little disciplinary power over their followers. In the summer tribal encampment, selected men's societies policed the camp. But throughout the greater part of the year, when the tribe was divided into separate hunting bands, tribal discipline simply did not exist. The individual who was wronged was expected to exact such punishment of the wrongdoer as he or his family was able to inflict. Not uncommonly, the criminal fled to another Blackfoot band or to a neighboring tribe. Theft customarily was followed by reclaiming of the stolen property. Murder was punished by the dead man's relatives, who usually took the life of the murderer. But if the murdered man was poor and the killer rich and powerful, the matter

[6] General Alfred Sully, Census of Blackfoot Indians, 1870, Indian Office Records.

97

might be ended by a payment of horses to the family of the deceased. Thus it was possible for a wealthy man literally to get away with murder, although he would not enhance his popularity by doing so.

Frequent changes in band allegiance brought together in one residential community people without blood relationship closer than that of second cousins. Marriage between such persons was permitted. In fact, the fathers and mothers of several of my older Blackfoot informants were members of the same band at the time of their marriages.

Young men enjoyed remarkable freedom in their sexual life. They accosted girls while they were alone gathering wood or water on the outskirts of camp. They bragged of their conquests, particularly if they had had an affair with a married woman. Chastity before marriage was more an ideal than a reality for many girls. Yet a girl who earned a reputation for being too free with her favors might have to be satisfied with marrying a poor boy whose future prospects were equally poor.

Faint-hearted lovers, or more aggressive ones whose advances were repulsed by the girls of their choice, sometimes employed love medicines to bring them success in their amorous endeavors. These were secret formulae concocted by specialists for a fee. Because the Cree Indians were famous for these medicines, the Blackfeet referred to love medicine as "Cree Medicine." There were many varieties. One such medicine called for making two little birch bark images, one representing a man and the other a woman. A stick was dipped in the liquid medicine, then touched to the hearts of the male and female figures. This magic was certain to make the girl long for the company of her as yet unsuccessful lover. So powerful were love medicines reputed to be that resistance to them was considered useless.

Fathers and mothers were ambitious for their daughters to marry well. It was not uncommon for the father of a little girl to tell a successful warrior, "When my daughter is old enough, she will be your wife." The marriage might not take place for a decade. Elk-Hollering-in-the-Water told me she was promised to Bear Chief when she was no more than seven. She married him when she was about seventeen. Some girls married before the age of twelve, but many reached their middle teens before they took this serious step. Few young men married before the age of twenty-one.

It was considered a family disgrace for an unmarried girl to become pregnant. The girl alone was held responsible for her actions. It was something of a disgrace to the families of both boy and girl if they eloped. The socially approved marriage was an important family function. It was arranged by a close friend or a relative of the boy with the girl's father or elder brother. Marriage was simply solemnized by an exchange of gifts between the families of the bride and groom. The first gifts could be offered by either the bride's or the groom's folks. Horses always were the most prized gift. One or more horses were invariably given, along with robes or blankets and household goods of lesser value. Relatives commonly chipped in to make the marriage gifts as imposing as possible. It was expected that the gifts returned by the spouse's family should be more lavish than those they had received. The bride went to live with her husband in a separate lodge or that of his family.

My elderly informants were very careful to remind me that white men who claimed the Blackfeet used to purchase their wives were misinformed. They stressed the importance of the exchange of gifts in the old-time Blackfoot marriage ceremony.

After marriage it was improper for the husband to speak directly to his mother-in-law. But his ties with the male members of his wife's family generally became very strong. He commonly gave horses to his elder brother-in-law after his return from a successful horse raid. He sometimes gave him choice buffalo meat after a hunt.

Polygamy was common among the Blackfeet because it was a practical means of caring for the excess of women created by heavy war losses. Women outnumbered men by two or three to one. Possession of several wives was one of the distinguishing marks of the successful man. A few of the leading chiefs had ten

99

or more wives. Probably more than half of the men had at least two. In these polygamous households the husband's favorite, his "sits-beside-me-wife," accompanied him to feasts and ceremonies and supervised the work of the other women in her husband's home. Cautious men tried to minimize the dangers of jealousy and friction at home by marrying sisters. A husband of an eldest sister could expect the younger ones to be offered to him as they reached marriageable age, although he did not have to accept them. Double-Victory-Calf-Robe had two elder sisters, both of them married to Iron Horn. One day her father said to her, "My son-in-law, Iron Horn, is very kind and good to us. You had better marry him and be with your sisters." Her family outfitted a travois, helped her mount the travois horse, and she rode over to Iron Horn's lodge. He accepted her as his third wife and gave horses to her father.

Men were the undisputed lords of their households. They expected their wives to wait upon them hand and foot, to bring them food when they wanted it, to light their pipes and remove their moccasins. Some men beat their wives unmercifully with their riding whips. If a wife found her husband's cruelty unbearable, her elder brother would take her back to her family. Any man who tired of his wife could send her back to her family. In either case the wife took her property with her and the marriage was dissolved.

An errant husband could bestow his favors where he wished, but an unfaithful wife, if found out, was in for real trouble. Even though her husband might forgive her, he knew he could not retain the respect of other men unless he took revenge upon her lover, either by killing him or taking his horses, weapons, and other valuables. More often the husband wreaked his vengeance upon his wife. If he was a member of a men's society, his fellow members helped him to shame her. They dragged her from his lodge out on to the plains at night and attacked her. Then they or her jealous husband cut off the end of her nose to mark her for the rest of her life as an unfaithful wife. In 1833, Maximilian observed that women with clipped noses were common in the

Blackfoot camps. "When ten or twelve tents were together, we were sure to see six or seven women mutilated in this manner."[7] However, this severe punishment for infidelity was discontinued by the middle 1870's.[8]

Stormy as their marital lives sometimes were, Blackfoot Indians were fond and indulgent parents. Large families were common. Some men claimed to have fathered more than a score of children by their several wives. The pregnant woman wore a broad, adjustable rawhide belt as her time approached. It supported and protected her when she rode horseback or engaged in active work. Sometimes an expectant mother's labor pains came while she was riding with a moving camp. She dropped out of the line of march and two or three hours later returned to the caravan with her newborn babe in her arms. Usually, however, the birth took place in a tipi. An elderly woman, experienced in midwifery, gave the mother a decoction of roots to drink to ease her pains and facilitate delivery. While the mother grasped one of the lodge poles and an assistant held her around the waist the midwife attended to the delivery, then laced the mother in her rawhide belt. Sometimes the mother resumed her household chores the next day.

A portion of the baby's navel cord was cut, dried, and preserved in a beaded buckskin case as the child's primitive health insurance. The cases for boys' navel cords were in the form of snakes; girls' were lizard-shaped. The Blackfeet believed that snakes and lizards were never sick and lived long lives. The child was bathed and wrapped in soft skin. Moss or a soft punk served in lieu of diapers.

A few days after the birth the father called upon some distinguished member of his band to name the child. The name was carefully chosen because it was believed to have an important influence on the child's life. Sometimes it was the name of a respected ancestor; at other times it commemorated a brave or generous act of the bestower or of the child's father. Lazy

---

[7] *Travels*, II, 110, 117, 136.
[8] Bradley, "Manuscript," *MHSC*, Vol. IX, 271.

Boy, the oldest living Piegan a decade ago, followed this traditional custom in naming my younger daughter. He gave her the name Many-Steals-Horses-Woman, explaining that as a young man he had been very successful in capturing horses from enemy camps so he thought this name would bring her good fortune in whatever she tried to do.

Elaborate cradles were luxury items, uncommon among the Blackfeet a century ago. When walking or riding on horseback, women commonly carried their babies on their backs, inside their robes or blankets. The mother stood with her back bent, grasped the infant by both arms, swung it over her shoulders, then quickly drew her robe about her own body and that of the child. Blackfoot mothers nursed their babies until long after they were able to walk. Indeed, some mothers continued to nurse their children until they were five or six years old, believing this would prevent another pregnancy until their youngest child was old enough to look after himself.

Children were taught the elements of good manners and respect for their elders. They were expected to sit quietly while adults were talking in the tipi, to perform their chores promptly, to observe the taboos of the family medicine bundles, and to help the aged and show particular respect to them. They were taught to take teasing gracefully. But if a child of about their own age struck them, they were to fight back to the best of their ability.

The mother was responsible for the education of her daughters. The little girl began to learn about women's responsibilities by watching her mother and grandmothers at their tasks. She imitated their actions in her childhood play. She began to help her mother in such light tasks as picking berries, and graduated to the heavier work of digging roots and carrying firewood and water for the lodge. As the girl grew older, she received instructions in dressing hides, preparing foods, making clothing, and in the women's crafts of geometric painting, porcupine quillwork, and beadwork. A girl was expected to become proficient in these crafts before she married. At the annual sun dance mothers explained to their daughters the honor bestowed upon the medicine woman because she had always been true to her husband.

Girls dressed in garments which were miniatures of those worn by their mothers. But small boys often went nude in the summer. Or, at most, they wore only a breechclout in warm weather.

Blackfoot children were accustomed to horses from infancy. As babies they rode on their mothers' backs atop a horse when camp was moved. When they were able to sit up, they rode on the travois or on horseback behind their mothers. At an early age, usually by their fifth year, they were taught to ride alone. The child was lifted into a high-horned woman's saddle on a gentle horse, and rawhide ropes were passed back and forth between pommel and cantle on each side and tied to prevent the child's falling. A parent led the horse around the camp at a slow walk. If the child was afraid, he could hold on to the saddle horn. As he gained in experience and confidence, he was led at a faster pace and was taught to use the reins to control his mount. When camp was moved, the child was tied in the saddle and the horse was led by an adult. Soon he was riding alone. By the time most children were six or seven years old, they were good riders. Some rode little saddles made for them by fond mothers or grandmothers. They also learned to ride bareback and to ride double, and they frequently competed in impromptu horse races.

Fathers looked after the education of the boys, but they were allowed much more freedom than were girls. Boys were taught to make miniature bows and arrows. They were encouraged to take part in rough, active body- and character-building games and sports. At the sun dance encampment fathers pointed out to their sons the great warriors of their tribe and cited the honors that came to men who were brave and successful at the arts of war. The hero-worshiping youth was told again and again the stirring narratives of the outstanding fighting men of his tribe, both past and present. He was reminded of the old Blackfoot proverb, "It is better to die in battle than of old age or sickness."

Boys of about ten years of age were entrusted with the daily care of the family horse herd. The boy herder rose before daylight to go after the horses in their night pasture and drove them to a near-by lake or stream for water. Then he drove them to good pasturage near camp and returned home to breakfast. He watched the grazing herd during the day and drove it to water at noon and again in late afternoon. Toward evening he drove the herd to night pasture and hobbled the lead mare to prevent the herd from straying.

Boys who had lots of nerve began to break horses for riding when they were twelve or thirteen years of age. The easiest and least dangerous way to break broncs was in a pond or stream. Two boys rode double on a trained horse, leading the bronc by a rope or halter. They rode into the water until the bronc was up to its shoulders. Then the front rider held the lead rope close to its chin while the other boy climbed on its back. The lad on the trained horse quickly passed the rope to the bronc rider. As soon as the bronc felt the weight of the boy on his back, he began to jump and buck, but as soon as his head got wet, he quieted down. He tired quickly, and the boy rode him out of the water. If the bronc still showed a lot of spirit it was led back into the water again for another session.

At other times boys led a bronco into a muddy or swampy area to break it. Then one of them jumped on its back. When the horse tried to buck, its feet sank into the mire. If the rider was thrown, he would not be hurt. The horse's spirit was broken before it could get out of this boggy training ground.[9]

Orphaned boys could find homes with wealthy families by looking after the large horse herds and assisting in the hunt. All boys began to hunt buffalo calves in their early teens, and not long thereafter they graduated to hunting adult buffalo and some of them began to join horse-raiding parties. Only the sons of wealthy men could look forward to a good marriage before they had begun to accumulate a herd of their own horses.

In their late teens a group of young men banded together to purchase membership in the lowest of the graded men's societies

[9] Ewers, "Horse in Blackfoot Indian Culture," B.A.E. *Bull* 159, 60–64.

at the tribal sun dance encampment. They selected a leader, who presented a pipe to the leader of the society. Each of the other youths gave pipes to other members of the society. If the pipes were accepted, the petitioners were expected to make other gifts of horses and valuable goods to those who relinquished their society membership to them and who taught them the ceremonial procedures of the organization. It was usual for societies to sell out to a group of younger men every four years.

There were seven of these age-graded men's societies among the Blackfeet in 1833. The youngest group was then the Mosquitos, the oldest the Buffalo Bulls. Two decades later the Bulls Society among the Piegans had become inactive on account of the death of many of its older members, but a new society, the Pigeons, or Doves, had been added to the bottom of the series.[10]

Because members of these societies belonged to different hunting bands, they were only active during the summer season when the tribal camp was organized. At that time the head chief called upon one or two of the societies, usually the younger of the mature groups, to police the camp and the tribal hunt. In the sun dance camp each society performed its peculiar ceremony. Collectively, the men's societies were known as the All-Comrades.[11]

There was another and even closer relationship between boys of the same band, that of partners. Two boys of about the same age became close companions. They played together as children, helped each other in courting girls, went to war together, and offered advice and assistance to each other whenever it might be needed. If a young man was wounded in battle, his partner risked his life to carry him to safety and stayed behind the rest of the war party until the disabled man was able to be helped home. In many instances this close friendship and mutual assistance between partners continued through the rest of their lives.

[10] Maximilian, *Travels,* II, 112–17.
[11] Clark Wissler, "Societies and Dance Associations of the Blackfoot Indians," American Museum of Natural History *Anthropological Papers,* Vol. XI, Part 4, 361–450. Includes detailed description of specialized paraphernalia and ceremonies of each society.

There was a women's society among the Blood and Northern Blackfoot tribes which was unknown among the Piegans. Its members were wives of the most highly respected men in their tribes. Prior to the sun dance in summer, members of this Matoki society built a ceremonial lodge which resembled a buffalo corral, and on the final day of their four-day ritual re-enacted the drive of buffalo into the corral. Some of the members wore buffalo headdresses and mimicked the actions of buffalo.[12]

The aged were no longer abandoned on the plains as had been the common lot of enfeebled old people before the Blackfeet acquired horses. If an old man or woman was too feeble to ride alone, he or she was carried on the A-shaped horse travois. If the head of a family knew he was about to die, he called his relatives together and told them how he wished his horses and other property divided among them. If he died without having made such a verbal will, the other people in camp made a run for his property as soon as they heard his relatives weeping and wailing. Men ran for his horses; women went for his household equipment. The men might take all his best horses and leave the poorest ones for his widow. Close relatives of the deceased, preoccupied with mourning his loss, made no attempt to prevent this raid on his property. Custom decreed that they should not do so. These raids were made with particular relish upon the property of a man of wealth who had had a reputation for miserliness during his lifetime.

No such action followed the death of a highly respected, generous leader. His lodge interior was carefully arranged just as it had been when he had entertained prominent guests. His body was dressed in his finest clothing and laid upon a raised platform of poles in the center of his lodge. Then his relatives painted simple representations of his brave war deeds on his favorite horse, braided its mane and tail and tied feathers in them, and placed his best saddle on the horse's back. In the presence of all the people of the camp this horse and others to be sacrificed were led to the door of the death lodge. Each in turn was shot

[12] *Ibid.*, 430–35.

with a gun. A close relative of the dead man pressed the gun against the horse's head and pulled the trigger. The bodies of the dead horses were left where they fell, but camp members were permitted to strip them of their valuable riding gear. The gear was of no more value to the deceased, for according to Blackfoot belief the spirit horse joined the spirit of its master wearing the trappings it bore at the moment of its death. The death lodge was left undisturbed. People of the dead man's camp feared to loot it lest his spirit return to haunt them.

Prominent chiefs sometimes expressed the desire to have their bodies taken to the fur posts when they died. It was then the responsibility of the fur company to bury them. Maximilian witnessed a double burial of two relatives of Bear Chief by the traders at Fort McKenzie in the summer of 1833.

> The two Indians were laid in the same grave, wrapped in a red blanket and buffalo skin, over which was laid a piece of colored stuff, given by Mr. Mitchell [the chief trader]. The bottom and sides of the grave were lined with boards; the body, too was covered with wood; his bridle, whip, and some other trifles, were thrown in, and the grave filled with earth.[13]

A number of prominent Piegan chiefs who died in the fifties and sixties were taken to Fort Benton for burial.

Women prepared bodies for burial. The deceased were usually dressed in their best clothes, their faces were painted, and the bodies were sewn in buffalo robes and deposited in the forks of trees. Sometimes they were placed on the ground in a ravine or on the summit of a hill, then covered with rocks and dirt to keep the wolves from molesting them. It was customary to kill a man's favorite horse—his trusted companion on the buffalo hunt and war party—near his burial place. Poor families who could not afford to sacrifice the dead man's horse cut its mane and tail short and considered that the animal was in mourning for its master.

[13] *Travels*, II, 141.

Widows donned old clothes, cut their hair short, and smeared their hair, faces, and clothes with white clay. In their anguish, mourning women scratched the calves of their legs with sharp pieces of flint, causing their blood to flow. Some widows chopped off joints of their fingers. For several weeks they made daily trips to a quiet place outside their camp and sang doleful mourning chants.

When men mourned the death of a loved one, they also put on old clothes, cut their hair, and smeared themselves with white clay. Sometimes, to appease his grief for a dead wife or child, a man took to the warpath, eager to perform a deed of reckless bravery without regard for the risk to his own life.

Blackfoot woman with nose cut off in punishment for adultry (*Courtesy Yale University Library*).

6: Artists and Craftsmen

In THE MIDDLE of the nineteenth century, Blackfoot men and women evidenced their handicraft skills in the making and decorating of a variety of useful articles. Some of their crafts differed little from those of their stone-age ancestors. Others made effective use of the sharp metal tools, cloth, glass beads, and other items received from the fur traders. Yet, even when they employed European-made materials, they produced handiwork such as was never known to Europe, reflecting the ingenuity and good taste of its Indian makers.

The trade in buffalo robes encouraged greater production in a craft that was old long before white men appeared in the Blackfoot country—that of skin dressing. The women who dressed buffalo robes for market played an even more important role in the fur trade than did their husbands who killed the buffalo. Theirs was harder work than buffalo hunting. Twenty-five to thirty robes a winter were about as many as an industrious woman could prepare. A good buffalo hunter could keep several wives supplied with all the hides they could process. Women who excelled at skin dressing were proud of both the quantity and the quality of their output. Older women bragged of the number of robes they had dressed for market and the number of lodge covers they had made. Girls were taught that skill in dressing skins was a desirable attribute in the eyes of a prospective husband.

Dressing a buffalo hide involved a series of processes that can be much easier described than performed. After the hide was removed from the dead animal, fragments of tissue and fat mixed with blood still adhered to its inner surface. The first task was to remove this matter by a process known as fleshing. A woman stretched the hide out on the ground, hair side down, and drove lodge pegs through it at intervals around the edge to hold it securely in place. Then she knelt over the hide and hacked away the undesired matter with short, vigorous strokes of a sharp-toothed implement held in her right hand. As in early times, the shaft of this tool was usually a buffalo legbone, but the keen iron blade had a much sharper cutting edge than the stone one of prehistoric times. Yet even with this improved blade a strong woman worked several hours fleshing a large buffalo hide.

After the hide was cured and bleached in the sun a few days, the woman scraped the inner surface to an even thickness with an adzelike tool. She stood on the hide and leaned over and chipped away the surface by moving her scraper, much as a skilled carpenter uses a plane. This tool had an L-shaped elk-horn handle hafted to a blade of iron. Scraping a hide occupied half a day. It would have taken longer with a primitive stone-bladed scraper.

Next, the woman thoroughly rubbed an oily mixture of buffalo brains, fat, and liver into the hide. Then she rubbed the inner surface with a stone, the heat of which distributed the oil through the hide. She placed the hide in the sun to dry, then saturated it with warm water and rolled it into a bundle. By that time the hide had shrunk in size, so that it was necessary for the woman to stretch it by pulling with her hands and feet.

Finally, she broke down the tissues and softened the skin by rubbing the surface vigorously with a rough stone, then sawing the skin back and forth through a loop of twisted rawhide tied to the under side of an inclined lodge pole. After two full days of hard work the buffalo robe was dressed and ready for market.

Buffalo robes were bulky, heavy things for a woman to handle in the successive stages of skin dressing. Many women preferred to dress half a hide at a time. They cut the hide in two from head to tail along the center of the back. After the two halves were dressed they sewed them together neatly with sinew thread.

The buffalo robes Indians used for their own outer garments and bedding received this same treatment. However, for most Indian uses the buffalo hair had to be removed. This was done with the scraping tool. If the hide was to be employed for making articles of rawhide, it was fleshed and scraped on the inner surface and the hair was knocked off with blows from a rock.

The thinner hides of smaller mammals—elk, deer, antelope, and mountain sheep—were dressed in the same manner as buffalo hides. But after the oil was worked into the skin, the hair side was scraped with a rib-bone beaming tool resembling a spokeshave, to make sure that all the fine hairs were taken off.

Among the Blackfeet, women were the experts in working buffalo rawhide. With sharp butcher knives they cut long lengths of rawhide rope, cut and fitted saddle covers, and cut out the outlines for a variety of containers of folded rawhide.

Because of its strength, flexibility, and durability the heavy hide of the buffalo bull made the best rope. In making rope a woman cut one long continuous strip from a green bull hide. Beginning at the outer edge, she cut a strip about four inches wide, working around the hide in a concentric circle. Then she cut a slit near one end of this strip and drove a lodge peg through the slit into the ground. She stretched the rope as tight as she could and drove another peg into the ground through a similar slit at the other end of the line. Later she pulled up one peg, stretched the strip farther, and pegged it down again. After the rawhide dried, she took it off her simple stretcher and began softening it by rubbing the inner (meat) side with a rock. Then she doubled the strip lengthwise, hair side out, and bit it to hold the crease. She passed one end of the strip through the eye sockets of a buffalo skull and, standing with one foot on the skull to steady it, used both hands to saw the strip back and forth through the eye holes to rub off the hair and further soften the hide. Then, with a rock, she knocked off any hair that remained. Taking her knife again, she cut the strip down the center lengthwise, dividing it into two ropes, each two fingers wide. She trimmed each rope carefully to make it an even width throughout its length. Any short pieces trimmed off were saved for whip lashes. After trimming, she oiled the ropes with back fat. A single bull hide provided two ropes, each about seventeen feet long. This rope was used for lariats, hackamores, bridles (single strand or plaited), picket lines, hobbles, saddle-rigging straps, stirrup straps, travois ropes, and cords for wrapping bundles and tying them to travois or pack saddles.

A buffalo hide to be used for covering a frame saddle was first soaked in a pond or stream for several days until it became green and foul smelling. It was then stretched on the ground, hair side up. Boiling water was thrown on it, and the hair was taken off with a rock. The saddlemaker then turned the hide over and scraped the flesh from the underside with a hide scraper. She then stretched the hide over the saddle frame, fitted it, cut it, and sewed it in place with rawhide cord. She took her stitches on the underside of the saddle, where they would not show when the saddle was in use. To prevent the wooden frame from warping as the rawhide dried and shrunk, she tied the saddle over a log about the width of a horse's back or forced an old rolled-up lodge cover between the side bars and wrapped a rawhide cord around saddle and cover to hold them in place until the saddle cover dried.

Of the several types of containers made from single pieces of rawhide—folded, and laced or tied with thongs—the most common was the parfleche. When folded like an envelope, the Blackfoot parfleche was a rectangle about two feet long and fifteen inches wide. Women made them in pairs, one parfleche for each side of a pack horse. A large buffalo hide would yield material for both cases. The craftswoman first soaked the rawhide, with the hair on it, in water, then she pegged it out on the ground, hair side down. She measured the outlines of the cases on the hide with peeled willow sticks. While the hide was still damp, she painted simple geometric designs on the end and side flaps which would show when the cases were in use. She did not bother to paint the backs, which would be hidden from view.

She used willow sticks for rulers in laying out the decorative fields, and as straight edges in painting the outlines of the geometric designs. She first outlined all the painted forms in a single color. Then she filled in the larger areas of the composition with the desired colors. Some women mixed their paints with hot water, which caused them to sink into the damp hide and become permanently fixed after the hide dried. Others applied to all the painted areas an overcoat of sticky glue, made by boiling the tail of a beaver or the clean, second-scrapings of buffalo hides. This thin coat of sizing gave the colors a glossy appearance.

After the paint dried, the craftswoman turned the rawhide over and removed the hair with a hide-scraper or a rock. Pounding the opposite side with a rock whitened the unpainted portions of the rawhide and made the colors stand out from the background. Finally, the woman cut the parfleches to their desired shapes with a sharp knife, folded them into envelope form, and burned the tie holes with a heated iron rod. The parfleches were finished.

Areas of rawhide remaining after the parfleches were cut out were not wasted. They were used for smaller containers or for resoles in repairing moccasins. Women made other rawhide cases in rectangular or cylindrical form and painted them. Those intended to hold sacred objects were decorated with long, cut-rawhide fringes.

Men made shields and drums of rawhide. To make a shield, the thick hide of a buffalo bull's neck was placed over a fire in the ground so that it would shrink and become still thicker and tougher. It was trimmed into a circular form about eighteen inches in diameter. Men painted on their shields sacred symbols such as buffalo, the sun, the moon, and stars, which they believed would protect them from their enemies' bullets and arrows. The belly hide of a horse was preferred for drumheads. It would not soften or stretch out of shape. To tighten a drumhead, they held it near a fire. Paintings on drums were also of sacred character.

Blackfoot painters used both native and trade pigments. Their own colors were mostly mineral ones. Several reds were obtained from colored earths or crushed rock. By baking a gray or yellowish clay over ashes, they obtained a reddish brown. The spring buds of pussy willows provided another red. Yellow was a colored earth commonly found in the valley of the Yellowstone River. Buffalo gallstones furnished another yellow. White was an earth, and black was either earth or charcoal. Although the Blackfeet knew how to obtain a blue from dried duck dung and a green from plants growing near lakes, they preferred the blue and green from the trading posts.

Pigments were ground to a powder in small stone mortars, stored in little buckskin sacks, and mixed with hot water or glue extracted from boiled beaver tail or the underscrapings of a hide. Paint brushes were pieces of porous bone cut from the edge of a buffalo shoulder blade or hipbone. Their honeycomb composition held the paint and permitted it to flow smoothly onto the surface of rawhide or soft skin. Outlines were drawn with sharp-pointed brushes. Colors were spread over larger areas with the sides of the same brushes or with rounded-edged ones. A separate brush was used for each color.

As a general rule women painted only geometric designs on rawhide cases, buffalo robes, and lodge linings. Men painted human or animal forms on their shields, drums, and lodge covers, and they recorded their successes at war on the inner surfaces of their buffalo robes.

The largest and most striking examples of Blackfoot Indian painting were the larger than life-size representations of animals and birds depicted on the outer surfaces of their conical lodge covers. These primitive mural paintings portrayed the creatures which the tipi owners regarded as the sources of their supernatural powers. Each was painted in strict accordance with the instructions the owner received in the vision or dream in which he obtained his power. The lodge owner called upon a man who was known to be a skilled painter. He told the artist what creatures to portray and where to locate them on the cover. The painter drew the outlines of the figures in black or dark brown while the lodge was standing. Then the cover was spread out on the ground and less skilled artists assisted the painter in filling in the outlines with colors designated by the owner. A buffalo tail or handful of buffalo hair was used to apply the color to the larger areas, and the paint, mixed with hot water, was rubbed onto the cover with considerable pressure.

Usually a single pair of the larger mammals, such as buffalo, deer, or elk, representing the mythical giver and his mate, appeared on a cover. If the subjects were smaller mammals, such as beaver or otter, several pairs were represented. A device symbolizing the home of the creature usually was painted on the back of the cover. The animal or bird figures faced the doorway, one or more on each side of the lodge. Usually the bodies of the figures were of one solid color—black, red, or yellow. On many of these animals the throat, heart, and kidneys were painted in contrasting colors. It was important to show them because they were regarded as the sources of the creature's power.

Most painted lodges also had two areas of geometric design. A banded area at the bottom, usually in red, represented the earth, while unpainted discs within this field symbolized fallen stars. The second area, at the top, was painted black, representing the night sky. Unpainted discs within this area indicated the constellations of the Great Bear and the Pleiades. Near the top and at the back of the cover a Maltese cross representing the morning star or butterfly was painted. It was thought to bring powerful dreams to the tipi owner.

Only a small proportion of the Blackfoot lodge covers bore these colorful, decorative paintings. However, the making of the cover itself was no mean achievement. From six to twenty buffalo cow hides were needed, the number depending upon the relative wealth of the lodge owner and the size of his family. An elderly woman experienced in cutting and piecing together hides laid them out on the ground and told her assistants where to cut and sew them together with sinew thread. At the end of this sewing bee the lodge owner feasted the women who took part in this work. Lodge covers were replaced at least every other year. Rather than discard its old cover a wealthy family might give it to a poor woman who would cut several feet off the bottom and convert it into a tipi for her family.

In the fall of the year women cut new tipi poles of lodgepole pine. After a woman had brought her poles into camp she made berry soup and invited young men who wished to help peel these poles to a feast. To remove the bark from a pole, a man secured a stick on the sharp end of his knife, grasped the stick with one hand and the knife handle with the other, and employed the knife as a draw shave.

Women painted geometric designs on the buffalo-skin draft screens which lined the lower portions of their conical lodges. The distinctive decoration on Blackfoot linings consisted of a narrow horizontal band near the top with broader bands extending downward at intervals of about fifteen inches.

Blackfoot Indian beds were simply made of dried grass or rawhide spread on the ground and covered with buffalo robes. Women displayed their craftsmanship in making and decorating the backrests set up at the head and foot of each bed. Some 125 or more peeled willow rods were tied together with sinew cord one above the other to form a flexible, comfortable, A-shaped seat back. The backrest was usually edged with red or blue trade cloth, and a flap of the same material tastefully decorated with porcupine quills or beadwork was suspended from the top. A pole tripod supported the backrest, and these poles, too, might be decorated by peeling off sections of bark in geometric patterns with a sharp knife and filling in the peeled areas with paint. It is doubtful that these picturesque house furnishings were known in prehistoric times.

Even though trade cloth was much used in Blackfoot clothing in the mid-nineteenth century, traditional styles of basic garments persisted. Some men did wear hooded coats made from Hudson's Bay blankets, copied from those worn by French-Canadian fur traders. And some members of both sexes preferred the trade blanket to the buffalo robe for their cold-weather outergarments. But buffalo robes were by no means passé. Some of these robes were decorated on their skin surfaces with series of horizontal parallel bands in painting or porcupine quillwork. The Indians called these "real decorated robes," suggesting that the decorative pattern was an old one. Successful warriors preferred to illustrate their deeds of valor with crude, stick-like figures of horses captured and men fighting painted on their buffalo robes.

A man usually wore his buffalo robe or blanket wrapped around his body, with his left shoulder covered and his right arm and shoulder uncovered. He held the garment in place by grasping the two ends with his left hand underneath the robe. In very cold weather or when courting, a man pulled this garment over his head like a shawl and kept both arms covered. Women generally belted their blankets or robes about their waists, allowing the upper part to fall free when they needed to use both hands in their work.

For daily wear, men dressed in calico or flannel shirts, blue cloth breechclouts, and cloth leggings, but their finest dress clothing was of skins. Women lavished much time and care upon making and decorating their husband's dress clothes. The finest shirts and leggings were of antelope or bighorn skin. Two animal skins were needed to make the sleeved shirt, which was put on over the head. One skin formed the front of the garment, the other the back, and the legs of the animals hung down as trailers at the sides. Usually a narrow flap of red flannel bordered the neck opening. Over the center of the chest was sewed a large rosette or rectangle of skin, covered with quillwork or beadwork. Over both shoulders and down both sleeves (covering the seams) were narrow bands of quill or bead embroidery about three fingers (two inches) wide.

Leggings made of the same material as the shirt extended from ankle to hipbone, where they were tied to a narrow rawhide belt in a common knot. The leggings of this period fitted the form of the leg rather tightly. The vertical seam on the outside of the leg was covered with a beaded or quilled band

to match those on the shirt. The most elaborate outfits were decorated with hairlock or weasel-skin pendants from the neck, and
sleeves. Sixteen or more weasel skins were required to decorate
both shirt and leggings. Worth three or more horses, such suits
were generally the property of rich men.

Some men painted black or dark brown horizontal stripes on
their shirts and leggings if they were instructed to do so in their
dreams. Indeed, many of the finest suits were made in fulfillment of dream instructions. They were regarded as personal
medicines endowing their owners with supernatural power and
were worn only in battle, in ceremonies, in dress parades, and
to be buried in.

The handsome eagle-feather bonnets worn by a few Blackfoot
leaders were reserved for the same occasions. These were not
of the familiar flowing type made by the Sioux, but were crowns
of eighteen to thirty upright feathers inserted in a folded rawhide headband. The headband was covered with red flannel and
decorated with little brass discs and pendants of white weasel
skin.

The woman's basic garment was a long, sleeveless dress reaching almost to the ankles. Ceremonial dresses differed from everyday ones primarily in their elaborate decoration. Some dresses
were made of calico, some of heavy blue trade cloth, but the
finest were of antelope or elkskin. One skin formed the front and
one the back of the garment. They were sewed together at the
sides, and both were sewed to a yoke of the same material which
covered the shoulders and upper arms. A handsome dress, collected by John James Audubon in 1843, has a narrow band of
trade beads bordering the neck opening, broader bands over the
shoulders, and a still broader meandering band below the border
of the yoke on both front and back. A row of elktooth pendants
hangs from the broadest band of beadwork.[1] Some wives of
wealthy men wore four rows of elkteeth on both front and back

[1] Specimen in Audubon Collection, American Museum of Natural History,
New York City.

of their best dresses. Decorative patches of black and red flannel were sewed to the lower portions of fancy dresses.

Dresses had considerable fullness below the waist to allow freedom of movement in mounting and riding astride. They were confined at the waist by a broad belt of rawhide, fastened with buckskin tiestrings. In addition, women wore knee-length leggings of skin or trade cloth, decorated with bands of beadwork. Women appeared to prefer beadwork to quillwork in the decoration of their own clothing.

Both sexes wore soft-soled moccasins of deer or elkskin in warmer weather, of buffalo hide (hair inside) in winter. One piece of skin, folded along the inner side of the foot, provided both sole and upper. The sinew-sewn seam ran from toe to heel around the outside of the foot and up the back of the heel. Ankle flaps were added. Although dress moccasins were tastefully decorated with porcupine quills or bead embroidery, common ones were undecorated.

The traditional craft of quillwork still flourished. Porcupine quillwork was considered a sacred craft. Young women were ceremonially initiated into the art of handling the sharp-pointed quills. Their first quilled articles were presented as gifts to the sun. It was thought that a woman who attempted to do quillwork without having been ceremonially instructed would go blind or suffer from swelling finger joints.

Most Blackfoot quillworkers preferred the medium-sized quills from the back and sides of the porcupine. They imparted red, green, or blue colors to quills by dampening a quantity of dye plant yielding the desired color in water, placing a number of quills on top of it, wrapping them together in a piece of buckskin, and placing the package under their bed. After the package was pressed by the weight of the woman's body for a couple of nights it was unwrapped and the dyed quills removed. Some women dyed their quills by boiling them in water with a quantity of colored trade cloth.

Quills were kept in cigar-shaped elk-bladder containers until they were used. The quillworker made holes in the skin article to be decorated with a metal awl and passed sinew thread through these holes to attach the quills. She held the quills in her mouth to soften them and drew them between her teeth to flatten them. Women most commonly applied quills to men's shirts and leggings and to buffalo robes in series of narrow parallel bands, each less than one-fourth of an inch wide. Quill-work designs were usually made up of small geometric elements such as squares, rectangles, equal-armed crosses, and stepped-triangles. After the quills were sewed down, the crafts-woman pressed them firmly with a buffalo-horn implement to make them lie flat.

This earlier technique of quillwork influenced Blackfoot bead embroidery. Women applied the beads in narrow bands and employed the same simple, blocky geometric designs in beadwork which they had been accustomed to use in quillwork. The embroidering beads of the period were about one-eighth of an inch in diameter, larger than those used in reservation days. Traders supplied these beads in six different colors—light blue, dark blue, dark red, deep yellow, white, and black. Blackfoot women showed a decided preference for the blue and white beads. They commonly alternated bands of blue and white beads in decorating their dresses. They used blue for background and white for designs in their beadwork on men's suits. At that time beads were expensive, and women used them more sparingly than in later years.

Men fashioned tobacco pipes from a grayish, calcareous shale quarried at sites beside the eastward-flowing rivers of the Black-foot country. With a sharp piece of metal a pipemaker marked the outline of the pipe on a block of stone about three or four inches square and an inch and a half thick. He drilled the stem and bowl holes with a metal tool resembling a sharp-edged screwdriver, and expanded the hole in the bowl with a broader metal reamer. Then he shaped the outside with a file and care-fully removed the file marks with a knife and a piece of sand rock. The form of the pipe resembled an acorn resting on a heavy, blocky base. The maker blackened the surface of the pipe by holding it over a fire of green buckbrush, greased its surface with animal fat, and then polished it with a piece of skin or a rag until it was shiny black.

Long, flat pipestems were made of ash wood. The long central smoke hole was burned out with a heated iron rod before the surface of the stem was smoothed with a sand rock. The bowls of women's pipes were either miniatures of the larger men's pipes or were small L-shaped ones. They were fitted to short, willow stems.

Both men and women made horn spoons, cups, and ladles, employing a technique which probably was used by their prehistoric ancestors. A buffalo horn or mountain sheep horn was thrown into a fire to fry out the gluey matter. It was removed from the fire and, as soon as it was cool enough to handle, trimmed to the outline of the utensil desired. Then it was softened in boiling water, withdrawn, and a stone of the desired shape forced into the bowl cavity. While still pliable the handle was bent to the angle or arc desired and weighted down with stones. The horn was wrapped in a piece of skin or cloth until it dried out and hardened. Then it was unwrapped, and the weights removed. Finally, the surface was smoothed with a sand rock and the utensil greased with animal fat and polished with the hand to give it a shine.

Wooden bowls were fashioned by another traditional crafts process. A woman who wished to make a bowl first located a large burl on an ash or cottonwood tree, cut it off with an axe, and carried it back to camp. Ash generally was preferred because of its attractive grain. She roughly hewed out the bowl cavity with an axe and finished hollowing out the interior by carefully removing small chips of even size and thickness with her ironbladed skin scraper. After smoothing the inner surface with a sand rock, she removed the bark from the outside with a knife and shaped it with her scraper. After the bowl had dried in the sun, she greased it inside and out and polished the surface to bring out the grain of the wood. Both circular and boat-shaped bowls were made in different sizes. The walls of some of them were less than three-eighths of an inch thick. These wooden utensils served for soup and serving bowls, dishes, and drinking cups.

Even though Blackfoot warriors had been carrying firearms for more than a century, the bow and arrow was still their favorite buffalo-hunting weapon. The flint arrowhead had been superseded by one of hoop iron, which the Blackfeet called "wide rope." A barrel hoop from one to two inches wide could be obtained from traders in exchange for a buffalo robe. The Indian arrowhead maker drove an old axe head into the ground and used its top surface for an anvil. He cut out the arrowheads from the hoop iron with a sharp chisel and sharpened their edges with a file. Completed arrowheads were either rounded or square-shouldered, in accordance with the maker's preference. They measured about two and one-half inches long. An expert could fashion fifty or sixty metal arrowheads in a day.

Arrowshafts were of sarvis berry, about five hands and two fingers long, measured fist over fist as we would do in choosing sides in a baseball game. Three feathers of the eagle, hawk, crow, or goose were attached to the rear of the shaft with sinew wrapping. The arrowhead was fitted into a slot in the front of the shaft and bound with sinew. To hold the sinew wrapping in place, the portions of the shaft to be wrapped were lightly scored with a knife, and a glue made from boiled pieces of buffalo phallus was applied to these areas with a stick. Arrow makers could tell their finished products by minor differences in construction, as well as by the number, widths, and colors of painted stripes under the feathering.

A length of chokecherry about the thickness of a man's wrist was the preferred wood for bowmaking. It was carefully shaved with a knife and bent to a proper double-curve while the wood was still green by tying it at each end and in the center to a sturdy pole and driving wooden pegs between bow and pole midway between each of the ties. In three or four days the bow dried out sufficiently to hold its shape. The bow was backed with sinew, which was glued in place with buffalo-phallus glue.

On some of the finest bows a rattlesnake skin was glued over the sinew. The grip was wrapped with buckskin cord. Twisted sinew served for a bowstring. It was tied around the nock at one end and looped over the nock at the other end. Bows were kept unstrung when not in use. Probably the majority of bows were thirty-six to forty inches long.

Blackfoot archers generally held the bow in a slanting rather than a vertical position. Methods of arrow release differed according to the preference of the individual and the strength of the bow. If the bow was stiff and hard to pull, the archer might hold the arrow between thumb and first finger and pull the bowstring with his second finger (the so-called secondary release). If the bow was limber, he might hold both arrow and bowstring between thumb and first finger (primary release).

Quivers of buffalo calfskin were lined with red flannel and decorated with blue and white beads. Some men owned handsome quivers of mountain lion or otter skin.

Most Blackfoot Indian men and women possessed a great deal of manual skill. Nevertheless, some individuals who specialized in particular crafts produced articles of such outstanding quality that they were sought by others. Men who painted tipis and robes were specialists. Older men who excelled as makers of bows and arrows or pipes could find ready markets for their products among their fellows. They might be paid a horse for a handsome pipe bowl and stem or for a fine bow and a quantity of arrows. Similarly, elderly women who were expert saddlemakers or dressmakers exchanged their handicrafts for horses or other desirable articles. The Indians were proud to own wellmade things, and they readily distinguished between shoddy workmanship and fine craftsmanship.[2]

[2] John C. Ewers, *Blackfeet Crafts*, U. S. Indian Service, *Indian Handicrafts Series No. 9*, 1944.

Painted lodges in the sun dance encampment near Browning, Montana, 1942 (*Courtesy Museum of the Plains Indian*).

7: Raiding for Horses and Scalps

THE BLACKFOOT TRIBES were at the height of their power in the middle of the nineteenth century. Their Indian enemies and the white fur traders knew them as the most formidable and warlike people on the northwestern plains. Edwin T. Denig, able trader at Fort Union, who knew all of the tribes of the region, called the Blackfeet "the most numerous and bloodthirsty nation on the upper Missouri."[1] Certainly they were the most aggressive.

Their theater of warfare was a vast area which included the valley of the Saskatchewan and the upper tributaries of the Columbia, as well as the upper Missouri. Of the surrounding tribes, only the Sarsis and Gros Ventres, their lesser allies, were safe from Blackfoot attacks. They raided eastward down the Saskatchewan into Cree country and down the Missouri past the mouth of Milk River into Assiniboin country. They raided southward into the land of the Crow Indians beyond the Yellowstone. Blackfoot war parties crossed the Rockies to attack the Flatheads, Pend d'Oreilles, Kutenais, and Shoshonis in their own country.

In 1854, James Doty learned that Blackfoot war parties frequently raided the Shoshonis "by way of a pass on or near the headwaters of the Yellowstone River. The Blackfeet seem to entertain an inveterate hostility toward the Snakes and it is difficult to say how far removed these Indians must be to prevent the

[1] *Indian Tribes of the Upper Missouri*, B.A.E., *46th Ann. Rept.*, 470.

Blackfeet from reaching them."[2] Doty's word "inveterate" certainly applied to this warfare. The Blackfoot tribes had been fighting the Shoshonis for at least a century and a quarter.

Eight years earlier Father De Smet found the gallant little Flathead tribe "greatly reduced by the continual attacks of the Blackfeet."[3] These relentless attacks, coupled with the demoralization of the Flatheads, forced the Jesuits to abandon their mission of St. Mary's in the Bitterroot Valley in 1850.

Four years later Denig observed that the Assiniboins "have had the worst of it" in their wars with the Blackfeet.[4] That same year the agent for the Crow Indians reported:

> Scarcely a day passes but the Crow country is infested with more or less parties of Blackfeet, who murder indiscriminately anyone who comes within their reach. At Fort Sarpy [the principal trading post among the Crows] so great is the danger that no one ventures over a few yards from his own door without company and being well-armed.[5]

So relentless were the Blackfoot attacks that the American Fur Company abandoned Fort Sarpy the following spring. For two years prior to 1856 the Crow Indians preferred to go without the annuities to which they were entitled under the terms of the Fort Laramie Treaty of 1851, "rather than run the risk of passing through a country beset by their deadliest enemies, the Blackfeet and Blood Indians of the north."[6] Denig feared that the Crows, caught between the Blackfeet on the north and the powerful Sioux on the east, might be exterminated.[7]

It is doubtful that any other western tribes were so genuinely feared by so many other tribes as were the Blackfeet in the middle of the nineteenth century. The Assiniboins, the western

[2] James Doty to Isaac I. Stevens, December 20, 1854, Indian Office Records.
[3] Rev. Pierre Jean De Smet, *Life, Letters and Travels of Father Pierre Jean De Smet*, III, 992.
[4] *Indian Tribes of the Upper Missouri*, B.A.E., 46th Ann. Rept., 399.
[5] Reports of the Commissioner of Indian Affairs, 1854, 85.
[6] *Ibid.*, 1856, 81.
[7] Denig, "Of the Crow Nation," B.A.E. *Bulletin 151*, 71.

bands of Crees, the Crows, Shoshonis, Flatheads, Pend d'Oreilles, and Kutenais all looked upon them as their greatest enemies.

Nevertheless, Blackfoot warfare was aimed at neither the systematic extermination of enemy tribes nor the acquisition of their territory. It was not organized and directed by a central military authority, nor was it prosecuted by large, disciplined armies. Rather, Blackfoot warfare was carried on primarily by numerous small parties of volunteers who banded together to capture horses from enemy tribes. Each raiding party was hastily organized before departure and disbanded immediately after its return home. It might never see action again as a military unit. Its members were motivated much less by tribal patriotism than by hope of personal gain—the economic security and social prestige that possession of a goodly number of horses would bring them. The killing of enemy tribesmen and the taking of scalps were not major objectives of these raids.

Many of the most active Blackfoot horse raiders were members of poor families who were ambitious to better their lot. They were inclined to take the most desperate chances. Some acquired horses, settled down, and became respected members of the middle class. A few became wealthy. Many lost their lives in actions with the enemy. Most sons of middle-class families needed more horses than their fathers could give them if they were to marry and set up their own households. A few cowardly fellows and some sons of wealthy men never went on horse raids. But there were also rich young men who loved the excitement of these raids and coveted the prestige that could be gained through success in war.

The raiding party itself offered the best training ground for the would-be warrior. Boys in their middle teens joined these parties to learn the arts of war. More than a century ago Doty observed:

> In one of these parties are generally found 3 or 4 young men, or mere boys, who are apprentices. They go without the expectation of receiving a horse, carry extra moccasins and tobacco for

the party, do all the camp drudgery, and consider themselves amply repaid in being permitted to learn the science of horse stealing from such experienced hands.[8]

Sometimes a childless wife, who preferred to share her husband's dangers rather than to stay home anxiously awaiting his return, accompanied a raiding party.

The seasoned Blackfoot raider was a courageous, alert, resourceful fighting man. Nevertheless, he did not attribute his success in war to these qualities. Rather he attributed it to the power of his war medicine. No leader or active member of a war party took the field without his war medicine. It would both protect him from harm and insure his success in his hazardous adventure. A young man might obtain war medicine in a dream in which a kindly spirit appeared, took pity on him, and gave him some of its supernatural power, together with complete instructions for making the sacred symbol of this power and for its use. However, it was more common for a young man to obtain his war medicine from an elderly man who had been a war hero in his youth and whose own war medicine had proved its potency by bringing him safely through many dangerous raids.

Before a young man embarked on a raid, he might take a pipe and other gifts to a noted old veteran and ask him for help. This older man might be his own father. Usually he was a relative. The young fellow made a sweat lodge for the older man, who prayed for him and who transferred to him some of his power and the sacred symbols thereof—a war song, face paints, a sacred object to be worn in action, and instructions for their use.

Of more than fifty Blackfoot war medicines known to me, the great majority were single feathers or bunches of feathers worn in the hair. Perhaps feathers were favored because they were light and compact—practical articles for carrying on long journeys afoot. But there were other war medicines—necklaces, bandoleers, headdresses, shirts, knives, and lances. Running Wolf's war medicine was a moon-shaped brass necklace with pendant

[8] James Doty to Isaac I. Stevens, December 20, 1854, Indian Office Records.

feathers. The figure of a horse was incised on the brass ornament. Before going into an enemy camp to capture horses, Running Wolf sprinkled water on his necklace. "In a short time clouds would gather and cover the moon, making it easier to take horses from the enemy without being seen."

The horse-raiding party was led by an experienced man whose war record and good judgment inspired confidence in his ability to lead a group of men to an enemy camp, capture a goodly number of horses, and return home without losing any member of his party. The leader (or partisan, as the fur traders often referred to him) might invite others to join him on a raid, or several young men might come to him and ask him to be their leader. No one was compelled to go on these raids. All participants were volunteers. Although the leader might be a mature man in his thirties (rarely more than forty years of age), most of his followers were young men in their late teens or early twenties. Often two young men who were close friends joined a war party together. As partners they would look after one another in the field.

Spring and summer were favorite seasons for horse raids. Rarely did the Blackfeet try to raid the tribes west of the Rockies in winter, when deep snows clogged the familiar mountain passes. However, some raiders preferred to take horses from neighboring plains tribes in winter because their enemies were less vigilant in winter and falling snow would quickly obliterate the tracks of captured horses, making it impossible for their enemies to follow them after they started for home.

Before setting out on a raid, the party was supposed to obtain permission of the band chief, who was thus informed of their destination and objective. They would not do it, however, if they believed he might object to their venture. On the evening before departure the prospective raiders walked around camp drumming on a piece of buffalo rawhide and singing their wolf (war) songs. Their friends and relatives gave them food and extra moccasins to take on their journey. Other young men, upon hearing their drumming, might ask to join the party. The leader would refuse their requests if he thought they were unreliable or if he believed his party was large enough. Most horse-raiding parties were small, comprising less than a dozen men. Many leaders did not want large parties, for they were too difficult to command and to conceal from enemy eyes. Occasionally, parties of fifty or more men did raid for horses. Rarely, too, two or three men set out on one of these perilous quests.

After drumming around the camp, members of the party agreed upon a location at some distance outside the village where they would muster later that night or in the morning. Because they did not want to attract a host of brash young neophytes or uninvited incompetents, they kept the time and place of their meeting secret.

The objective of the horse raid was neither to kill enemies nor to take scalps but to capture horses. Like the World War II Commando raid, it was a stealthy operation in which the little attacking group tried to take the enemy by complete surprise, to strike quickly and quietly, in darkness or at dawn, achieve its limited objective, and be off before the enemy learned of its loss.

The raiders' dress and equipment were limited to the bare essentials. Because a group of footmen could conceal themselves easier than could horsemen on the outward journey, they usually set out on foot. In warmer weather they wore plain buckskin shirts and leggings, breechclouts, and moccasins. In winter they preferred Hudson's Bay blanket coats with white backgrounds which provided a practical camouflage against snow-covered ground and overcast skies. Hair-lined moccasins and mittens and a fur cap with earflaps protected their extremities from the cold.

Each man carried a light pack containing several pairs of moccasins, one or more rawhide ropes for catching, riding, or leading horses, an awl and sinew for repairing moccasins, a small pipe with a short willow stem and some tobacco for an occasional smoke en route, and the raider's personal war medicine. These things were wrapped in a blanket roll carried on the back by a rawhide strap over the chest. Each man also carried his food for the early stages of the journey—some dried meat or pemmican in a rawhide case suspended by a shoulder strap or tied on top of his pack. Each also carried a sharp, heavy-bladed knife in a rawhide sheath at his belt. It served both as a tool and as a weapon. With it he cut firewood and timbers for temporary shelters, butchered animals killed for food, and, if the need arose, silently killed an enemy and lifted his scalp. Each also carried another weapon—either a short bow and quiver of arrows or a muzzle-loading flintlock with shot pouch and powder horn.

The raider's complete equipment probably weighed less than twenty pounds, including a gun weighing a little over four pounds. With this light load he set out on an expedition that might take him six hundred or more miles, at least half that distance on foot. In the early part of the outward journey, when danger from the enemy was not great, the raiders traveled in daylight. Moving at a steady pace and stopping now and then to rest and smoke, they made about twenty-five miles a day. But as they neared the enemy country, they traveled at night and hid during the day.

On approaching enemy territory, the raiders stopped to kill enough game to provide food for the remainder of their journey. Usually they built a war lodge in a heavily timbered bottom or on a thickly wooded height, or repaired an old one built by some earlier party. If a new lodge was needed, all set to work gathering fallen timbers or cutting new ones to erect a conical framework of poles. This they covered with bark or brush. They then laid heavy logs around the base and built an angled, covered entrance way. Working industriously, a war party could complete the lodge, large enough to sleep a dozen men, in two hours. It was built well inside the edge of timber, where it could not be seen from the open plains. But it was on dangerous ground. All hands were needed to speed the work.

A lazy fellow who refused to perform his share of the labor— who was content to let the others gather materials for the war lodge or who would not go after firewood when the leader asked him to do so—made himself very unpopular. Sometimes the others deliberately left a small hole in the side of the lodge over the place where he was to sleep, to let the rain, snow, or wind in on him. If the war party enjoyed a favorite dish of Crow-guts (buffalo intestines turned inside out and stuffed with meat), the cook secretly filled one end of the intestine with a piece of tough rawhide. After the other members were served the delicious meat-filled portion, the unpalatable rawhide end was given to the idle fellow. This treatment might make an indolent man so angry he would leave the party and return home. If the others were successful in their raid, the lazy fellow who went home in advance of the others became an object of ridicule.[9]

Under most circumstances desertion of a raiding party was considered a cowardly act. Aged veterans of many raiding parties frankly told me that there were times on the outward journeys when they grew homesick for their wives or sweethearts and fearful of the dangers ahead. They were tempted to turn back, but instead they quietly sang their war songs, which helped them to regain their courage. However, if a member of a party had a bad dream in which he was warned of disaster ahead, he was privileged to turn back. So great was Blackfoot respect for the messages received in dreams that they said any man who accused another of cowardice because he heeded his dream warning and went home would surely be killed on the expedition.

The war lodge not only provided shelter from rain, snow, and cold, but concealed the fire of relatively smokeless willow branches built inside and served as a fortress in case of enemy attack. It was a base of supplies, where some food could be left to be picked up on the return journey, and a base for scouting operations.

From the war lodge the leader sent several picked men ahead to locate the enemy camp. Thus he avoided the danger that could arise from the entire party's searching for a nomadic foe in enemy country. The scouts moved with utmost caution, fearful of encountering enemy war or hunting parties. Wearing wolfskin disguises, they surveyed the surrounding country from high

[9] John C. Ewers, "The Blackfoot War Lodge: Its Construction and Use," *American Anthropologist,* Vol. XLVI, No. 2, 184–85.

ground to make sure they could proceed with safety. They examined burned-out campfires and horse tracks, as well as tracks made by travois and footmen, to determine their recency and direction of movement. They were alert to any sudden movement of birds or animals that might indicate the nearness of other humans.

Meanwhile, the other members of the raiding party left at the war lodge hunted buffalo, deer, elk, or any other game that might provide dried meat for the remainder of their journey. They butchered the animals, dried the meat, and filled the men's provision bags. Sometimes they prepared an additional meat packet—a small rawhide container that could be fastened to the belt, holding enough concentrated dried meat to provide an occasional mouthful for the raider hastening homeward with captured horses. One of these packets was made for each man. It was called "war lunch."

When the scouts located the enemy camp, they watched it from a concealed position long enough to determine its size, the number of men, and the number and quality of horses. They then returned to the war lodge as rapidly as they could. As they came in sight of their waiting comrades, they approached in a zigzag course, signifying that they had found the enemy. While the leader went to meet them, the others set up a pile of sticks near the lodge. Returning with the scouts the leader kicked over this pile of sticks, and all the men scrambled for them. Each stick a fellow retrieved was considered a prophecy of a horse he would take from the enemy.

Guided by their scouts, the party then moved toward the enemy village, traveling by night and hiding during the day, until they reached a concealed spot overlooking or in sight of the enemy. The leader closely observed how the enemy picketed their choice horses near their lodges and where they drove their less valuable horses for night pasture. Then he explained his plan of attack.

As the zero hour approached, each party member opened his pack, prayed for success, sang his war song, painted himself, and donned his war medicine. Usually his prayers were addressed to the sun or the moon (who in Blackfoot belief was sun's wife) and consisted of a simple, direct appeal for help in taking horses and reaching home safely. These long moments before going into action were tense, even terrifying ones for the inexperienced younger fellows. One of them might ask a more experienced comrade for some of his medicine. Or a young man might make a solemn vow to give a feast for the owner of some sacred bundle back home or to undergo the agonizing self-torture in the sun dance of his tribe if he accomplished his mission.

The attack usually was scheduled for daybreak. Then the leader and a few of his bravest and most experienced men walked noiselessly into the enemy camp. If dogs barked, they threw bits of meat to them, waited, circled the camp, and approached it from another direction. Sometimes these men rubbed cottonwood sap on their hands and bodies. Its odor tended to quiet the horses and make them more willing to follow strangers. Quickly they approached the best horses, which were picketed in front of the lodges of their sleeping enemies, cut the picket lines with their sharp knives, and led the prized animals away. If there was no noise within the camp, no indication that any of the enemy had been roused, these adept horse thieves left the horses they had taken with a boy or inexperienced member of their party outside the camp and returned for more picketed animals. Sometimes the other members of the raiding party drove off some of the range herds while their leader and his most able men were after the picketed animals.

Whether or not the raiders' movements woke their enemies, it was important that they make a quick getaway in order to get as much head start on their pursuers as possible. Sometimes, in their haste to get away, a member of the party was left behind without a horse to ride. He had to shift for himself—find a hiding place in the brush until the next evening and get home alone as best he could.

It was always dangerous for a raiding party to be too greedy. To stay too long in the enemy camp or to try to run off too many horses was asking for trouble. Driving loose horses at a fast pace over uneven country, through timber and across streams for hundreds of miles, was a difficult task. Sometimes loose horses had to be abandoned to prevent the party from being overtaken by the enemy. Not infrequently an overambitious raiding party was overtaken and its men had to fight for their lives. My older Blackfoot informants, men who had raided for horses, could not recall that any Blackfoot party had brought home as many as one hundred horses, although they knew of parties that had driven off more than that number from enemy camps. Forty to sixty horses was considered a very good haul.

On the first leg of the homeward journey the raiders set a fast pace. For two or three days the men rode day and night, changing from one mount to another as the horses tired. Then the men stopped for a good overnight rest. Next morning they divided the captured horses. Unless the party had decided upon an equal distribution of the animals taken, each man could claim the horses he had led out of camp or the range stock he had run off. Bitter arguments over the ownership of range horses jointly run off by several Indians sometimes followed. It was the leader's duty to settle these disputes as equitably as possible. Some leaders gave fine horses they themselves had taken to members of their parties who could claim none. A leader's generosity helped him to maintain a reputation as a popular leader who would not want for followers in the future.

From this point the raiders rode homeward at a more leisurely pace. When near their camp, they stopped to paint their faces and decorate their horses. Then they rode triumphantly toward camp, firing their guns in the air to signal their return. After they were welcomed home, successful raiders gave horses to their relatives, most commonly to their fathers-in-law or brothers-in-law. Nor did the young warrior forget the old man who had prayed for him and given him his war medicine. He invited his benefactor to his lodge, fed him well, and gave him one or more of the animals he had taken on the raid.

This was the pattern of the successful Blackfoot horse raid—

one which accomplished its limited objective without loss from action with the enemy. Many parties were not so lucky. The artist Paul Kane, in 1847, learned of an outward-bound horse-raiding party of seven men, led by the Blackfoot Big Horn, which had the misfortune of meeting a formidable Cree force.

This small band, seeing their inferiority to their enemies, attempted flight; but finding escape impossible, they instantly dug holes sufficiently deep to entrench themselves from which they kept up a constant fire with guns and arrows, and for nearly twelve hours held at bay this large war party, bringing down every man who ventured within shot, until their ammunition and arrows were entirely exhausted, when of course they fell an easy prey to their enemies, thirty of whom had fallen before their fire. This so enraged the Crees that they cut them in pieces, and mangled the dead bodies in a most brutal manner, and carried their scalps back as trophies. It is said that Big Horn frequently sprang out from his entrenchment, and tried to irritate his foes by recounting the numbers of them he had destroyed, and boasting his many war exploits, and the Cree scalps that then hung in his lodge. So exasperated were they against him, that they tore out his heart from his quivering body, and savagely devoured it amongst them.[10]

Alexander Culbertson told of three Blood warriors and a woman who were en route to a Crow Indian camp to capture horses. While they were stopping to smoke, they were attacked by thirty mounted Crow fighting men. Two of the Blood men were killed instantly. The third, though wounded, knocked one of the horsemen from his saddle, jumped on the horse, and escaped to Fort McKenzie. The lone woman was taken prisoner, stripped of her clothes, and kept under constant watch. One stormy night her captors relaxed their vigilance, and she escaped. Five days later she was seen by Culbertson in the bushes near Fort McKenzie. Naked, barefoot, and without food, she had made her way to the fort.

[10] *Wanderings of an Artist*, 284–85. Father De Smet doubtless referred to this same action (De Smet, *Life, Letters and Travels*, II, 520–21).

She was in a sad plight, being entirely naked except for the little protection afforded by bunches of sagebrush tied about her person, with feet lacerated by days of travel over stones and prickly pear, and worn down with exposure, fatigue and starvation . . . She was at once clothed and fed, and speedily recovered from the effects of her painful experience.[11]

Such were the hazards of horse raiding and the courageous ways in which the Blackfeet faced them. It is not possible to estimate the number of these small-scale actions in which the Blackfeet were involved. But the testimony of veteran horse raiders indicates that they were not uncommon. The first impulse of a small raiding party on sighting a superior enemy force seems to have been to run for shelter in timber or thickets if such refuge was near. The enemy was loath to approach wooded areas in which their opponents could not be seen. In woods or brush a gallant little group of men might hold off a much larger enemy force until nightfall and escape under cover of darkness.

If they were overtaken on the open plains at a distance from timber, the smaller party hastily dug foxholes with their knives and prepared to sell their lives dearly. The attacking force, if it was on foot, moved forward, keeping constantly in motion, jumping from side to side to prevent the men in the foxholes from taking careful aim. Those men who had the greatest confidence in the protective powers of their war medicines led the attack. They might storm the fortification and wipe out the defenders, but not without heavy losses among their own men.

The killing of one or more of their beloved leaders or of a number of their warriors roused the Blackfeet to seek revenge not only upon the killers but upon their entire tribe. On such an occasion they organized an expedition in force with the avowed object of taking enemy scalps. Sometimes presents of tobacco were sent to other tribes of the Blackfoot group accompanied by a request for assistance in raising a large war party.

This large-scale scalp raid differed markedly from the much

[11] Bradley, "Manuscript," *MHSC*, Vol. III, 211–12.

more common horse raid in many ways. Prior to its departure, all the warriors who volunteered to participate rode for a distance outside the camp, where they mustered, dismounted, donned their war clothes and face paint, and decorated their horses, then mounted and converged upon the camp, carrying their weapons. While the mounted warriors circled the camp, several old men and women stood in the center of it, drumming and singing a lively song. The riders shouted, dismounted, and danced on foot beside their horses, imitating the prancing of spirited horses. This "riding big dance" was an impressive show of tribal solidarity and determination. It roused the fighting spirit of the entire group and sent the warriors off on their mission with the encouragement of those who remained behind. It might be likened to a modern football pep rally before a football team departs for a crucial game on the opponent's field.

Usually the raiding party was led by a prominent chief whose war experience and success in battle qualified him for leadership in the eyes of his followers. Its members rode ordinary saddle horses and led their prize buffalo horses to save their strength for the battle ahead. The warriors set out wearing their ordinary clothes, but carried their war medicines and fancy war clothes (if they were prosperous enough to own them) in bundles tied to their saddles. They carried their fire weapons (flintlocks or bows and arrows), shock weapons (war clubs and knives), and defensive shields of rawhide. Scouts were sent ahead to search for enemy camps and wandering enemy war parties.

If the scouts were lucky enough to find an inferior force, the Blackfeet lost little time in changing to their war clothes, putting on their war medicines, mounting their best horses, and attacking. Thus, in the year 1849, a large Blackfoot party (estimated, perhaps too highly, at eight hundred men) fell upon a party of fifty-two Assiniboin horse raiders and annihilated them.[12]

When seeking revenge for earlier losses at the hands of the enemy, the Blackfeet wreaked terrible revenge upon their vic-

[12] Edwin T. Denig to Alexander Culbertson, December 1, 1849, Missouri Historical Society Library.

tims. A Blackfoot warrior whose father, brother, or best friend had been killed by the tribe he was fighting was not content merely to take the scalp of a fallen enemy. He mutilated the body of his foe—cut off his hands, feet, and head, or even literally hacked him to pieces.[13]

In 1848, Paul Kane heard a report of a Blackfoot massacre of a party of Crees. Among "the slain was a pipe-stem carrier, whom they skinned and stuffed with grass; the figure was then placed in a trail which the Crees were accustomed to pass in their hunting excursions."[14]

If these actions on the part of Blackfoot warriors appear bloodthirsty, it is well to remember that they received no softer treatment from their enemies when the tables were reversed. Cruelty bred more cruelty. The reliable reporter Edwin T. Denig recorded this incident in the year 1854:

> some Blackfeet stole horses from the Cree camp, were pursued and 11 out of 12 of which the party consisted were killed. The remaining one was taken, scalped, his right hand cut off, and thus started back to his own nation to tell the news. Now as this man was leaving the camp he met a Cree boy whom he managed to kill with his remaining hand, was pursued and taken the second time, and was tortured to death by slow mutilation.[15]

In the spring of 1853 the Crow Indians pursued five Blackfoot warriors who stole horses from their camp near Fort Union.

> The Crows surrounded them and by constant firing killed all except one who was shot through the leg. This man they took out alive, scalped, and cut his hands off, gathered their boys around and shot into his body with powder, striking him in his face with his own scalp, and knocking on his head with stones and tomahawks, until he died. Afterwards the five bodies were carried

[13] See Maximilian's description of the mutilation of a fallen Assiniboin which he witnessed in 1833, pp. 62–63 this book.
[14] *Wanderings of an Artist*, 289.
[15] *Indian Tribes of the Upper Missouri*, B.A.E., 46th Ann. Rept., 492.

to the camp, the heads, hands, feet and privates cut off, paraded on poles, and thrown around the camp, some of which found their way to the fort and were presented to the Cree Indians then there.[16]

Scalping an enemy, so elderly Blackfoot Indians who performed this feat in their youth have told me, was quickly accomplished by leaning over the victim who was lying on the ground face down, grasping his hair with the left hand, using the right hand to cut around his crown with a sharp knife, and jerking off the hair with skin attached, removing a section of the scalp about three inches in diameter. Some warriors who had been scalped alive recovered and lived to fight again. My aged informants corroborated Maximilian's observations that survivors of scalping generally wore caps to cover their bald spots.[17]

The Blackfoot Indians graded war honors on the basis of the degree of courage displayed in winning them. They recognized that a man might scalp an enemy who had been killed by another and that a man might kill an enemy from a considerable distance with bullet or arrow. Their term for war honor, *"namachkani,"* meant literally "a gun taken." The capture of an enemy's gun ranked as the highest war honor. The capture of a bow, shield, war bonnet, war shirt, or ceremonial pipe was also a coup of high rank. The taking of a scalp ranked below these deeds, but ahead of the capture of a horse from the enemy. The capture of a horse was too common an accomplishment to receive a higher rating.

After collecting their trophies, the successful scalp raiders rode homeward. As they neared their camp, they began to sing and proudly display their trophies. The wife or other female relative of each man who had brought home a trophy carried it in the post-raid scalp dance. The hands, feet, scalps, or even the heads of fallen enemies were raised on poles borne by the women as they danced in a circle. These gruesome trophies proved to the

[16] *Ibid.,* 491–92.
[17] Maximilian, *Travels,* II, 120.

entire camp that Blackfoot warriors had revenged their past losses at the hands of their enemy. Usually they were thrown away after the scalp dance. They had served their purpose.

Battles between large Blackfoot forces and sizable enemy ones were rare. However, during the 1840's and 1850's, the Blackfoot tribes repeatedly attacked the small Flathead, Pend d'Oreille, and Kutenai tribes when they crossed the Rockies to hunt buffalo on the plains. The Jesuit missionary Father Gregory Mengarini, who accompanied the Flatheads to the plains in the spring of 1846, graphically described one of these actions:

> When the enemy is sighted, word flies from mouth to mouth, and all is hurry and bustle for a few minutes. Some strip themselves naked. These are poor men from whom the enemy can expect little. Others clothe themselves in calicos of flaming colors to show their riches and invite the attack of such as dare to face them. One thing remained to be done; the women and children and the missionary must be taken to a place of safety.
>
> Firing had already begun on both sides, and the plain was covered with horsemen curvetting and striving to get a chance to kill some one of the enemy. An Indian battle consists of a multitude of single combats. There are no ranks, no battalions, no united efforts. Every man for himself is the ruling principle, and victory depends on personal bravery and good horsemanship. There is no random shooting, every Flathead or Blackfoot always aims for the waist.[18]

Although this battle lasted nearly all day, only four Flathead Indians were killed. They claimed the Blackfeet lost twenty-four men. However, Indians commonly exaggerated both the numbers and the casualties of their opponents.

In large-scale battles, when the size of the opposing forces was nearly equal, Blackfoot tactics suffered from weakness of organization and command and the relative independence of the individual warriors. Blackfoot fighting men were not soldiers but

[18] *Mengarini's Narrative of the Rockies*, Montana State University, *Sources of Northwest History No. 25*, 17.

gladiators. True, they sometimes formed a line and charged the enemy on horseback, bending low over their horses' necks and weaving their bodies from side to side. A boy learned the difficult feat of protecting his body by hanging on the side of his horse, but men in combat rarely employed this trick-riding technique. It was too dangerous to expose the entire side of one's horse to enemy fire.

If their enemies were afoot, the Blackfeet tried to ride them down. Upon overtaking a mounted enemy, the rider tried to unhorse him with his war club. Then he dismounted and tried to finish him off with his war club or knife. A favorite shock weapon was a broad, sharp, double-edged knife known to the Blackfeet as a "stabber" or "beaver tail knife." Grasping the handle so that the steel blade protruded from the heel of his fist, the warrior employed a powerful downward motion to strike his opponent above the clavicle, or a sidewise sweep to stab him between the ribs or in the stomach. This knife was useful in finishing off a wounded or disabled enemy and for taking his scalp.

If the initial ferocious charge was repulsed, the warriors were apt to fall back and continue the battle from a distance of one hundred yards or more with their fire weapons. The muzzle-loading flintlock, which had been so frightening to their enemies in the early years of its use, proved a relatively ineffective weapon after both sides became armed with these guns. Because it was difficult to reload on a running horse, riders commonly dismounted to employ it. Their well-trained horses stood near by. To speed the loading process the warriors held the bullets in their mouths. They quickly measured two fingers of powder from the horn into the barrel, lifted the barrel to the mouth and dropped a ball into it, gave the stock a couple of hard blows with the hand to settle the charge and eject some powder into the pan, lifted the gun, aimed, and fired. But without wadding, both range and velocity of fire were impaired.

Governor Isaac I. Stevens called the Indians' firearm "an inferior kind of shot-gun." He regarded the bow and arrow as "a much more efficient weapon in the hands of an Indian than a gun."[19] This was one good reason why many of the Blackfeet continued to fight with bow and arrow. Some poor young men could not afford a gun. Others carried both gun and bow and arrows to war.

In the intertribal warfare on the northwestern plains a century ago, the accent was placed upon offensive operations. The Blackfeet suffered almost as much as their neighbors from repeated thefts of valuable horses by small raiding parties. Nevertheless, they normally went to bed without posting night guards. Only when they discovered signs during the day that led them to believe enemy raiders were in the neighborhood did they take special precautions to protect their horses. Then they might build a crude corral of cottonwood posts connected by crossrails lashed to the posts with rawhide rope, and place a guard near by. Some nights the men and women of a lodge took turns staying awake listening for any unusual restlessness among the picketed horses or any sound that might indicate the presence of an enemy horse thief in their camp. More rarely, when they believed an enemy horse raid was imminent, young men set a trap by concealing themselves in the tall grass surrounding the camp, lying flat on their stomachs with their loaded guns beside them. When the unsuspecting enemy approached they jumped up and opened fire at close range. Sometimes the men lying in ambush picketed a handsome horse near them, hoping to lure a horse-crazy enemy into their trap.

Older men and chiefs tired of incessant warfare with neighboring tribes and the terrible losses suffered in numerous engagements both large and small. Sometimes they managed to negotiate a peace with like-minded chiefs of an enemy tribe. But their peace usually proved to be only a short breather between hostilities. Their efforts were nullified by their own ambitious young men who needed enemy horses and war honors to gain economic and social status.

[19] Reports of the Commissioner of Indian Affairs, 1854, 205.

Father De Smet learned of a Crow attempt to make peace with their old Blackfoot enemies. The principal Crow chief sent twenty-five warriors, guided by a Blackfoot captive who had been offered his freedom, to present a pipe of peace to the Blackfeet. As they neared the large Blackfoot camp on the Marias River, they met two Blackfoot hunters. Two men of the Crow party, whose brothers had been killed by the Blackfeet a month before, killed them and hid their scalps in their bullet pouches.

When they reached the Blackfoot encampment, they found the leaders willing to accept the Crow peace offer. That night a curious Blackfoot woman found one of the scalps in a Crow bullet pouch and took it to her chief. He recognized the hair as that of one of the young hunters who had failed to return. After telling her to keep quiet about her find, the chief ordered his best warriors to be armed and ready at daybreak.

The following morning the chief showed the Crow delegation the scalp and asked who among them had taken it. When no one claimed it, the woman who had found it pointed out the man in whose pouch it was. He then manfully acknowledged it.

Unwilling to commit murder on the ground where they had smoked the peace pipe with the Crow delegates only the day before, the Blackfoot chief offered the Crow warriors a chance to start for home—as far as a near-by hill. When they reached it, the Blackfoot warriors went after them. The Crows hid in a deep ravine and fought off several sporadic Blackfoot advances. From their protected position they killed a number of the Blackfoot attackers without loss to themselves.

The Blackfoot chief then appealed to his men to follow him in a mass assault. They rushed into the ravine and killed every man of the Crow delegation with knives and war clubs. Angered by the treacherous actions of this Crow group, as well as by the killing of members of their own avenging party, the Blackfoot women cut the bodies of the slain enemies into small pieces and carried them on poles around the camp, amid "chants of victory, yells of rage, and howling and vociferations against their enemies. There was also a general mourning caused by the loss of so many warriors fallen in this horrible engagement."[20]

So the war with the Crow Indians continued. And at the same time the Blackfoot tribes fought the Crees and Assiniboins and the many small tribes from west of the Rockies who dared to hunt buffalo on the plains.

[20] De Smet, *Life, Letters and Travels*, III, 1037–43.

Blackfoot woman with horse travois (*Courtesy Smithsonian Institution*).

8: All in Fun

T HE BLACKFOOT INDIANS were a far cry from those strong, silent, dead-pan caricatures of Indians commonly portrayed in the white man's western fiction and his motion pictures and television programs. They were really a fun-loving people who enjoyed funny stories, practical jokes, and a wide variety of games and sports. It is significant that they looked upon Old Man not only as the creator but as a humorous little fellow who went around trying to play tricks on people and animals and whose tricks sometimes backfired. Many Napi stories are not only funny, but obscene.[1]

The Blackfeet loved to poke fun at strangers, especially members of other bands. When a number of men gathered in a lodge to welcome a guest it was common for some of them to make indecent remarks about him. Should the guest appear annoyed at their jibes, they only intensified their efforts. It was the host's duty to prevent the joking from going too far. One Piegan band was noted for annoying visitors by a mock family row. The host began a quarrel with his wife. Neighbors rushed in and took the woman's part. In the general row which followed all fell upon the guest and roughed him up without doing him any serious injury.[2]

[1] Clark Wissler and D. C. Duvall, "Mythology of the Blackfoot Indians," American Museum of Natural History *Anthropological Papers*, Vol. II, Part 1. A selection of Napi stories appears on pages 19–39.
[2] Clark Wissler, "The Social Life of the Blackfoot Indians," American Museum of Natural History *Anthropological Papers*, Vol. VII, 53.

A measure of the fun-loving nature of the Blackfeet may be judged from the great number and variety of their games and amusements for young and old. Children's play varied with their ages, with the sexes, and with the seasons. It had real educational value. In their play children imitated many of the activities of their elders and so painlessly prepared themselves for the responsibilities of adult life. At play girls learned the rudiments of baby care, craftwork, housekeeping, and moving camp. Boys' competitive sports were rowdy enough to toughen their bodies and varied enough to develop their agility and skill in the use of weapons. This play helped to improve their bodily co-ordination and gave them valuable practice in making quick, sure decisions in the midst of action—excellent training for the future hunter and warrior. Adults found relaxation from the cares and tensions of daily life in games of skill or chance and in spectator sports. The common custom of gambling on the outcome intensified their interest in these activities.

Older children made their own playthings and gaming equipment. Little children's toys were made for them by their elders. A little girl of six or seven years who accompanied her grandmother into the brush to collect firewood might beg the old woman to make her a birch doll. The grandmother would cut a section of a birch limb about one foot long and four inches in diameter with her axe. She used her butcher knife to cut a groove around the piece about four inches from one end. This formed the doll's shoulder line. Above this line she whittled a crude, knob-like head and bored little holes in one side of the knob to suggest eyes, nose, and mouth. The simple doll had no ears, hair, or legs. The body retained the unaltered form of the birch cylinder below the shoulder line. Little girls clothed these dolls by simply wrapping a piece of buckskin or trade cloth around the cylinder.

As girls grew older, they wanted more realistic dolls. Then their mothers or grandmothers made them dolls with arms and legs as well as heads of skin or trade cloth stuffed with grass. The facial features were delineated with thread or trade beads.

These well-proportioned dolls were clothed in miniature garments very much like those worn by women of the tribe—skin dresses, leggings, moccasins, and robes. Human or horse hair was sewn to the head to complete the illusion of reality.

Adults made an ingenious hobbyhorse for small boys and girls to ride. A fairly heavy tree with a double bend in it was selected and felled. The bark was peeled off, and the thick, lower end placed in a hole in the ground deep enough so that the bend in the trunk would appear about thirty inches above the ground. Sometimes a carved wooden horse head was attached to the front and a stick or bundle of horsehair tied to the rear of this hobbyhorse to make it look more like a real animal. The child mounted astride the horizontal bend in the log. He might throw a piece of buffalo hide or an old saddle over the bend in the log, tie rawhide reins to the upper projection, and carry a stick for a whip while he rode as fast and furiously as his fertile imagination would permit. This toy was known as "crooked-buttocks shape."

Little boys themselves made toy horses from willow branches more than a foot in length. One end of the branch was split along the center; half of this split portion was turned up to form the head and neck, the other half turned down to make the forelegs. The other end of this branch was similarly split, and one half bent to make the tail, the other to provide the legs. In summer small boys playing along a stream bank made miniature horses of clay. While the clay was soft, they placed sticks in the end of each leg. When the modeled clay hardened in the sun, they could stand their horses in the earth. Boys swimming in summer sometimes collected flat stones and set them up in the sand beside the river. Pretending the stones were horses, they moved them about and confined them in little stick corrals.

In spring, small boys and girls played house. The boys snared gophers, peeled off the skins, turned them inside out, and filled them with grass to dry. Girls gathered sticks for foundation poles and sewed the skins together to make miniature tipi covers. Gopher skins were placed inside the lodges much as buffalo robes were used in their parents' homes for seats and bedding. Girls

147

also made miniature travois, parfleches, and other containers for use in playing at moving camp. They tied the luggage on the travois and attached the travois to a long forked stick. This stick played the role of the travois horse. The sharp lower end was pushed into the ground to hold up the travois when camp was "on the move." A doll rode in the fork of the stick like a woman astride her travois horse.[3]

Children made other crafts solely for their own amusement. In summer they pulled long strands of tough "earring grass" and wove them into little cups and baskets. In fall, when the leaves were changing colors, little girls collected cottonwood leaves and folded and tore them into the form of little tipis. They placed the brightly colored "tipis" in a circle and imagined them to be a great sun dance encampment of painted lodges. In early winter girls gathered silverberries, boiled them, and strung their gray seeds on sinew cords for necklaces.

Occasionally girls played a kind of crack-the-whip. Seven or eight girls formed a line, each girl holding on to the one in front of her by the waist. As the leader walked along she sang "Skunk with no hair on the backbone." Then she ran and tried to swing the line so that she could turn and tag the last girl in line. The girl at the back of the line could not let go of the one in front of her, but she could duck or move her body to avoid the outstretched hand of the leader. If this girl was tagged, she became the leader, and the girl in front of her became the last one in line.

Boys' play was both more active and more varied. Boys played at mimic hunting and warfare. When there was plenty of fresh meat in camp after a buffalo hunt, a group of boys tied a piece of meat to a long rawhide rope. One of them dragged the meat along the ground while the others ran after him with their bows and arrows, shooting at the meat. From time to time the lead boy stopped and pawed the ground with his feet, imitating the actions of a buffalo bull. Then he swung the meat in a circle around his head while the other boys continued to shoot at it.

[3] Ewers, "Horse in Blackfoot Indian Culture," B.A.E. *Bull.* 159, 225–27.

If a boy was accidentally hit by a blunt-headed arrow, he fell down groaning, and the other boys squeezed the juices from weeds and pretended to doctor him.[4]

In winter, boys hunted rabbits; in early summer, gophers and birds. When hawks were hatched in June or July, boys took the baby birds from their nests. They made a woven cage of willow withes about eighteen inches in diameter and hemispherical in shape. Sometimes they kept the hawks in the cage all winter, feeding them on gophers and other small animals. When camp was moved, the hawk cage was placed on top of a travois load. The next spring, boys used the hawk feathers for fletching their arrows.

In spring, boys played the "clay war game." They went to a river bank where there was plenty of soft, wet clay. Each boy cut a willow stick about six feet long. They divided into two groups of equal numbers. Each group made a supply of clay balls about two inches in diameter. Then the opposing groups faced each other about seventy-five yards apart. The object of the game was to fit a ball of wet clay to the end of the willow rod and swing it with such force that the pellet flew through the air and hit one of the opponents. Older men who played this game in their boyhood said the pellets traveled "like bullets" and "they sure hurt if they hit you."

At the summer sun dance encampment boys held another throwing contest. Each boy cut himself a willow rod a little thicker than a lead pencil and a little over two feet long. He peeled the bark off and hardened the stick in a fire. These sticks were thrown for distance, the stick sliding along the ground as far as possible. Each boy held the back of his stick between his thumb and two fingers. Informants claimed some boys could make one of these "sliding sticks" travel about one hundred yards. The boy who threw his stick the farthest took all the sticks of his competitors. In a variant of this game, boys threw their sliding sticks toward a distant stake placed in the ground. The one whose stick came to rest nearest the stake was the winner.

[4] Joseph K. Dixon, *The Vanishing Race*, 111.

Boys bet arrows on another throwing contest called "humpies." The missile was a section of willow branch with a piece of the trunk or larger branch attached to it. The boy who could throw this piece of wood the greatest distance was the winner.

Archery contests were popular and consumed much of the boys' playtime. One contest, usually held in spring, consisted of shooting at an arrow placed upright in the ground below the crest of a hill from a distance of about fifty yards. The boy whose arrow was closest to the target won the arrows of his rivals. Another archery competition, known as "walking arrow shooting," was begun by one boy shooting an arrow and all the others using it as a target. They did not return to their starting place, but, instead, a second target arrow was shot from the site of the first target and the contestants shot again. Again arrows were bet on each shot, with the understanding that the winner took all.

The winner of a stationary target contest took the arrows he had won and shot them at a moving target. This was a packet of buckbrush about five inches long tied with rawhide cord. He threw the target into the air, raised his bow, and shot before the buckbrush dropped to the ground. Each arrow that failed to hit the target was returned to its original owner.

The period of the summer encampment, when all the boys of the tribe were together, was a specially active time for them. About sunset two groups of boys sat down opposite one another. A large flat stone was placed on the ground in front of each group. The boys spat on the stone, placed a hot coal from a fire on top of it, then hit the coal a solid whack with a stone maul. This made a report like the crack of a gun. It was important to keep the big rock moist with saliva, because a dry rock would not make as loud a report as a wet one. The only object of this contest was to see which group of boys could make the loudest noise. This was simply called the "fire game."

Wrestling also was popular in the summer encampment. Sometimes all the boys living in tipis on the south side of the camp circle challenged the boys living on the north side of the circle. The leader of one group called upon a certain lad from the other to come out and wrestle any member of his side that boy might choose. The challenged boy stepped forward and pulled the fellow he wished to wrestle to his feet by the hair of his head. They struggled until one of them was knocked off his feet. Wrestling continued until one boy defeated four successive opponents. Then all the boys of both sides joined in a general melee. They tried to strike members of the opposite side by kicking backwards like horses. One old informant recalled, "If you got kicked in the thigh, you really knew it."

Winter brought an end to fair-weather games and sports, as well as to swimming in the rivers or lakes near camp, all of which Blackfoot children loved. But boys and girls had no less fun on the snowy hills and ice-covered rivers near their winter camps. Coasting down the steep slopes and out on the valley floor was always popular. Girls rode on raw buffalo hides. It is said that their mothers watched these hides closely. If a girl returned home with a hide that had become worn soft, her mother took it from her to cut up for moccasin soles or rawhide rope. Boys used cleverly made sleds with five to ten buffalo rib-bone runners. The ribs were separated from the backbone and reassembled in exactly the same order. They were tied together tightly at each end by a rawhide rope that wound around a crosspiece of split willow. The seat was a piece of the leg skin of a buffalo, tied at each end to the willow crossbars. A buffalo-tail ornament was sewed or tied to the rear of the seat. A rawhide rope, tied to the front end, served to pull the sled uphill and to guide it in sliding down. Before riding on the sled, the owner pulled it around in the snow until the runners were coated with ice. In coasting, the boy sat on the hide seat, leaned well back, and balanced his weight by extending his legs forward and upward at an angle. He held the rawhide rope in his hands and jerked it to one side if he wished to turn his sled. The buffalo-tail decoration trailed behind, flopping crazily in the breeze.

Sometimes boys tried to see who could coast the greatest distance down the slope and into the valley. At other times, when the snow was well packed on the ground, they pushed their riderless sleds down the slope to see which one could travel the greatest distance. Sometimes, too, a group of boys and girls of about the same age played "hunting the buffalo." First a group of girls started coasting downhill on buffalo hides. They were the buffalo. Then boys, representing hunters, followed on their sleds. When all piled up at the bottom of the hill, each boy would poke a girl in the pit of the stomach and shout, "I kill you now."

There were several other children's games played in snow. The children tried to see who could hop the farthest on one leg in deep snow. In another contest, boys on one side tossed a small boy from the other side in a buffalo robe or blanket. They tried to toss him so high he would cry out that he had had enough. If they could make him do that, they won; if they could not, the other side was declared the winner. A variation of that game was one in which boys of one side held a buffalo robe stretched tightly, on which a small boy of the other side stood. At the same time a boy on the ground took a deep breath and repeated the sound "tups, tups, tups." If the boy fell off the shaky buffalo robe before the other one was out of breath, his side lost. If he remained standing after the other boy lost his breath, his side won.

Boys spun tops on the snow or ice. Each boy had a birchwood top about two and one-half inches high, tapering from a diameter of one and one-half inches above to a point at the base. He started his top spinning with a quick twist of the wrist and kept it turning by stroking it occasionally with the deerskin lashes of a willow-handled whip. Tops were spun on hard-trampled snow or, more often, on a thin covering of snow on the river ice.

A favorite top game was played on a circular track of packed snow about twenty feet in diameter. At intervals, little cross trenches were dug in the snow. Two boys tried to see which of them could spin his top the greatest distance around the circle. It required considerable skill to whip the moving top so that it would jump one of the trenches and keep spinning after it landed on the other side of it. The winner took the loser's top as a forfeit.

Another top game was played on smooth river ice, substituting round stones about the size of a man's fist for the wooden tops. Two boys started their stones spinning rapidly, then whipped them together as hard as they could. The boy whose stone cracked the other one or continued to spin the longest after the collision was the winner.

When it was snowing, boys and girls enjoyed sliding on the river ice. They ran and, as they began to slide, started to repeat the phrase, "Man, it's sure true." They tried to say this phrase (in Blackfoot, of course) as many times as they could before they came to a stop. When there was snow on the river ice, girls cleared a long path in a large oval. Sometimes it followed the river around a bend and back. Then the best "skater" started sliding over the ice on moccasined feet. The others fell in behind. Round and round they skated, vying with one another to see who could go the fastest.

On clear, cold, moonlight nights boys and girls gathered on the river. Boys sat on their rib-bone sleds and the girls pulled them over the ice. At other times boys broke off chunks of ice or sat on old metal frying pans while they held the girls' dresses and were pulled about on the river ice. Then boys took turns pulling the girls.[5]

As boys and girls grew into teen-agers, they gave up children's amusements, but they did not abandon their love of sports. Young men and women played a kind of shinny, called "batting ours," with a hair-stuffed, skin-covered ball about the size of a baseball and curved sticks of wild cherry. On a field of play more than one hundred yards long there was a goal at each end marked by upright stakes about four feet apart. There were usually ten to fifteen persons on each side. To start the contest, the ball was tossed into the air at midfield, and play continued

[5] John C. Ewers, "Some Winter Sports of Blackfoot Indian Children," *The Masterkey,* Vol. XVIII, No. 6, 180–87.

until one side succeeded in hitting the ball between the goal posts defended by their opponents. It was a fast, rough game. Sometimes the teams struggled for hours, hitting the ball all over the field before a goal was scored. Boys sometimes took advantage of this game to do a bit of playful flirting with the girl contestants. Food was prepared before the game. At game's end it was served to members of the winning team.

Another teen-agers' ball game played by both sexes together or by girls only was known as the "Cree Women's game." The players stood in a circle about twenty feet in diameter. One of them threw a hair-stuffed ball, a little larger than the one used in the shinny game, toward a player on the opposite side of the circle, who hit it back with his or her fists. The object was to keep the ball in the air. As soon as it fell to the ground all the players scrambled for it, trying to pick it up and put it back in play as quickly as possible. This primitive volleyball game demanded both speed and agility of those who played it well.

Mature women preferred less strenuous and more sedentary games. The "travois game" was their favorite. It was played by two women, seated opposite each other, with five flat pieces of buffalo bone, each about six inches long and three-fourths of an inch wide and tapering to blunt ends. Four of these bones were marked on one side with meandering, incised lines, called "snakes." The fifth bone bore incised bands near each end. To start the game one woman cast the four snake-marked bones from a hollow shank-bone shaker on the ground or a blanket. If all four bones landed snake-side up, she was declared the winner. However, that rarely happened. If one or more of the bones remained plain-side up, the player was allowed eight attempts to turn them all snake-side up by casting the fifth bone at them spear fashion. Then a count was kept of the upturned snake-marked bones and the opponent took her turn. When one of the players gained a point total agreed upon in advance, she won the game.

When two expert players matched their skill and luck in the "travois game," they usually were surrounded by men and women who bet robes, parfleches, travois, weapons, horses, and other valuables on their favorite.[6]

Another popular women's gambling game was seen among the Piegans more than 150 years ago by David Thompson. Small pieces of wood, each marked to represent different counts, were placed in a wooden bowl, thrown into the air, and caught in the bowl. Then the marks on the upturned surfaces of the rude dice were counted. The bowl passed from contestant to contestant until one of them gained the number of points they had decided would be required to win the game.[7]

A variant of our children's guessing game of "button, button, who's got the button" has been a very popular gambling game among the Blackfeet for more than a century and a half. The Blackfeet called it "fancy gambling." In its most simple form this game was played with two short cylindrical lengths of bone small enough to be completely hidden in a man's clenched fist. One bone was unmarked, the other had a narrow band of rawhide wrapped around its center. The contestants sat facing each other, with a lodgepole on the ground between them. A member of one side was chosen to hide the bones. While his teammates sang and beat upon the lodgepole with short clubs, he swayed with the music and moved his hands back and forth in front of or behind his body, passing the bones from hand to hand to confuse the opposition further. One of his opponents had to guess which hand held the marked bone. If he guessed wrong, the first side scored a point and continued to hide the bones. If he guessed correctly, his side scored a point and gained the right to hide the bones. Twelve willow sticks served as counters, and the game continued until one side won them all.

In the old days this was one of a series of games played between men's societies during the summer tribal encampment.

[6] Wissler, "Social Life of the Blackfoot Indians, AMNH *Anth. Papers*, Vol. VII, 60–61. Describes a more complex variant of "the travois game."

[7] Thompson observed this game before 1800, and Bradley mentioned it in the 1870's, but Wissler's informants did not describe it to him in the first decade of the present century (Thompson, *Narrative*, 359–60; Bradley, "Manuscript," *MHSC*, Vol. IX, 277).

Both contestants and onlookers bet on the outcome. The stakes were horses, robes, guns, and even the clothing on their backs. Some heavy betters lost everything they owned.[8]

The men's societies also competed in the wheel game. One society challenged another by sending tobacco to its leader. If he accepted the tobacco, his society accepted the challenge also. If he feared the skill of the rival society at this game, he might return the tobacco to the challengers. They then presented the tobacco as a gift to the sun.

The playing field was a level stretch of ground about thirty feet long, with a log placed across the course at each end. Before the game began, members of each society gathered around one of the logs and sang their ritual songs. Each society carefully selected as its representative one of its members who possessed an outstanding war record and who was adept at this game.

The wheel used as a moving target in this game was a small hoop, about three inches in diameter, made from the fire-hardened neck cord of a buffalo. Inside the hoop were five or more spokes of rawhide cord and a small opening in the center. The spokes were strung with beads, a different color being used for each spoke, and each color representing a different kind or color of horse (red for sorrel, copper for bay, yellow for buckskin, white, and black). Each contestant carried an arrow-like pole about three feet long with a metal head and feathering.

Spectators lined the sides of the course, many of them betting on the outcome of the contest. They were silent as the two players stepped on the course. Each of these contestants raised his pole toward the sun and offered a short prayer in such words as, "See me. See this arrow. See how it is painted. That is how my arrow was painted when I killed a Crow. I shall shoot to win because what I say is true." Each man then declared his target on the wheel in terms of his own war experience. One might call out, "I took a white horse from the Flatheads. I shall

[8] Thompson, *Narrative*, 360–61. A century and a half later this is still a popular gambling game among the Blackfoot Indians. It is now commonly referred to as "the stick game."

shoot for the white beads." The other might say, "I took a sorrel horse from the Crows. I shoot for the red beads." If a player lied in proclaiming his coup, he would surely lose.

The players agreed between themselves which of them was to roll the hoop. If they couldn't agree, the one with the better war record was given his choice. Some men preferred to roll the wheel so they could know its course and speed. Others preferred to let their opponent roll the hoop so they could concentrate upon casting their pole. Before rolling, each man spat upon the head of his pole. The roller then lifted the wheel to the sun and rolled it toward the log at the far end of the course. Both men ran after it and hurled their weapons before the hoop struck the log. If one man pierced the center of the hoop with his pole, he won. If neither pole hit the center, that man won whose pole was in contact with the colored beads of his choice when the wheel stopped after rebounding from the log barrier. The game continued until one player either pierced the center hole of the wheel or scored his point. Usually it was not necessary to roll the wheel more than twice. Judges representing each society were stationed at both ends of the course to determine the winner.

Some young men played this hoop-and-pole game informally as a means of gambling. In these contests there were no recountings of war exploits or prayers to the sun before rolling the wheel. The players merely declared their targets.

Boys played this game with a larger wheel for a target. It was a sarvis-berry-wood hoop with a rawhide webbing inside and a small hole in the center which the boys called "the belly button." The blunt-ended poles were as long as the players could reach with outstretched arms. Boys pretended they were lancing buffalo when they threw their poles. They called it the "bull game." Certainly hurling poles at a moving target was good training for the future hunter and warrior.

The Blackfoot Indians look upon the hoop-and-pole game as a very old one. They claim that Napi once played it against a Kutenai on Oldman River. The stakes were control of the buffalo.

According to the legend, Napi was the winner, and "that is why there were no buffalo west of the Rockies."[9]

Foot racing was another popular sport among boys and young men. Boys who could run faster than their playmates were proud of this accomplishment. More formal foot races were run between young men of the men's societies during summer encampments. Each society selected its fastest runner. Clad only in moccasins and breechclouts, they ran a course of half a mile or more. The challenged society had the right to determine the distance to be run.

Most exciting of the series of contests between men's societies during the summer encampments was horse racing. The horse entered by each society had to belong to one of its members. The entries were determined in secret trials held some distance from the camp by each society. Jockeys usually were relatives of the owners—light, adolescent boys who were smart, expert riders. They rode bareback with only a war bridle and whip to control their mounts. The jockeys wore only breechclouts and tied their hair behind their heads to keep it from blowing in their faces.

Presenting a challenge to an intersociety horse race followed a formal procedure. The challenging society selected one of its most successful warriors, who dressed just as he had when he had won a signal war honor and decorated his horse as it had appeared at that time. He mounted, rode around the camp circle to the lodge of the leader of the rival society, sang his war song, lifted his gun, and fired at the lodgepoles just above their crossing. Then he shouted his society's challenge to a horse race. The rival society's leader rushed out of his lodge, gun in hand, and fired into the air, shouting his acceptance of the challenge with some such boast as, "I killed an enemy and I scalped him. You aren't going to scalp me." Later that day delegations from the two societies met to decide upon the time and the details of the race.

These were usually match races run over a level stretch of plains near the encampment. Generally the course was about

9 *Ibid.*, 359.

two to four miles in length. On the day of the race the competing horses were watched very carefully lest a horse medicine man approach one of them and employ his secret formula to cause it to tire or falter in the stretch. The finish line was marked on the day of the race. It might be merely a furrow scraped in the earth across the course or two piles of rocks erected about sixty feet apart by society members who had used rock fortifications to defend themselves against an enemy attack.

Shortly before race time the two competing horses were led to the finish line where the crowd of spectators gathered to look them over and to place their bets. Horses were commonly wagered, the animals bet against each other being tied together and held by a youth. Guns, robes, blankets, and food were other common stakes. A man might wager his pad saddle against another's bow and quiver of arrows. Even painted lodges, together with all their sacred accessories, sometimes were bet on horse races. Men did not wager their wives' possessions. The women bet among themselves. Before race time great piles of articles wagered stood near the finish line.

While the jockeys walked their horses toward the starting point, members of the competing societies drummed, sang their ceremonial songs, and engaged in good-natured horse play. They pretended to re-enact their war exploits against members of their rival society. A man who had scalped an enemy would run up to a member of the rival group, knock him down, and pretend to take his scalp. A man who had captured a horse of the same color as the one entered by the rival society in the race might cry out, "I stole a horse just like that one of yours. I had complete power over it. This horse of yours will be tamed too."

Two men, one from each society, served as starters. The jockeys walked their horses in a wide circle around them. As they came abreast of them, facing the finish, the starters shouted "Ok'i" [now], and the jockeys whipped their horses into a run. The race was on.

At the finish line there were also two judges, one man from each society. But usually there was nothing to judge, for the winning horse was often fifty to one hundred yards in the lead. Sometimes one horse played out and was not able to finish. Rarely was it a close race all the way.

After the race the gleeful winners claimed the articles they had won. If a loser protested that the race had not been fair, men of the winning society knocked him down and rubbed dirt or manure on him. With the winning horse in the lead, the victorious society marched back to camp, once around the camp circle, and stopped at the lodge of the leader. The winning horse was entrusted to the care of an old man, who picketed it near the lodge and sang to it. The men of the winning society sang, danced, and rejoiced late into the night.

Members of the losing society might consider this a good time to organize a raiding party in quest of a fast horse from an enemy camp—one that would enable them to turn the tables on their rivals the next summer.[10]

Certainly the fun-loving Blackfeet had no dearth of recreational opportunities, active or sedentary, summer or winter. Nor were their activities confined to the daytime. At night the Indians gathered for social dances. Usually the women sat on one side, the men opposite them, with three or four drummers in the center. As the drummers beat a lively rhythm on their tambourine-like instruments, individuals rose and danced about, bending their knees, stomping their feet, and swaying their bodies gracefully in time to the music.

They whiled away the long winter nights with story-telling. Many of the older men were masters of the art of telling a good story, and their repertory was both extensive and varied. There were myths of the stars, of Napi's amusing adventures, and of the origins of sacred rituals and common customs. There were tales of animals and of the heroic deeds of Blackfoot warriors in their conflicts with many enemies. Some of these stories were humorous, even vulgar; some were educational and inspirational.

[10] Ewers, "Horse in Blackfoot Indian Culture," B.A.E. *Bull. 159*, 227–34. The popular intersociety horse races ended with the breakdown of Blackfoot men's societies in the 1870's.

They had one quality in common—they were all fascinating. As the old storyteller talked on into the night, his listeners might become drowsy. It was considered good etiquette for members of his audience to interrupt him with an occasional "ah" to show their appreciation and to let him know they were still awake.

Stick game in progress at sun dance encampment near Heart Butte, 1944 (*Courtesy Museum of the Plains Indian*).

9: The Old Time Religion

T HE BLACKFOOT INDIANS lived in a world of uncertainty. Their lives were plagued by the fear of death from starvation, from sickness, or at the hands of their many human enemies. If they had less cause to fear starvation in the middle of the nineteenth century than had their prehistoric ancestors, they had more reason to fear sickness. Their old men and women could recall the disastrous losses their tribes had suffered in two smallpox epidemics. They were still surrounded by hostile tribes, any of which might send a mobile raiding party against one of their isolated hunting camps without warning.

Yet the Blackfeet did not face these dangers alone. They believed they were surrounded by supernatural powers much stronger than human ones which they could call upon for protection from evil influences and to aid them in their own undertakings. These powers resided in the skies and in the waters, as well as on land. Sun and thunder were the most powerful sky spirits. Beaver and otter were potent underwater ones. Buffalo, bears, elk, horses, snakes, eagles, crows, and other animals and birds of the Blackfoot country also could communicate their powers to humans.

Supernatural power invariably was given to men in dreams. Rarely did a man experience a dream of power while he was sleeping at home in the lodge of his family. Dreams of power did come to some young men when they were alone and separated from fellow members of a war party. But more commonly a young man actively sought supernatural aid by going out alone on foot to some isolated spot at a distance from camp. There, on a bare hilltop, beside a lake, or in some other rarely frequented place, the young man fasted and called upon all the powers of sky, earth, and water to have pity upon him. "Hear, Sun; hear, Old Man; Above People, listen; Underwater People, listen." There he remained without food or water until he was exhausted and fell asleep. Then, in response to his supplications, an animal, bird, or power of nature (such as thunder) appeared to him. This spirit in human form spoke to him and expressed pity for him and the desire to give him "some of its power." The spirit then showed him certain objects sacred to it and told him how they should be made and cared for, and how they should be manipulated to bring the man success and to protect him from harm. The spirit also gave him the songs, face paint designs, taboos, and the ritual associated with the use of its particular "medicine."

Soon after the young man returned home, he made the articles given him in his dream in accordance with the instructions he received from the spirit. They comprised the contents of his personal medicine bundle. It should be made clear that the Blackfeet regarded these sacred objects as important symbols of power. They were not the power itself. If a medicine bundle was lost or captured by the enemy, the power was not permanently lost. He who was possessed of the power could remake the bundle. Unless he relinquished this power to another through formal transfer, he retained it until his death.

Naturally, some of these medicine bundles came to be more highly respected than others. If a man prospered and obtained outstanding success as a warrior and wealth in horses, his fellow tribesmen came to consider his power to be unusually potent. Others wished to share in its benefits. The Blackfeet believed that just as a man received his power or medicine from a spirit helper, so he could transfer this power to some other human. When a man wanted to obtain the power represented by the medicine bundle of another Indian, he approached the owner and offered him a pipe and the promise of horses and other valuables in exchange for his power. Should the owner not wish to part with his sacred possession, or should he feel the offer too small, he refused the pipe. If he accepted the pipe, he agreed to the transfer.

Although the details of transfer rituals differed with particular medicine bundles, the ceremonies associated with the transfer of the more important bundles had a number of general features in common. Before the formal transfer, the petitioner and bundle owner purified themselves by taking a sweat bath together. The two men, both naked, entered a sweat lodge, which was a temporary structure composed of a framework of arched willows covered with buffalo robes. Attendants heated stones in a near-by fire and placed them inside the sweat lodge. The two bathers sprinkled water on the hot stones, producing a steam which caused them to perspire freely in the little enclosure. Meanwhile, they sang and prayed. At the conclusion of this purification rite they ran to the cool waters of a near-by lake or stream.

The bundle transfer took place inside the owner's tipi. His wife assisted him in the ritual of transfer. Usually a smudge of sweet-smelling grass or other fragrant plant was made on an earth altar in front of the owner's seat. He opened the ceremony by narrating in detail the story of the origin of the bundle. Then, very slowly and deliberately, often making three feints toward an object before touching it, he proceeded to open the sacred bundle. He untied the knots in the rawhide cords surrounding the bundle, unwrapped the outer covering of skin and the inner ones of trade cloth, and reverently picked up each of the sacred articles in the bundle. He accompanied his actions with prayers and songs, singing a different song for each article handled. Smoking a pipe, dancing, and painting the face of the bundle purchaser were also parts of the ritual of transfer of the more important bundles. Many hours were required to transfer a complex bundle.

The purchaser watched and listened intently, for he had to learn every detail of the bundle ritual. He also had to learn the taboos associated with the care of the bundle. Most bundles had to be hung on tripods behind the owner's lodge during the day and brought inside at night. Other taboos were more varied. The owner of a medicine pipe bundle must not let anyone pass in front of him when camp was moved. A beaver bundle owner dared not show fear of water in any form. The owner of a snake-painted tipi must not break a bone in his lodge.

Frequent transfer of medicine bundles was encouraged by the Blackfoot belief that having owned important bundles added to a man's prestige and social position. Men of distinction were proud to recount the various bundles they had possessed during their lifetime, just as they were proud to tell of their brave deeds in war. Everyone knew that purchase of an important bundle required sacrifice of considerable property and that learning the ritual of the bundle was an intellectual accomplishment.

Many articles associated with successful achievements in war came to be regarded as medicine bundles. Among them were headdresses, shirts, shields, knives, and lances. These more important war medicines were usually the property of the well-to-do members of the tribe.[1]

The most common of the more important classes of medicine bundles were the painted lodges. There were more than fifty of them among the three Blackfoot tribes. The handsomely painted lodge cover was not a sacred entity in itself. Rather it was part of a complex of sacred objects received by its original owner in his dream of power.

According to Piegan tradition some of the oldest painted lodges are the bear ones. Their origin is explained in the following legend: Long ago a young Piegan determined to obtain some secret power which would bring him success in war. While traveling through heavy timber in search of a fasting place, he came upon a cave. He entered it. When his eyes became accustomed to the darkness he saw the cave was occupied by a mother bear and her cubs. When he pleaded with the bear mother not to harm him, she quieted down and even let him fondle her cubs.

[1] War medicines are described on pages 127–28 of this book.

For four days and nights he stayed in the bear's den without food or water. Meanwhile he prayed to the bear to give him of its power.

On the fourth night he fell asleep. In his dream a male and female bear appeared. They took pity upon him. The female bear gave him her home, a handsome lodge with three red bears painted on each side and red circles on the front and back representing the bears' den. The doorway was covered with a bearskin. She also gave him incense to be burned in the lodge day and night, a blackstone pipe bowl carved in the shape of a bear, and a song, "Underneath there is a bear which is very powerful. With her protection I shall always be spared in battle."

Then the male bear spoke. "My son, I give you my lodge too." Two black bears standing on their hind legs were painted on this lodge, one at each side of the entrance. The father bear also gave him a pipe and a drum.

Then the mother bear gave him a knife with a bear-jaw handle. She threw the knife at him, and he grabbed it before it could harm him. The bears gave him a song to go with it. "A knife is just like dirt thrown against me."

The bears then drove their children back into the brush and painted themselves. They painted their faces red and made long vertical stripes on their faces by scratching off the paint with their claws.

They told him, "This is how you should paint for battle. This painting will protect you."

When enemies of the bears came through the brush and attacked them, the male bear charged and killed the attackers. Then he told the boy, "See. That is the way. Always charge in battle as I just did."

The next day the young man left the bears' den. Not long afterward he joined a war party. In battle he carried a bear knife, painted himself, and charged as the bears had taught him. He took several scalps, but was himself unharmed. After he returned home, he made the two bear lodges just as the bears had shown them to him in his dream.[2]

The bear knife became a coveted Blackfoot war medicine. It had a sharp double-edged iron blade. Bear jaws and feathers were bound to its wood or bone handle. There were more than a half-dozen bear knives among the three Blackfoot tribes. In 1847, the missionary Father Nicholas Point met a Frenchman who had lost all his horses in a fight with the Blackfeet. But he was proud to have captured "a bear knife, which is for the Indians what a floating flag is for civilized man."[3]

Only a very brave man dared to purchase a bear knife from its owner because the transfer ceremony was a dangerous ordeal. After they had purified themselves in a sweat lodge, the man who wished to acquire the bear knife and the owner entered the latter's lodge naked. A bed of thorns was in the lodge. The owner made a smudge of parsnip roots, donned a bearclaw necklace, sang his bear songs, and imitated a bear pawing the ground. Then he jumped upon the petitioner, pushed him on to the bed of thorns and painted him in the bear manner.

After that he said, "Now, I shall give you the bear knife. If you don't take it, I shall keep it. If you get hurt with it, don't blame me."

He crawled four times around the lodge interior growling like a bear. Then, holding the knife by the end of its sharp blade, he hurled it at the initiate. If the latter caught it, he became the new owner and the former owner congratulated him. "You gave your life for that knife. It will make you powerful."

The daddy of all Blackfoot medicine bundles was the beaver bundle. Indian traditions refer to the beaver bundle as the oldest type of medicine bundle. It was by far the largest. Owners of beaver bundles, known as beaver men or "those who have power over the waters," were the tribal calendar keepers. With sticks in their bundles they kept count of the passage of the months

[2] This origin legend was told me by Fish Wolf Robe, a Piegan, at the time I negotiated the purchase of a bear-painted lodge for the Museum of the Plains Indian.

[3] Nicholas Point, "A Journey on a Barge on the Missouri River from the Fort of the Blackfeet [Lewis] to that of the Assiniboin [Union], 1847," *Mid-America*, Vol. XIII, 247.

and they foretold the return of spring each year. These men and their bundles played important roles in calling the buffalo and in planting and harvesting sacred tobacco. The sun dance bundle is thought to have been derived from the beaver bundle.

There were several beaver bundles among the three Blackfoot tribes. Several different legends account for their origin. According to one Blood Indian version, the beaver bundle originated in this way: Once a man and his wife camped alone by the shore of a lake. In their lodge were the skins of almost every kind of animal and bird, for the man was a very good hunter. One day, while he was away hunting, a beaver came out of the water and made love to his wife. The beaver continued to visit her daily. Then one day he persuaded her to go with him to his home in the water. When the woman's husband came home, she was gone. He searched the neighborhood for her until he found her tracks leading into the water. Then he gave up his search.

At the end of four days his wife came out of the water and returned to the lodge. In the course of time she gave birth to a beaver child. She told her husband of her affair with the beaver, but he did not harm her. He became very fond of the beaver child.

When the beaver learned of the man's kindness to the beaver child, he took pity upon the man and decided to give him some of his medicine power in exchange for the bird and animal skins in the man's lodge. One day, when the woman was getting water from the lake, the beaver met her and told her he wished to visit her husband. He requested that incense be burned in the lodge to purify it before his arrival and that her husband give him all the things he asked for in his songs.

When the beaver entered, the lodge was scented with burning incense. He and the husband smoked together. Then the beaver began to sing a song in which he asked for a particular bird skin. When the song was ended, the man rose and gave it to him. Then one by one the beaver sang his songs. Each time he asked for the skin of a certain bird or animal, until he had obtained all the skins in the man's lodge. But meanwhile the man learned all the songs of the beaver medicine and the bird and animal skin that went with each song.

After the beaver returned to his home in the lake, the hunter collected the skins of all the different birds and animals and made them into his sacred bundle. Thus the beaver medicine bundle came to be.[4]

The great size of this bundle and the variety of its contents caused the beaver ritual to be the most complex of all Blackfoot Indian rituals. It required years for a man to learn the several hundred songs of this ceremony, the animals to which each referred, and their proper sequence in the ritual. Consequently, ownership of a beaver bundle was not transferred very often. As a beaver man grew old, he taught the ritual to a younger man so that he could carry on the ceremony after the old man's death.

The beaver bundle was opened and the ritual performed in response to an Indian's vow to feast the beaver man and to give him valuable property if he or one of his family should recover from a serious illness or be saved from imminent danger on the warpath. In early times, when food was scarce and the people were hungry, they called upon the beaver man to open his mighty bundle and perform his ritual to call the buffalo. The beaver man and his wife danced, shaking the hoofs and tail of a buffalo which were taken from the bundle. He prayed and sang his potent buffalo-charming songs to change the direction of the wind and drive the buffalo toward camp. The next morning buffalo would be found close by and would be driven into the pound made by the people of the village. In gratitude for his service in preventing starvation, the people gave the beaver man choice morsels from the buffalo impounded and killed.

Seeds of the sacred tobacco planted by the Blood and Northern Blackfoot tribes were preserved through the winter in the bundles of beaver men. At planting time in May they gave a

[4] This origin legend was told me by Frank Red Crow, a Blood, in 1951. Four variants of the beaver medicine origin legend appear in Wissler and Duvall, "Mythology of the Blackfoot Indians," AMNH *Anth. Papers*, Vol. II, Part 1, 74–78.

feast and prepared the seeds by mixing them with deer, antelope, and mountain sheep dung, sarvis berries, and water. The soil was readied for planting by spreading brush over the field, burning the brush, and sweeping the ground with brush brooms. Each planter and his wife then dug a small plot about three feet square with a digging stick, dropped tobacco seeds in the holes, and covered them.

The beaver men believed the tobacco spirits were dwarfs no more than a foot high. Before leaving the garden for the summer hunt, each planter placed a little crooked stick in the center of his plot. Tied to this stick were a miniature pair of moccasins and a tiny pouch containing tobacco seeds—gifts to the "little people." In fall when the tobacco was ripe for harvest, the nomadic Indians returned to their little tobacco garden. The beaver man again performed his ritual before the tobacco was harvested.

Another type of medicine bundle which was of respectable age and great importance to the Blackfoot tribes was the medicine pipe. David Thompson learned of the medicine pipe among the Piegans before 1800. Alexander Henry, in 1809, was told of the Blackfoot belief that the medicine pipe was a gift from the thunder.

> Thunder is a man who was very wicked and troublesome to the Indians, killing men and beasts in great numbers. But many years ago he made peace with the Blackfeet, and gave them a pipestem in token of his friendship; since which period he has been harmless.[5]

In 1943, Makes-Cold-Weather, an elderly Piegan Indian, transferred his Blood Medicine Pipe to me for the collections of the Museum of the Plains Indian. At that time he recited the following legend of the origin of the medicine pipe:

« « « In the fall of the year three sisters went to pick berries on some hills near their camp. A storm came up quickly, and hail began

[5] Henry and Thompson, *New Light*, II, 366.

to fall. The two younger sisters ran back to camp, but the eldest stopped, looked up, and called out, "Oh, Thunder, stop this hail and I shall marry you." The storm ended, and the sky cleared.

Before she reached camp, the eldest sister saw a strange, handsome man walking toward her. When he drew near, she said to him, "Get away from me. I want nothing to do with you."

The man replied, "But you said you would marry me. I am the Thunder."

Then the girl recalled, "You are right. That is what I promised."

The young man said to her, "Now, close your eyes until I tell you to open them." She did as he told her. When she was told to open her eyes again, she found herself in a strange country. There were many lodges. The young man led her to one of them and told her to enter it. Inside the lodge he introduced her to his mother and father. She looked around the lodge and saw a large pipe hanging near them.

After the girl had lived in her new home for a while she became homesick. She went out into the hills and cried. When her husband went looking for her, he found her in tears. He asked her what was wrong, and she replied, "I'm lonesome for my own people—my father and mother, my brothers and sisters, whom I never see any more."

Then he promised her, "Stop crying and I shall take you back to your family."

When they returned to their lodge, her husband told his father that his wife was homesick. The father replied, "Yes, I was going to tell you to send her home. When she goes, tell her to take this pipe."

That evening the father showed her how to perform the medicine pipe ceremony, and explained, "In the spring of the year you will hear me thunder. Then you must give a feast, unwrap this pipe, and perform the ritual and dance I have taught you. I give you this lodge that goes with the pipe. Tell your medicine men to carry this pipe and dance out of the lodge so I can see them."

Then Thunder stood up, put the pipe on his back, and showed the girl how it should be carried when camp was moved. He also showed her how the bundle was to be supported on a tripod behind the lodge during the daytime while in camp. Then he said, "Now, close your eyes until I tell you to open them again." When she opened her eyes Thunder said, "Now I must leave you." She stood alone in the lodge.

Next morning a young Indian, who rose early, was surprised to see a strange painted lodge in the camp. He reported its presence to the chief, who asked him to go see what the strange people were doing in his camp. When the young man looked into the lodge, he saw the girl, recognized her as the one who had been lost some time before, and hurried to tell her parents of her return. When her father saw the new lodge and the strange bundle, he asked her, "What are these?"

She explained, "They are Thunder's lodge and his medicine pipe. They are presents to you from my father-in-law, Thunder." » » »

Each year thereafter the medicine pipe was opened shortly after the first thunder was heard in spring. In his ritual the medicine pipe man carried his sacred pipe out of the lodge, raised it toward the sky, and prayed for the welfare of his people and that no one in his camp would be killed by thunder (lightning) that year. The pipe bundle also was opened when a camp member, in fulfillment of a vow to have the ritual performed should a dear one recover from sickness or survive dangers on the warpath, made a payment of valuable possessions to the medicine pipe man. It was opened when the tobacco in the bundle was renewed and when it was transferred to a new owner.

The highly respected medicine pipe men were easily recognized by their peculiar hairdress. Each let his hair grow long and wore it gathered in a large forward-projecting coil over his forehead. These men played an important role in camp movements, always leading the moving camp. Their pipes had a unique function in oath taking. A Blackfoot Indian who swore upon the medicine pipe made as solemn a pledge of speaking the truth as the Christian who swore upon the Bible in a court of law. These Indians believed that any man who violated his oath taken upon the medicine pipe would surely die.

There were nearly a score of medicine pipe bundles among the three Blackfoot tribes. The most sacred object in each bundle was a long wooden pipestem elaborately ornamented with plumes and such other decorations as eagle feathers, hair or weasel-skin pendants, trade beads, bells, or ribbons. The stone pipe bowls, wooden food bowls, sacred stones, and other accessories in the bundle were employed in the ritual. But they were secondary in importance to the pipestem. Although the ritual of the medicine pipe was less complicated than that of the beaver bundle, it involved the singing of a lengthy series of songs and prayers as well as dancing with the pipe.

Some medicine pipes were carried by war parties as powerful war medicines. One of these was the "children's pipe," which originated in the dream of a Blood Indian named Middle Calf while he was on his way home alone from a horse raid. In this dream an old man appeared who assured Middle Calf he would reach home safely. The old man gave him a pipe to take to his children, saying this pipe would bring them luck and good health. When he reached home, Middle Calf made the sacred pipe just as he had seen it in his dream. Its stem, less than eighteen inches in length, was much shorter than that of most other medicine pipes. It was decorated with pendant feathers, trade beads, and an obsidian arrowhead.

At the sun dance encampment Middle Calf offered to transfer his sacred pipe to any child who wished to own it. A wealthy Indian sent word that he wished to purchase it for his eldest son. The transfer ritual was unusually simple, involving the singing of but four songs. First the owner took some balsam needles between his fingers and raised his hands, while singing, "The above ones gave me this incense which I hold." Then he held up his right hand with the thumb extended and sang, "The holy one above, he is holy." He touched the ground with the same thumb and sang, "The earth persons are holy." Finally he took the pipe stem in both hands, raised it, and sang the fourth song. "My pipe is holy. My pipe hears me." Then he stood up, holding the sacred pipe, and danced to the accompaniment of drums.

This medicine pipe had two functions—to bring health and to foster success in war. The father of a sick child might make a vow to purchase this pipe so that the child might regain his health. When going into battle or into an enemy camp to capture horses, the owner of this sacred pipestem tied it in his hair on the top of his head.[6]

One of the greatest mysteries in the history of the Blackfoot tribes is that of the origin of their tribal sun dance. Alexander Henry referred to their high regard for the sun when he wrote in 1811, "The greatest oath a Slave [Blackfoot] can possibly utter is that the earth and the sun hear him speak."[7] But he made no mention of a tribal sun dance among the Blackfeet. Prince Maximilian was at Fort McKenzie and visited the Indian camps near by at the sun dance season, but he did not describe the ceremony. Many years later Lieutenant Bradley reported that some of the white employees at Fort McKenzie witnessed the Piegan sun dance in 1832. And the winter count of the Blood Indian called Father of Many Children recalled the year 1818 as the one in which "The Blood Indians had their Sun Dance in the winter time."[8] Possibly the ceremony was new to the tribe at that time.

In any event, it seems improbable that the Blackfoot tribes originated the sun dance. It was the major tribal religious ceremony among nearly a score of Plains Indian tribes. It was most highly elaborated among the Arapahoes, Cheyennes, and Western Sioux. Probably the Blackfeet derived this ceremony from the Arapahoes, either directly or through their neighbors, the Gros Ventres, who were close relatives of the Arapahoes. Whether the Blackfoot tribes borrowed some of the features of the sun dance of an alien tribe before the beginning of the nineteenth century is questionable. It may very well have been an early nineteenth century innovation.

Certain it is that by the middle of the nineteenth century the sun dance was the great tribal religious festival of the Blackfeet. It is equally certain that their sun dance was not a carbon copy of the ritual of any other tribe. It was modified and adjusted

[6] The story of the children's pipe was told me by Jim White Bull on the Blood Reserve in 1951. The pipe itself is in the collection of the Denver Art Museum.

[7] Henry and Thompson, *New Light*, III, 731.

[8] Bradley, "Manuscript," *MHSC*, Vol. IX, 268.

to the existing Blackfoot ceremonial pattern of the medicine bundle. The beaver medicine men in particular contributed both to the symbolism and the sacred paraphernalia of the Blackfoot sun dance.

A woman, the medicine woman, played the leading role in the Blackfoot sun dance. Only a woman who had lived a virtuous life, one who had always been true to her husband, could qualify for this part. She assumed this sacred role by making a solemn vow to the sun at a time of crisis in her family. She promised the sun that if her sick loved one should regain health or her warrior son or husband return home safely from a perilous raid, she would undergo the sacrifice of serving as medicine woman in the sun dance of her tribe. This sacrifice involved not only the purchase of a costly natoas bundle worth many horses, but also the observance of a fatiguing fast and the personal responsibility for the success of the complex ceremony. She knew full well that should anything go amiss during the ceremony, she alone would be blamed, and both her veracity and her virtue would be denounced by her fellow tribesmen.

If her appeal to the sun was answered, the woman's promise was formally proclaimed to the people of her camp. She faced the sun, and a man experienced in the sun dance ritual publicly declared that this woman, whose prayer to the sun had been answered, promised to give the sun dance. In some years more than one woman in a tribe made this sacred promise. Each was required to purchase a bundle and assume the medicine woman's role. Perhaps this accounted for the existence of several natoas bundles in each Blackfoot tribe. Other virtuous women pledged themselves to assume the less demanding roles of "coming forward to the tongues" and assisting the medicine woman.

In the spring of the year a messenger was sent from the camp in which a woman had pledged to serve as medicine woman to the other scattered bands of the tribe. He presented tobacco to the chief of each band and informed him of the woman's promise. After the bands assembled in early summer to form the tribal camp circle and begin the summer hunt, relatives of the medicine woman began to collect buffalo bull tongues to be used in the ceremony. When a sufficient number of tongues were supplied—several parfleches full—the camp announcer called upon all those who had served as medicine women in previous years and the women who had vowed to "come forward to the tongues" to come with their husbands to the lodge of the medicine woman, which was pitched a little inside the great camp circle. There a medicine woman of a previous year who was to instruct the neophyte in the role she was assuming lifted one of the tongues and called upon the sun, professing her steadfast loyalty to her husband. Each woman in the assembly then made a similar confession. Then the sacred tongues were cut up, boiled, and placed in parfleches in the medicine woman's lodge.

Movements in Blackfoot rituals commonly were repeated four times. In the sun dance the entire camp moved four times on as many successive days. On the morning of the first day the medicine woman began to fast. Each day the camp moved she led the way, riding a horse with travois attached, on which were placed the sun dance bundle and the parfleches filled with sacred tongues. On each of the four days her husband and the male instructor wise in the ritual of the sun dance purified themselves in a sweat lodge made from one hundred willows, which were cut, brought in on horseback, and made into a lodge by members of one of the men's societies. Finally, on the fourth day, the people of the tribe arrived at the site selected for the erection of the great medicine lodge.

The major action and the climax of the sun dance occurred on the fifth day. It was on that day that the medicine lodge was built. Its most sacred architectural feature was the center pole, a tall tree trunk of cottonwood, forked near the top. A man famed as a scout for war parties was sent to select the center pole. When he found a suitable tree he returned to camp and reported his discovery. Then he led a party of seasoned warriors to the tree. A man who had killed an enemy chopped the tree down and, as it began to fall, shot at the trunk with his gun. As soon as the tree hit the ground all the warriors charged it. Each broke off a limb and counted coup upon it just as they would have done upon a fallen enemy. The party dragged the pole into camp and laid it in the center of the camp circle with the base facing the east. Other men gathered posts, poles, and brush needed in building the medicine lodge.

The design of the medicine lodge appears to have changed about the middle of the nineteenth century. According to Indian tradition and one published account, the older form of this structure resembled a huge tipi with long poles leaned against the tall center pole.[9] This conical structure was like the Crow Indian sun dance lodge of later years. In more recent years the Blackfoot medicine lodge has been a polygonal edifice of forked, upright cottonwood posts connected by stringers laid in their forks. There was one peripheral post for each band of the tribe. Each band was responsible for cutting, hauling, and setting its post early on the fifth day of the ceremony. Certainly this type of medicine lodge, resembling the one used in the Arapaho sun dance, has been common since the 1870's.

In the forenoon of this day the complicated ritual of transferring the natoas bundle to the medicine woman was begun in her lodge west of the unfinished medicine lodge. The medicine woman of a previous year and her husband were on hand to transfer their bundle. Either her husband or another man well versed in the intricate transfer ritual served as master of ceremonies. Also in the lodge were the medicine woman's female assistants.

Slowly and deliberately the natoas bundle was opened and its sacred contents revealed. A long series of prayers and songs accompanied the opening. The most important articles in the bundle were the sacred garments and accessories of the medicine woman. One by one her assistants helped her to put them on. The garments included an elkskin dress, a robe of the same material, and an elaborate headdress. This was a buffalo-hide headband in the form of a lizard, with pendants of weasel skins and upright feather plumes. Attached to the front of the headband

9 *Ibid.*, Vol. IX, 266.

was a crude skin doll containing tobacco seeds and a weasel skin stuffed with human hair. A flint arrowpoint hung from the doll's head. The Blackfoot Indians believed this peculiar bonnet and the elk garments had been given to a beaver medicine man long ago by a bull elk. The elk, in turn, had received them as presents from another elk who had run off with his wife. The primary costume accessory was a sacred digging stick similar in form to the ones commonly used by Blackfoot women for unearthing prairie turnips. Another legend tells of the origin of this religious symbol. A woman married the Morning Star and went to live with him in the lodge of his father, the Sun. One day the woman used this tool to uproot a sacred turnip. She looked down through the turnip hole, saw her own people on earth, and became homesick. Morning Star then permitted her to descend to earth through the turnip hole.

One by one the long series of songs recited the mythological origin of each object in the bundle. After the medicine woman was outfitted, her husband's body and face were painted black with charcoal, a half-moon was painted on his breast and a circular sun on his back, and lines representing sun dogs were made on his cheeks, chin, and forehead.

During this ceremony in the medicine woman's lodge an altar was constructed near the lodge door by stripping off the sod in an area about three feet square, covering it with a thin layer of light-colored earth, and executing a symbolic dry-color painting on this prepared surface. A central circle (Sun) was flanked by representations of two sun dogs (Sun's face painting), a crescent moon (Sun's wife), and a disc (Morning Star, their son). Before the medicine woman's party left her lodge, this altar was destroyed, symbolizing the obliteration of the scar on the face of the legendary Blackfoot hero, Scar Face. In the Scar Face myth his face was healed during his visit to the Sun.[10]

[10] The fact that three legends—the Beaver Medicine, the Woman Who Married a Star, and Scar Face—are required for the symbolism of the Sun Dance is further indication of the composite character of this ritual. Clark Wissler, "The Sun Dance of the Blackfoot Indians," American Museum of Natural History *Anthropological Papers,* Vol. XVI, Part 3.

It was late afternoon when this private ceremony in the medicine woman's lodge ended. In single file the occupants emerged from the tipi, led by the master of ceremonies. Following him in order were the medicine woman's husband, the former medicine woman who had transferred her bundle, the medicine woman herself, wearing her sacred headdress, elkskin dress, and robe and carrying the sacred digging stick on her back, and, finally, her assistants, carrying the parfleches containing the buffalo tongues. The procession slowly moved halfway around and back through the unfinished medicine lodge, the members halting and praying as they went, to an open-faced sun shelter set up west of the medicine lodge.

Then children and adults of the tribe who had been in poor health or wished to receive the blessings of the holy ones came forward with gifts of cloth or clothing. Males took their gifts to the ceremonial leader, girls and women to the medicine woman. Each petitioner was prayed for, and his or her face and wrists were painted. The medicine woman's helpers who had vowed to "come forward to the tongues" proceeded to open the parfleches containing the tongues. Each of them in turn took a piece of the dried tongue in her hand, faced the sun (now low in the western sky), held up the tongue, and earnestly prayed for the welfare of her relatives gathered around her. The remaining tongues were distributed among the great number of spectators, who consumed them in the same prayerful spirit as Christians experience when they partake of holy communion. It was a solemn and a sacred act.

The remainder of the public ceremony on the climactic fifth day of the sun dance was devoted to completing the erection of the medicine lodge. First the buffalo hide which was to be cut in narrow strips for use in binding the rafters in place was spread out on the ground. Then successful warriors who had purchased the privilege came forward to cut the hide. Each in turn held his knife high while he recounted four of his brave exploits, then cut several of the thongs.

Shortly before sunset four groups of men carrying pairs of

long poles connected by rawhide lines converged upon the medicine lodge from the four cardinal directions. They sang as they advanced. Then, using their poles as props, they carefully raised the center pole into position so that it stood upright in the hole dug to receive it. The medicine women stood by, praying that this pole raising might be accomplished successfully. Should the pole fail to stand upright, people would surely accuse her of being less virtuous than she proclaimed to be.

Raising the center pole provided the dramatic climax to the medicine woman's role in the sun dance. Once this pole was firmly planted, her assistants led her to her lodge, where she broke her fast on berry soup. Her husband took a final sweat bath to purify himself. Meanwhile, the other men of the great encampment completed the medicine lodge as quickly as possible by binding the rafters with the prepared hide thongs and covering the sides of the lodge with green cottonwood boughs.

Early the next morning a booth of cottonwood boughs was erected on the west side of the medicine lodge. This booth was occupied by two or more men who periodically left it to dance to the accompaniment of several old men who sang and beat upon a buffalo rawhide with rattles. Wearing only breechclouts and moccasins, the dancers faced the sun and blew upon eagle-bone whistles. Their dance consisted primarily of raising and lowering themselves on their toes in time to the music. These dancers were spoken of as "weather dancers" because they were responsible for preventing rain and insuring sunny weather through the remaining days of the ceremony. They usually performed for four days, during which they refrained from eating. At intervals during this period persons approached the weather dancers to be painted and prayed for.

On the first of the four days a fire pit was dug between the center pole and the entrance to the medicine lodge on its east side. Then, one by one, victorious warriors entered the medicine lodge, hung offerings to the sun on the center pole, and recounted their war exploits. After reciting each brave deed, a warrior placed a stick on the fire. Those who could add enough sticks to make the fire blaze high were greatly admired for their prowess. The warriors dramatized their accounts by re-enacting their accomplishments—the killing of an enemy, the capture of a weapon or a horse, or the taking of a scalp. They achieved considerable realism in these performances by such acts as firing their guns in the air and riding around the lodge with stick horses between their legs.

However, by far the most dramatic of all the warriors' actions in the medicine lodge were the excruciating self-tortures undergone by young men who had made vows to torture themselves in the sun dance of their tribe. In 1947 the Blood Indian Heavy Head, one of the last of the Blackfeet to submit to this painful ordeal, described his experience to me.

« « « My partner, Buffalo Teeth, and I went to war to take horses. At Medicine Hat we found a small camp of Cree half-bloods. It was moonlight when we sighted their camp. I looked up at the moon and prayed to it, "If I have good luck and get home safely I shall be tortured at the sun dance." Then I stole into the camp and got one bay that was picketed in front of a lodge without any of the enemy waking. Buffalo Teeth got a roan.

When I reached home, I told my story to my father, Water Bull. The old man got up and sang his encouraging song. Then he told me, "My son, you have done something worth doing. You have made a vow that you will be tortured at the sun dance. You must do it this coming sun dance."

A short time after that the bands began to come together for the summer encampment. I filled my pipe and went to Little Bear, a relative of mine who had been through the torture years before. I gave him the pipe and a buckskin horse, and said, "Here is a horse for you. Keep this pipe too. I want you to look after me in the torture." Little Bear went to the next lodge and got two old men, Green Grass Bull and Red Bead, both of whom had been through the torture. They came to Little Bear's lodge, smoked my pipe, and prayed for me.

The day before the torture I ate and drank nothing. Next day I had nothing until after the torture. However, the three old men gave me some sagebrush to chew.

I was the last and the youngest of the three Blood Indians to undergo torture that day. Inside the medicine lodge, on the west side of the center pole and north of the weather dancers' arbor, a shelter was built of sticks covered with willow leaves. I went in there before noon of the day of the torture. I was laid on my back with my head pointed north. I was barefoot and wore only a breech-clout of red trade cloth. There was a little bowl of white paint and another of black paint near by. The three old men painted four black dots, one below the other, under each of my eyes. This was called "tear paint." If I cried, the tears would run down there. Then they painted a double row of six black dots on each arm. They painted the symbol of the moon, points up, on my forehead in black. On the outside of each leg they painted a double row of six black dots. The rest of my body and my face were painted white. They took some broad-leafed sagebrush from the ground inside the sweat lodge and bound it together, placing a wreath of it around my head and bands of it around each wrist and ankle.

I was taken from the shelter and laid upon a blanket on the ground at the north side of the center pole. Other men were told to keep back away from me. Then an old man named Low Horn was brought forward. He counted four war honors. While Little Bear and Green Grass Bull held my arms, Red Bead took a sharp, iron arrowhead in his hand and asked me, "How do you want me to cut them, thick or thin?" I said, "Thin." (I learned later that the man doing the cutting always did just the opposite of the young man's request. So when I told him "thin," Red Bead knew to make his incisions deep.) Red Bead recited four war honors. Then he pierced my breasts with the sharp arrowhead and inserted a sarvis berry stick through each breast. These sticks were not sharp but flattened at the ends. Blood flowed down my chest and legs over the white paint. Then Red Bead pressed the sticks against my body. They turned me around to face the sun and pierced my back. To the skewers through my back they hung a miniature shield with feathers on it.

Rawhide ropes were brought out from the center pole and tied to the skewers in my breast—right side first, then left side. Red Bead grabbed the ropes and jerked them hard twice. Then he told me, "Now, go to the center pole and pray for your vow to come true." I walked up there. I knew I was supposed to pretend to cry. But oh! I really cried. It hurt so much. Coming back from the center pole, I was shouting. Then, before I started to dance, I jerked the shield off my back.

I leaned back and began dancing, facing the center pole. It felt just like the pole was pulling me toward it. I danced from the west toward the doorway of the lodge and back. Then, when the skewers didn't break loose, the old men realized that the incisions had been made too deep. Red Bead cut the outside of the incisions so they would break loose. As I started dancing again the left side gave way and I continued dancing with only my right side holding. Then an old man, Strangling Wolf, got up from the crowd and called out four war honors, then jumped upon me. The second rope gave way and I fell to the ground.

The three old men cut off the rough pieces of flesh hanging from my breasts. They told me to take these trimmings and the sagebrush from my wrists, ankles, and head and place them at the base of the center pole as my offering to the sun. This I did.

Then I took my robe and walked out of the medicine lodge alone. I went to a lonely place and fasted for a night. I wanted to dream. But I couldn't sleep at all because of the pain. At sunrise I prayed to the sun.

When I got back to my lodge my mother gave me some food. I had to stay in the lodge for several days. My breasts were so swollen I could hardly move. Indian doctors used herb medicines to take the swelling away and cure my wounds. » » »[11]

Nevertheless, six decades after this event Heavy Head still bore the scars of his torture.

There is a Blackfoot tradition that the custom of self-torture was introduced from the Arapahoes through the Gros Ventres. It was never as common among the Piegans as among the Blood tribe. Nevertheless, all three Blackfoot tribes made other sacrifices of flesh and blood to the sun. Sometimes warriors on their way to meet the enemy cut off bits of their skin and gave them to the sun along with their prayers for success in their dangerous mission. Women as well as men chopped off one or more fingers and offered them to the sun. An elderly Piegan woman once showed me the stump of a finger on one of her hands and ex-

[11] John C. Ewers, "Self Torture in the Blood Indian Sun Dance," *Journal Washington Academy of Sciences,* Vol. XXXVIII, No. 5, 168–70.

Young man undergoing the self-torture at a Blood Indian sun dance. From a photograph by R. N. Wilson in 1892 (*Courtesy American Museum of Natural History*).

plained, "My parents had several children before I was born. All of them died. When I was a baby, my mother cut off this finger and gave it to the sun so that I might live and enjoy long life. That I have done."

In the medicine lodge at sun dance time each of the men's societies danced and presented gifts to the sun. The varied ceremonies in the medicine lodge usually consumed four or more days. The lodge itself was left standing when the great camp broke up and the several hunting bands went their separate ways for the fall hunt.

Like other peoples, the Blackfoot Indians employed simple home remedies for minor ailments, but when someone was seriously ill they called upon a man or woman who had magic powers with which to cure the sick. The Blackfeet believed disease was caused by an evil spirit entering a person's body and that it could be cured by a doctor who possessed the power to expel the spirit. As Blackfoot doctors received their detailed instructions for curing the sick in dreams, their methods differed. Many, however, employed singing, drumming, and calling upon their supernatural helper for assistance. Not uncommonly, the doctor appeared to extract some small object from the sick person's body as proof that the cause of illness had been removed. Some doctors were specialists in treating broken bones, snake bites, or battle wounds. Many of the most renowned doctors were women. It was customary to pay the doctor one or more horses for his services. The family of a victim of a prolonged illness might give all their possessions to the Indian doctor.

The Blackfoot Indians believed that after death the soul traveled to the Sand Hills, a desolate country south of the Saskatchewan River. There the deceased entered upon a new life similar to the one he or she had lived on earth. The dead were invisible to the living. Nevertheless, Indians who traveled through the lonely sand hill country claimed they heard strange noises and saw the trails and deserted camp circles of the dead. The Blackfeet claimed that the ghosts of the dead sometimes returned to communicate with the living in weird, whistling sounds.

10: Black Robe Medicine Men

T HE LARGEST of the Piegan bands prior to 1846 was the Small Robes. Indians of this band kept to themselves and seldom met with the other bands of their tribe. George Catlin and Father De Smet even considered the Small Robes a separate Blackfoot tribe.[1] Before the great smallpox epidemic in 1837, this band may have numbered as many as 150 lodges, of which about half survived that great plague. The Small Robes usually hunted near the Three Forks and south of the Missouri. This was the country visited by the Flatheads when they crossed the Rockies on periodic buffalo-hunting excursions. The strong and independent Small Robes dared to make friends with the little Flathead tribe, enemies of the other Piegan bands. They hunted with the Flatheads on the plains and occasionally journeyed over the mountains to visit and trade with them in their Bitterroot Valley homes. At these times they sent scouts ahead to inform the Flatheads of the approach of a friendly party.

Probably the Small Robes were the first Blackfoot Indians to find out that the Flatheads were acting very strangely. They were reciting peculiar prayers in an odd language. They were making peculiar signs, crossing themselves in front of their chests. They were setting aside one day in every seven as a rest day, on which hunting, fishing, trading, and moving camp were forbidden. Each seventh morning the Flatheads assembled to listen to a moral talk by Old Ignace Lamoose, an elderly Iro-

[1] Catlin, *Letters and Notes*, I, 52; De Smet, *Life, Letters and Travels*, III, 949.

quois Indian who had settled among them. His speeches were interspersed with singing and dancing in a great circle. Yet the remainder of this Flathead holiday was spent in traditional enjoyments—gambling and horse racing. It was those morning performances that were so strange.

Old Ignace had been the leader of a little group of Iroquois, probably Mohawks, who had made the long trek westward from the valley of the St. Lawrence prior to 1830. Perhaps they had been encouraged to migrate by earlier Iroquois travelers who had gone west as canoemen for the fur traders. Ignace's party settled among the friendly Flatheads and tried to teach them some of the elements of the Christian religion they had learned at the Jesuit Mission of Caughnawaga, near Montreal.

But Old Ignace was not satisfied with his own imperfect efforts to interpret Christianity to the pagan Flatheads. He encouraged the Flatheads to sponsor delegations to the Jesuit headquarters in St. Louis to ask for a missionary. In the summer of 1835, Ignace took his two sons on the long overland trek to St. Louis, where he asked that a priest be sent to his western Indian friends. When two years passed and no priest came, Old Ignace again led a deputation toward St. Louis. Journeying eastward from Fort Laramie in company with a party of white men, they met a Sioux war party. The Sioux ordered the whites to stand aside, then killed Ignace and his four Indian comrades. Possibly the murderers mistook them for Shoshonis, their enemies.

Two more years passed. The original Iroquois contingent among the Flatheads was reduced to four. But they would not abandon their quest for a missionary to their friends. In the summer of 1839 two of them, Peter Lefthand and Young Ignace, volunteered to make the long trip to St. Louis. They journeyed through hostile Indian country down the Yellowstone and Missouri rivers, in company with friendly fur traders. This time the Iroquois were successful. After receiving assurances that a priest would be sent to the Flatheads the following spring, Peter set out alone to carry the joyous news to his adopted people. Young Ignace accompanied Father Pierre Jean De Smet, a brave and vigorous Jesuit who had been selected by his order for this assignment, across the plains and mountains in the spring of 1840. De Smet met the Flatheads and was impressed by the opportunities for missionary work in this virgin field. Then he returned to St. Louis.[2]

In the fall of the following year Father De Smet was back in the Flathead country, bringing with him two black-robed assistants and three lay brothers. Among the Flatheads they founded the first Roman Catholic mission in the great northwest. There, on Christmas Day in the year 1841, the first Blackfoot Indian converts to Christianity were received in baptism by Father De Smet. He said they were "an old chief of the Blackfeet nation . . . with his son and little family, five in all."[3] The chief received the Christian name of Nicholas. We don't know his Indian name, but it is most probable that he was a member of the friendly Small Robes band of the Piegans. Later that winter about twenty Blackfoot Indians visited the Flatheads, and Nicholas aided in instructing them in Christian teachings.[4] Nicholas, the enthusiastic convert, spread the word among his people on the plains. In February, 1842, De Smet wrote:

We are informed that he and his companions have spoken so favorably of prayer and the Blackrobes, that already the Sunday is religiously observed in the camp where Nicholas resides, and that a great chief, with the people of sixty lodges, intend shortly to make our acquaintance and attach themselves to the Flatheads.[5]

Perhaps the good priest's enthusiasm caused him to underrate the animosity of the other Piegan bands toward his Flathead friends. He was to learn that even among his beloved Flatheads, the power of the Prince of Peace was strangely interpreted. These

[2] John C. Ewers, *Gustavus Sohon's Portraits of Flathead and Pend d'Oreille Indians, 1854*, Smithsonian Institution *Miscellaneous Collections*, CX, No. 7, 54–63.

[3] De Smet, *Life, Letters and Travels*, I, 338.

[4] *Ibid.*, I, 364.

[5] *Ibid.*, I, 364.

Indians looked upon Christianity as a war medicine more powerful than any they previously had possessed. A series of seemingly miraculous victories by small Flathead parties over larger enemy forces, following Flathead conversion, appeared to strengthen the Indians' faith in the practicality of this new medicine. And even their Blackfoot enemies were beginning to think that "the medicine of the Blackrobes was stronger than theirs."[6]

Father De Smet had great admiration for his Piegan friends of the Small Robes band. It must have been a great shock to him when he received word of their disastrous defeat at the hands of the Crow Indians. In October, 1846, De Smet wrote, "The year 1846 will be a memorable epoch in the annals of the Blackfeet nation. . . . The Crows have struck them a mortal blow—fifty families, the entire band of the Little Robe, were lately massacred and 160 women and children have been led into captivity."[7] It was this action the fur trader Denig probably referred to in 1854:

> The Crow Indians a few years since, after killing all the men and boys of 50 lodges of the Blackfeet, took prisoners upward of 200 women and children. One of our gentlemen now in charge of that nation was with the Crow camp when the battle took place, and for two or three months afterwards, during which time he sought occasions to liberate about 50 women and send them home to their people.[8]

Serious as this loss to the Small Robes was, the massacre was not as complete as De Smet's first report indicated. Either part of the band was not engaged or many escaped with their lives, for the Small Robes band survived. It numbered some thirty lodges in mid-century and was mentioned by a number of later observers. However, the Small Robes never regained a position of prominence in the tribe.[9]

[6] *Ibid.*, II, 589.
[7] *Ibid.*, II, 524, 593.
[8] Denig, *Indian Tribes of the Upper Missouri*, B.A.E., *46th Ann. Rept.*, 551–52.
[9] John C. Ewers, "Identification and History of the Small Robes Band of the Piegan Indians," *Journal* Washington Academy of Sciences, Vol. XXXVI, No. 12.

Father De Smet recognized that the continuous state of war between the Flatheads and the Blackfeet was a threat to the survival of the much smaller Flathead group and an impediment to the civilization of both Indian peoples. He was delighted by an opportunity to arrange a peaceful meeting of these warring Indians in the fall of 1846. That summer Chief Victor led his Flathead tribe to the plains to hunt buffalo. There they were joined by twelve lodges of Small Robes. While on this hunt they encountered and defeated a superior force of Crow Indians. The Small Robes fought valiantly to revenge the recent massacre of their kinsmen. But after the battle they attributed the victory to the prayers of their Flathead comrades. They begged Father De Smet to let them become his followers and presented all their children to him for baptism.[10]

Flushed with success, the Flatheads met the host of Blackfeet in the great camp of Big Lake, Piegan chief. During the ensuing peace council, Chief Victor spoke of his achievements in war, modestly attributing his successes to the assistance and protection of the Black Robe's God.[11] His recent victory over the Crow Indians was confirmed by the Small Robes. The words of this small, middle-aged man must have made a strong impression on the many stalwart Blackfoot warriors who listened to them.

On September 15, Father De Smet held mass in the Piegan camp, where more than two thousand lodges were assembled, including Piegans, Bloods, Northern Blackfeet, and Gros Ventres of the Plains, and Flatheads and Nez Percés from west of the Rockies. The next day he composed a chant for the Piegans which he had translated into the Blackfoot language:

> *God Almighty;*
> *Piegans are all his children*
> *He is going to help us on earth;*
> *If you are good, he will save your soul.*

From a Blood Indian leader De Smet learned that there were

10 De Smet, *Life, Letters and Travels*, II, 574–80.
11 *Ibid.*, II, 593.

already a number of baptized children in that tribe. He was told that some sixty children among the Northern Blackfeet had been baptized by a Black Robe from Red River and that they wore crosses at their necks.[12] They were probably converts resulting from the labors of Father Thibault, who four years earlier had accepted an invitation from John Rowand, chief factor of the Hudson's Bay Company, to come to Fort Edmonton to serve the Crees and half-blood residents in that vicinity.[13]

Confident he had concluded a lasting peace between the Flatheads and Blackfeet, De Smet returned to the east. He left his associate, Father Nicholas Point, to continue missionary work among the Blackfoot tribes. This French priest, a gifted artist as well as a zealous churchman, worked diligently among the Blackfeet for eight months. Making his headquarters at Fort Lewis, the American Fur Company's post on the Missouri, Father Point baptized twenty-two Blackfoot children, then extended his labors to the camps of the hunting bands, spending several weeks in each. Through his skill in portraiture he won the interest and friendship of the chiefs. He held daily classes in Christian doctrine for each of three groups—men, women, and children. With the help of an interpreter he translated the ordinary prayers into Blackfoot and taught them to these groups so that they could recite them from memory. He wrote Father De Smet, "There is scarcely any camp among the Blackfeet in which the sign of the cross is not in veneration."[14]

Although Father Point performed and recorded no fewer than 651 baptisms among the Blackfeet, all but 26 of that number were children. Only 4 were men.[15] Point found that the adult Indians looked upon him and his new religion much as they had always regarded their own medicine men and their magic. They believed he could cause disease or make thunder to roll if he became angry. They thought that baptism, like the native sweat lodge, would insure bodily health. They believed he possessed

[12] *Ibid.*, II, 593–94.
[13] MacInnes, *In the Shadow of the Rockies*, 268.
[14] De Smet, *Life, Letters and Travels*, III, 950.
[15] Gilbert J. Garraghan, *Chapters in Frontier History*, 149.

the power to cure sickness and implored him to treat them. Father Point found the prominent men unwilling to accept his criticisms of their polygamous marriages. Ambitious young men, accustomed to seeking economic security and social advancement through raids on enemy tribes, would listen to his pleas for peace with neighboring peoples only if he could "immediately make Great Men of them." Sadly, he wrote to Father De Smet:

> I could have baptized a great number of adults; they even seemed to desire it ardently; but these desires were not yet sufficiently imbued with the true principles of religion. I could not content myself with the persuasion generally existing among the savages, that when they had received baptism they can conquer any enemy whatsoever. The courage and happiness of the Flatheads have inspired them with this belief. This explains why some wretches, who seek only to kill their neighbors, were the first to petition for baptism.[16]

The good Father would not compromise with his high principles. The stubborn Blackfeet were not convinced of the error of their heathen ways. So matters stood between the advocate of the Prince of Peace and the warlike Blackfeet when Father Point left the trading post by barge to return down the Missouri to civilization on May 19, 1847.

It was twelve years before the "Black Robe Medicine Men," as the Blackfeet called the Roman Catholic missionaries, returned to found a more permanent mission among these Indians. Meanwhile, the Blackfeet continued their raids on the camps of their neighbors—Crows, Assiniboins, Crees, Pend d'Oreilles, and the peacemaking Flatheads as well. Peace-minded chiefs could not prevent their young warriors from crossing the mountains to make life miserable for the small western tribes. Even before Father Point had left the Blackfoot country, warriors were fighting the Pend d'Oreilles, and soon thereafter they resumed raiding the Flathead camps.[17]

[16] De Smet, *Life, Letters and Travels*, III, 953–54.
[17] *Ibid.*, III, 951.

Blackfoot medicine man attending his patient at Fort Union in 1832. From a drawing by George Catlin (*Courtesy New York Public Library*).

Their failure to obtain the Black Robe's powerful war medicine did not shake the Blackfoot warrior's faith in their own. Nevertheless, at least one young man found a way to gain the advantages of the forbidden power on his own.

Big Plume (born about 1830) accompanied a war party to capture horses. He was one of the youngest members of the group. When they neared the enemy camp, the older men told the younger ones to wait outside the camp while they stole into the village to get horses for the entire party. While he waited outside the field of action, Big Plume fell asleep. When the veteran horse thieves led horses from the camp, all the young men except Big Plume ran to join them.

When Big Plume awoke and realized he had been left behind, he began to cry. But he saw it was nearly daybreak. So he jumped up and ran to get away from the hostile camp as fast as he could. At dawn he crawled into a badger hole, where he hid for the rest of the day. When night came, he started running again in the direction of his distant home camp. Running and walking, he covered as much ground as possible. Toward morning he came to some thick brush and hid in it the following day. There he fell asleep.

As Big Plume slept, a handsome white man wearing a canvas shirt appeared to him and comforted him, saying, "Don't be afraid. Don't cry any more. You will get home safely."

That night he traveled on. Again, as morning approached, he hid in some brush and went to sleep. The same man came to him, wearing a blue shirt, and said, "Don't worry. You'll get home safely." On the day following another night's travel this man came to him once again in his dreams. This time he was wearing a red shirt. He seemed to smile as he spoke his assuring words. Big Plume thought he looked like the Lord.

Another night's journey brought Big Plume to the Yellow Mountains. A fourth time he saw the man in his dreams. This time the man was wearing a skin shirt with holes in it and crosses painted on it. He said, "Don't be afraid. I am the Lord. I am sorry for you. You will get home and you will live to be an old man."

After Big Plume reached home, he made the skin shirt just as he had seen it in his dreams. He wore this perforated shirt with the red crosses painted on it to war. Big Plume was successful and became a leader among his people. When Big Plume grew old, his brother-in-law, Bear Chief, asked him for this shirt. Four times Bear Chief made this request before Big Plume said to him, "Make me a sweat lodge. I shall pray to the Lord and tell Him I am giving Bear Chief his shirt because I'm too old to use it."

After he had transferred the shirt to Bear Chief, Big Plume told him, "This summer you will go to war and will meet the enemy. All the others in your party will run away. You will have to fight them alone."

That summer Bear Chief's war party sighted a lone enemy in the distance. All his comrades ran away. Bear Chief put on his sacred shirt and prayed to the Lord for help. He sang the song Big Plume gave him, "All the other Indians are babies." Then he charged the enemy. His shirt was shot through front and back, but Bear Chief was not even scratched. Later Bear Chief carried this shirt on horse raids. When he wore it into the enemy camps, they could not see him. One time he wore the shirt in a battle with the Crow Indians. They shot at him but could not hit him.

This famous shirt became one of the most coveted garments among the Piegans. Although the original shirt is said to have been sold to George Bird Grinnell by Bear Chief, it was remade at least three times. One of these versions, owned by the late Albert Mad Plume in 1951, is shown in one of the illustrations in this book.[18]

In 1859, with the active encouragement of Blackfoot agent Vaughan, himself a Protestant, a Jesuit mission was founded on

---

[18] Chewing Black Bones, a Piegan, owner of the second version of this garment, told me the origin and history of The Lord's Shirt in 1951. The third version is Cat. No. LB1–1–p in the Denver Art Museum.

the Teton River near present Choteau. It was moved several times in the next few years and abandoned in 1866, because of Blackfoot hostilities toward the whites. In 1875, Father Imoda, who had been associated with this mission since its founding, summed up its meager achievements thusly:

> Some two thousand have been baptized in the various bands, some marriages solemnized, and in a few isolated cases a slight impression made upon their religious convictions, but except these slight results, the state of religion among the Blackfeet is about where it was when they first came under the notice of white men.[19]

North of the International Line, Father Lacombe labored tirelessly and fearlessly in the years following 1865. He lived in the camps of both the Blackfeet and their Cree enemies, ministering to their physical needs through epidemics and to their spiritual ones even in the midst of their intertribal battles. In 1871 he devised a picture chart to help explain Christianity to the Blackfeet. It proved so useful that Pope Piux IX had several thousand copies of the chart printed for use in Roman Catholic missions among primitive peoples in different parts of the world.[20]

The Roman Catholics were not alone in their efforts to bring Christianity to the Blackfeet. These Indians readily distinguished between the "Black Robe Medicine Men" (Catholics) and the "Short Coat Medicine Men" (Protestants) on the basis of their clerical garments. It was much more difficult for them to understand the significant differences between Roman Catholic and Protestant doctrine. They were confused by the competition between Christian missionaries of different sects.

If the progress of the Black Robes was slow, that of the Short Coats was no more rapid. Rev. Robert T. Rundle, a Methodist, went west to Fort Edmonton in 1840 to minister to the Blackfeet,

[19] Bradley, "Manuscript," *MHSC*, Vol. IX, 315–16.
[20] Katherine Hughes, *Father Lacombe, The Black-robe Voyager*, 201–203.

Assiniboins, and the half-bloods and whites at the trading post. He made little impression on the adult full-blood Indians.

In the summer of 1856 the Presbyterian Board of Missions sent thirty-year-old Rev. Elkanah Mackey to Fort Benton. His advent was long remembered by the Blackfeet, primarily because he brought his wife with him. She was an object of great curiosity among the Indians, for she was the first white woman to appear in the Blackfoot country. Rev. and Mrs. Mackey were provided quarters at the fort and began to make arrangements for establishing a mission. The Indians treated Mrs. Mackey with kindness and respect. But she was unhappy in the wilderness, so far from any other woman of her own race. Besides, she was pregnant, and there was no trained doctor within many hundreds of miles of Fort Benton. After a stay of one month the couple returned to the East.[21]

Thirty-seven years passed before a permanent Protestant mission was established among the Blackfeet in present Montana. Meanwhile, Rev. J. W. Tims inaugurated mission work for the Anglican church among the Northern Blackfeet in Canada. He made a thorough study of the Blackfoot language and published a pioneer book on the subject. But he was nine years in obtaining his first convert.[22]

Why was progress in Christianizing the Blackfeet so slow? Surely it was not due to any lack of zeal on the part of the early missionaries. Nor were the Indians unfriendly toward them. Certainly the Blackfeet did not lack serious interest in religion. Religious symbolism permeated many of their activities, and they actively sought supernatural aid to help them in their daily lives as well as in times of crisis. But a wide gulf separated the alien religious symbols and moral concepts of the missionaries from the familiar ones of the Indians. The Blackfoot Indians could not readily abandon the faith of their fathers for this strange new religion.

21 Guy S. Klett, *Missionary Endeavors of the Presbyterian Church Among the Blackfeet Indians in the 1850s,* Presbyterian Historical Society, 338–41.

22 Rev. J. W. Tims, *Grammar and Dictionary of the Blackfoot Language in the Dominion of Canada.*

11: Travelers Far Afield

For FORTY-SEVEN YEARS after the Lewis and Clark expedition, no official government exploring party entered the Blackfoot country. One could almost count on his fingers the number of white men, other than fur traders and trappers, who set foot on Blackfoot hunting grounds in that interval of nearly a half-century. None of them were soldiers or settlers.

Nevertheless, despite the isolation of their homeland from the westward movement of white settlers, it would be a mistake to assume that the Blackfeet remained ignorant of the world beyond their own hunting grounds and the territory their war parties traversed in their raids against neighboring tribes. Time and again prior to 1850, small parties of adventurous Blackfoot Indians journeyed far beyond the camps of their neighbors to more distant regions. In their travels they learned much about the extent and character of the western country and the customs of alien tribes. Long before their own country was invaded by white settlers, they learned of the Spanish settlements in the Southwest, of the Santa Fé trade, and of the growing numbers of white-topped emigrant trains that passed up the valley of the Platte River, over the Rockies, and on to Oregon, California, and Utah.

As early as 1787, David Thompson was told of a large Piegan war party which traveled southward in search of the Shoshonis. Finding no enemy and being unwilling to return home empty handed, they continued southward near the eastern base of the

Rockies until their scouts brought word of a long file of horses and mules led by "Black Men" (Spaniards). The Piegan warriors prepared to fight the white men, but the Spaniards, fearing to risk a battle with such an imposing force, rode off, leaving their loaded pack animals. The Indians threw the bags of white stones (silver) from the backs of the horses and mules and drove the animals home. Thompson, who was the most able geographer among the fur traders of his time, estimated that this contact with the Spanish miners was made at about 32 degrees north latitude, which would have been nearly fifteen hundred miles south of the Piegan party's home camp near present Edmonton.[1] A trek of this distance by a primitive Blackfoot war party seems almost incredible. Nevertheless, it was only the first of a number of long Blackfoot journeys southward that have been recorded.

About the year 1825 a group of Blackfoot warriors joined the Gros Ventres in attacking and plundering Chesterfield House, a Hudson's Bay Company trading post on the South Saskatchewan near the mouth of Red Deer River. Fearing the traders' revenge, eighteen or twenty Blackfeet joined their Gros Ventre allies in flight southward to the Arapahoes and Cheyennes near the Black Hills. There the Blackfoot warriors boasted of their skill as horse thieves. To prove their prowess, they continued southward, stole horses from the Kiowas and Comanches on Red River, and returned to the Arapaho and Cheyenne camps. Their descriptions of the fine buffalo country south of the Platte and of the large herds of wild horses they had seen there encouraged part of the Cheyennes and Arapahoes to move southward. Their Gros Ventre friends and the little group of Blackfoot adventurers went with them.[2]

This explains the strange presence of Gros Ventre and Blackfoot warriors on the Arkansas, about eight hundred miles south of their usual hunting grounds, where they were encountered

[1] Thompson, *Narrative,* 370.

[2] George Bent letters to George E. Hyde. I am indebted to Mr. Hyde, of Omaha, Nebraska, for copies of Bent's statements regarding the Blackfoot Indians who found refuge among his people, the Cheyennes.

197

by the David Jackson and William Sublette trading party en route to Santa Fé in the summer of 1831.[3]

Four years later, Colonel Henry Dodge, leader of a dragoon expedition ordered to the plains to impress the wild tribes with the strength of the United States, met the Cheyennes and Arapahoes in council at Bent's Fort on the Arkansas. Dodge noted that Gros Ventres were present and "also a small band of the Blackfeet proper, consisting of about fifty, who live with the Cheyenne and Arapahos."[4] Probably this number included the Cheyenne and Arapaho wives and children of the group of Blackfeet who moved south a decade earlier. Whether any of these Blackfoot Indians returned to their northern homeland, we do not know. They may have been content to remain in their adopted country. Perhaps they were represented in the ten lodges of Blood Indians living among the Arapahoes whom Alexander Culbertson met at the Fort Laramie Treaty Council in 1851. "They were unknown to him, and he did not learn how long they had been there or whether they ever returned."[5]

Both the Blood and Piegan Indians have a tradition of a party who journeyed south to the Arapahoes prior to 1850 and did come back. Piegan members of this group brought back the "Southern Gros Ventre" (Arapaho) medicine pipe. Tradition says they also returned with the "big rock" painted tipi and other sacred objects given them by the Arapahoes.[6]

In 1854, James Doty learned of another long Blackfoot trek southward.

About Ten Years ago a party of five chiefs, two of whom are still living, followed the Eastern slope of the Rocky Mountains until

[3] H. C. Dale (ed.), *The Ashley-Smith Explorations and the Discovery of a Central Route to the Pacific, 1822–1829*, 309.

[4] Colonel Henry Dodge, *Journal of a March of a Detachment of Dragoons under the Command of Col. Dodge, in the Summer of 1835*, 24 Cong., 1 sess., *House Document 181*, 25.

[5] James H. Bradley, The Bradley Manuscript, Book A, p. 184 (in the Montana Historical Society Library, Helena).

[6] Wissler, "Ceremonial Bundles of the Blackfoot Indians," AMNH *Anth. Papers*, Vol. VII, Part 2, 160–61. In 1947 the "Southern Gros Ventre" (Arapaho) pipe was owned by my Piegan interpreter, Reuben Black Boy.

they reached Taos and other Mexican Towns, between that and Santa Fe. The party committed no depredations in that country and indeed were traveling more for the pleasure and to see the world than with a view to war. They were absent from the nation three years and appear to have been the only Blackfeet to have been so far from home.[7]

This party may have taken the same route followed by the Piegan war party which brought back Spanish loot in 1787. Probably both groups of travelers followed the Old North Trail, described more than sixty years ago by the aged North Piegan chief, Brings-Down-the-Sun, as running southward from present Calgary "along the eastern side of the Rockies, at a uniform distance from the Mountains, keeping clear of the forests, and outside the foothills. It ran close to where the city of Helena now stands and extended south into the country [Mexico] inhabited by a people with dark skins, and long hair falling over their faces." At that time the Piegans showed Walter McClintock traces of this old trail. He observed that "the old horse trail and travois tracks were still plainly visible, having been worn deep by many generations of traveling Indians."[8]

More recently the late H. P. Lewis, an amateur archaeologist of Conrad, Montana, may have seen portions of this old Indian trail some twenty-five miles southwest of Choteau. It was marked by travois ruts, occasional stone piles, and stone tipi circles, the sites of overnight encampments en route. Lewis understood that "evidences of this trail following the foothills, just east of the main Rockies, are to be found for many miles."[9]

At its northern extremity, present Calgary, Alberta, the Old North Trail connected with two trails leading northward to Fort Edmonton.[10]

Just above Fort Benton, so the old Indians have told me, was

[7] James Doty to Isaac I. Stevens,, December 20, 1854, Indian Office Records.
[8] Walter McClintock, *The Old North Trail*, 435–40.
[9] H. P. Lewis, manuscript, Bison Kills of Montana. (Typescript copy in Missouri River Basin Archaeological Survey Offices, Lincoln, Nebraska), Chapter X, 6–7.
[10] Hugh Dempsey, *Historic Sites of the Province of Alberta*, 50–51.

an ideal fording place where the Missouri River could be crossed in waters little over knee deep. Many trails led southward from Fort Benton. In the summer of 1853, Governor Isaac I. Stevens questioned Blackfoot leaders about these travel routes.

> Those Indians whom I interrogated had frequently crossed over to the upper waters of the Platte and Snake Rivers, and they informed me that the whole country was open, and that there would be no difficulty in moving from Fort Benton, over quite a number of trails, to the emigrant route from the States, via Fort Laramie and South Pass to Salt Lake; and they described the country as being, for the most part, a very desirable one, excellent for voyaging, and abounding in wood, water and grass.[11]

Certainly the Blackfeet knew their way to the Oregon Trail well. Some years earlier, on a journey southward to this "Great Medicine Road" of the whites, the courageous Piegan chief Little Dog, led an attack on an emigrant train. In the valley of the Snake River, Little Dog and his men selected a favorable position along the trail to Oregon and awaited the approach of white men's wagons. Unaware of any danger ahead, a wagon train moved into the Indian ambush. The Indians fired, rushed upon the emigrants, massacred the men, and plundered the wagons. They found a box filled with strange objects which Little Dog thought were "brass buttons without eyes." The Blackfoot raiders were perfectly familiar with brass buttons. They had obtained them from traders in their own country. But of what value were heavy, glittering, metal buttons without eyes? The Indians cached them in the rocks overlooking Snake River and proceeded homeward with their more useful booty.

Years later, when Little Dog became familiar with American gold coins, he realized his folly in leaving those "brass buttons without eyes" buried far away in the valley of the Snake River. He told his story to the traders at Fort Benton, and they encouraged him to go after his cache of coins. But Little Dog, then

[11] Stevens, "Narrative," *PRR*, XII, 101.

renowned as a great friend of the whites, could not be persuaded to return to the scene of his savage attack on the emigrant train.[12]

Although the Small Robes paid friendly visits to the Flatheads west of the Rockies, the other Piegan bands and the Blood and Northern Blackfoot tribes knew the overmountain country only through the observations of their war parties. A favorite route of Blackfoot war expeditions against the Flatheads followed the Dearborn River upstream, went over Cadotte's Pass, and then down the river on the west side of the divide which still bears their name—Big Blackfoot. Farther west, Blackfoot war parties occasionally ambushed the Flatheads as they passed through a narrow defile on their way eastward to hunt buffalo on the plains. This canyon, near present Missoula, the traders named the Hell Gate, because "it was as safe to enter the gates of hell as to go into that pass."[13]

The Marias Pass, which connected the headwaters of the Marias River and those of the Flathead River on the western side of the continental divide, afforded the most gradual crossing of the Rockies. However, Little Dog told Governor Stevens in 1853 that the Blackfeet had not used this pass for many years and that it had become overgrown with underbrush. Stevens attributed its disuse to "some superstition of the Blackfeet."[14] My older informants gave a more practical reason for its avoidance by their war parties. Marias Pass was long, meandering, and indirect. They preferred the steeper but quicker short cut over Cut Bank Pass at the head of Cut Bank Creek and down Nyack Creek and the middle fork of the Flathead River on the west.

North of the Canadian boundary, Crow's Nest Pass was much used by war parties en route to the camps of the Kutenais, even though game was more scarce along this trail than in the favored passes farther south.

Some Blackfoot Indians journeyed down the Missouri, through the territory of their Assiniboin enemies and beyond Fort Union,

[12] Bradley, "Manuscript," *MHSC*, Vol. IX, 335–40.
[13] Father De Smet knew this gap as "Devil's gate" in 1846 (De Smet, *Life, Letters and Travels*, II, 582).
[14] "Narrative," *PRR*, XII, 106.

to visit the "Dirt Lodge People," the Mandan and Hidatsa earth-lodge dwellers at the mouth of Knife River in present North Dakota. Prince Maximilian noted that two Blackfoot Indians boarded the fur company's steamer *Yellowstone* at the Hidatsa villages in the summer of 1833 to return to their own people. One of them, Left Handed Bear, left behind a Hidatsa wife and small child. The other, Beautiful Hair, was shot and killed by a Cree Indian at Fort Union a few days later.

On August 7, when within two days' journey of the Blackfoot trading post of Fort McKenzie, Maximilian's keelboat party met two Blood Indians, a man and his wife, who were returning from a visit to the Hidatsas and Mandans. The German Prince recalled having seen them in the Hidatsa villages earlier that summer and observed that "the man was well made and both were very neatly dressed."[15] This handsome couple must have been Seen-From-Afar and his wife, whose visit to the Mandans and Hidatsas in the early 1830's is still known to elderly Blood Indians. Seen-From-Afar is credited with having brought back the Mandan pipe and its ritual, a medicine bundle still owned by the Blood tribe. His wife brought back a buffalo headdress of a Mandan or Hidatsa women's society and introduced it into the buffalo-calling ceremony of the Blood Indian women, the Matoki.

Nearly two decades later, Seen-From-Afar, then head chief of the Blood tribe, and his wife again visited the Hidatsas at Fort Berthold. They traveled downriver to Fort Union to greet Seen-From-Afar's brother-in-law, Alexander Culbertson, when he arrived on the fur company's steamboat from St. Louis. They reached Fort Union some days before the steamboat was due, and James Kipp, in charge of that post, sent his guests on to Fort Berthold, where they would be safe from hostile Crow Indians encamped near Fort Union. This precaution was well taken, for the courageous chief, who was "splendidly dressed," wearing "a magnificent bonnet of war-eagle feathers falling to his feet," would have made a conspicuous and inviting target for ambitious

[15] Maximilian, *Travels*, I, 363–64; II, 82–83.

Crow warriors eager to avenge the many depredations of Blood Indians upon their people.[16]

Doubtless a great many visits of adventurous Blackfoot Indians to far-off tribes prior to 1850 have never been recorded. At the very beginning of the nineteenth century David Thompson learned that there were young men among the Piegans who, wishing to distinguish themselves, "mix with other tribes and learn their languages, and become acquainted with their countries and their mode of hunting."[17] This primitive equivalent of travel abroad must have had educational value not only for the participants but also for their entire tribes. The few examples of visits to distant tribes I have cited clearly indicate that Blackfoot travelers brought back more than knowledge of geography and of the languages and hunting methods of alien peoples. Some of them returned with sacred objects and rituals which enriched the religious life of their own people.

Around their own campfires at night they must have retold for the edification of their stay-at-home friends and relatives many beautiful legends they had heard from the lips of members of far-off tribes. Probably the common elements in the mythology of many Plains Indian tribes were the result of the repetition of tales or episodes learned and retold by such traveling storytellers. It would have been strange indeed if Blackfoot material culture and crafts were not also enriched by the detailed observations of keen-eyed and quick-witted Indian travelers who had opportunities to take mental notes on the daily lives of other tribes.

Nor was the lack of a common spoken language a serious barrier to communication of ideas between distant tribes. Through the sign language the Algonkian-speaking Blackfoot traveler could converse with Siouan-speaking Mandans and Hidatsas, with Salish-speaking Flatheads, or with such distant Algonkian tribes as the Arapahoes and Cheyennes, whose oral dialects differed markedly from that of the Blackfeet. The gestures of an

16 Henry A. Boller, *Among the Indians: Eight Years in the Far West, 1858–1866*, 302–303.
17 Thompson, *Narrative*, 366.

accomplished sign-talker were precisely made and readily understood by men of other tribes. The vocabulary of signs was rich
enough to permit strangers who understood scarcely a word of
each other's speech to exchange information and ideas in mean-
ingful silence for hours on end.

Medicine Snake Woman, Blood Indian wife of the trader Alexander Culbertson (*Courtesy Montana Historical Society*).

12: Lame Bull's Treaty

O<small>F</small> the many Indian tribes who lived on the Great Plains south of the forty-ninth parallel, the last to negotiate a treaty with the United States were those the government referred to as "The Blackfoot Nation," which included the Piegans, Bloods, Northern Blackfeet, and their allies, the Gros Ventres. It was fifty-two years after the Louisiana Purchase before the United States made a formal treaty of peace with these Indian inhabitants of the extreme northwestern portion of that vast region.

Undoubtedly the warlike nature of the Blackfoot tribes was a factor of importance in the postponement of official government relations with them. The first treaties with western tribes generally were made to safeguard the lives and possessions of white settlers or emigrants who passed through tribal hunting grounds. Certainly no white man would have considered settling in or near the country of the warlike Blackfeet so long as there was plenty of fine land available elsewhere. The reputation of the Blackfeet as hostile and bloodthirsty people also discouraged emigrants from following the natural highway of the Missouri River during the growing migration to Oregon in the 1840's. The well-worn Oregon Trail passed far to the south of the Blackfeet, through the hunting grounds of the powerful Western Sioux, Cheyennes, and Arapahoes. As the number of emigrant trains moving over that trail increased during the middle and late forties, the Indian tribes living along the route became increasingly restless. The white transients were killing off the buffalo or frightening them away from their hunting grounds. Fear of Indian attacks upon the emigrants mounted as mid-century approached. Even the establishment of military posts at wide intervals along the route did not relieve this anxiety. The government knew that the Oregon Trail was the thin thread that connected the settled East with the growing settlements of the Far West. That thread could not be broken.

In the fall of 1849, David D. Mitchell, superintendent of Indian Affairs in St. Louis, recommended that the government call a great council with all the Plains tribes living between the Missouri River and Texas to make formal arrangements to indemnify the Indians for their losses and to define intertribal boundaries. He pointed out, "The boundaries dividing the different tribes have never been settled or defined; this is the fruitful source of many of their bloody strifes; and can only be removed by mutual concessions, sanctioned by the Government of the United States."[1]

On May 26, 1851, the Commissioner of Indian Affairs authorized Mitchell to hold a council and to treat with the "Indian tribes of the Prairies." The names and number of tribes to be invited to this council, the choice of the council site, and the details of the proceedings were left to Mitchell's judgment.[2]

Mitchell proceeded to make preparations for a great council to be held at Fort Laramie on the Platte River the following September. He instructed his former colleague in the American Fur Company, Alexander Culbertson, to select delegations from all the Upper Missouri tribes and to conduct them to Fort Laramie. Word reached Culbertson at Fort Union too late to permit him to obtain delegates from the Blackfoot tribes and the Gros Ventres. But he did have time to assemble delegates from the Assiniboins, Hidatsas, Mandans, and Arikaras, who accompanied him to the treaty ground.[3]

So the Blackfeet were not a party to the Treaty of Fort Lar-

[1] D. D. Mitchell to Commissioner of Indian Affairs, October 13, 1849, Indian Office Records.
[2] L. Lea to D. D. Mitchell, May 26, 1851, Indian Office Records.
[3] Bradley, "Manuscript," *MHSC*, Vol. III, 266.

amie. Nevertheless, because part of their country was located south and east of the Missouri, their lands within that area were defined in the treaty. A formal description of this portion of the Blackfoot country appears on the sheepskin copy of the Treaty of Fort Laramie, preserved in the National Archives in Washington:

> The territory of the Blackfoot Nation. Commencing at the mouth of the Muscle-shell river, thence up the Missouri river to its source,—thence along the main range of the Rocky Mountains, in a Southern direction to the head waters of the northern source of the Yellow Stone river,—thence down the Yellow Stone to the mouth of Twenty five Yard Creek,—thence across to the head waters of the Muscle-shell river,—and thence down the Muscle-shell river to the place of beginning.

The treaty was signed by prominent chiefs of two tribes hostile to the Blackfeet, as well as by two white men who were their old friends. D. D. Mitchell, the senior United States commissioner at the council, had founded Fort McKenzie among the Blackfeet nineteen years before. He had traded with the Blackfeet for seven years. Alexander Culbertson, husband of a Blood woman, had traded with the Blackfeet for seventeen years. Father De Smet, who prepared the official map on which the tribal boundaries agreed upon at the treaty were indicated, was another old friend of the Blackfeet.[4] Thus, even though there were no tribal delegates from any of the Blackfoot tribes at the Fort Laramie council, their interests were protected by intelligent, knowledgeable, and sympathetic white men.

Even before the ink was dry on the Fort Laramie treaty, easterners were agitating for a much more rapid means of transportation across the plains and Rockies than that afforded by the lumbering wagon train. Proposals for a railroad to the Far West were debated in Congress. In 1853, Congress appropriated $150,-000 for making field explorations and surveys to ascertain the

[4] De Smet, *Life, Letters and Travels*, IV, 1497–98. Father De Smet's original map is in the Map Division, Library of Congress.

most practicable and economical route for a railroad from the Mississippi River to the Pacific Ocean.

One of these explorations, along a route from St. Paul, Minnesota, to Puget Sound, would pass through the Blackfoot country. It was led by Isaac I. Stevens, newly appointed governor of Washington Territory and ex officio superintendent of Indian Affairs. An honor student at West Point, Stevens' military career had been a brilliant one. In 1853, at the age of thirty-five, he was assigned the triple responsibilities of leading a railroad survey, governing a large, newly established territory of the United States, and inaugurating official negotiations with some of the most formidable and warlike Indians on the North American continent.

Governor Stevens had never met the Blackfeet, but he knew that their "warlike and treacherous character was proverbial." Wisely, he secured the appointment of Alexander Culbertson as special agent to introduce him to these Indians. Stevens acknowledged, "I placed the more reliance upon the favorable influence which Mr. Culbertson might exert upon the Indians, as he had married a full-blood Blackfoot woman."[5]

When the Stevens party, exploring overland, reached Fort Union, 715 miles west of St. Paul, on August 1, 1853, they were met by Mr. and Mrs. Culbertson. Then, in traditional Indian fashion, Culbertson sent presents and tobacco to the Blackfoot chiefs with this message from Governor Stevens:

> I desire to meet you on the way and to assure you of the fatherly care and beneficence of the government. I wish to meet the Blackfoot in a general council at Fort Benton. Do not make war upon your neighbors. Remain at peace, and the Great Father will see that you do not lose by it.[6]

History has strange ways of almost repeating itself. Just as the Shoshoni woman, Sacajawea, had been of inestimable service

[5] Reports of the Commissioner of Indian Affairs, 1854, 195.
[6] Stevens, "Narrative," PRR, XII, 85.

to Lewis and Clark in introducing them to her own people forty-eight years earlier, so did Medicine Snake Woman (Mrs. Culbertson), daughter of a Blood Indian chief, play a major role in establishing friendly relations between this second government exploring party through the northwest and her people, the Blackfeet. Fearful of the expedition's reception by the warlike Blackfeet, Culbertson had planned to leave his wife at Fort Union. But she insisted upon going with him, saying:

> My people are a good people but they are jealous and vindictive. I am afraid that they and the whites will not understand each other; but if I go, I may be able to explain things to them, and soothe them if they should be irritated. I know there is great danger; but, my husband, where you go I will go, and where you die will I die.[7]

While Governor Stevens lectured his men upon the "importance of pursuing a conciliatory course towards the Indians," Mrs. Culbertson "was in constant intercourse with the Indians, and inspired them with perfect confidence." She listened to what the Indians said and reported it through her husband to Governor Stevens. Knowing well her people's love of good stories, she entertained them with accounts of the whites she had seen in far-off St. Louis. "As she described a fat woman she had seen exhibited, and sketched with great humor the ladies of St. Louis, it was pleasant to see the delight which beamed from the swarthy faces around her."[8]

Mrs. Culbertson probably helped to induce the Piegan band chief, Little Dog, reputed to have been her cousin, to accompany John Mix Stanley, the artist of the expedition, to the great camp of Piegans near the Cypress Hills to persuade their chiefs to come to Fort Benton to the council with the Governor. Stanley himself won the admiration of the Blackfeet by taking daguerreotype portraits of them. "They were delighted and astonished

[7] Reports of the Commissioner of Indian Affairs, 1854, 196.
[8] *Ibid.*

to see their likenesses produced by the direct action of the sun. They worship the sun, and they considered that Mr. Stanley was inspired by their divinity, and he thus became in their eyes a great medicine man."[9]

On September 21, Governor Stevens met some thirty chiefs, braves, and warriors from the three Blackfoot tribes in council in a large room at the trading post of Fort Benton. He observed that these Indians were dressed in their finest clothing "of softly prepared skins of deer, elk or antelope . . . ornamented with beadwork" and that they carried Northwest guns and bows and arrows.

In his opening address to the Indians, the Governor stressed their need to make peace with their enemies, saying:

> Your Great Father has sent me to bear a message to you and all his other Children. It is, that he wishes you to live at peace with each other and the whites. He desires that you should be under his protection, and partake equally with the Crows and Assiniboines of his bounty. Live in peace with all the neighboring Indians, protect all the whites passing through your country, and the Great Father will be your fast friend.[10]

Chief Low Horn, answering for the Piegans, spoke of the peaceful intentions of the Blackfoot chiefs. But he explained that the chiefs "could not restrain their young men, but their young men were wild, and ambitious, in their turn to be braves and chiefs. They wanted by some brave act to win the favor of their young women, and bring scalps and horses to show their prowess."[11]

Governor Stevens exacted the promise of the Indians at the council to cease making war upon the Flatheads and Nez Percés,

[9] Stevens, "Narrative," PRR, XII, 104–105. Unfortunately, none of these first photographic portraits of Blackfoot Indians have been preserved. One of my elderly Blood informants said he had heard of portraits made at the time of the Lame Bull Treaty which were given to the Indian sitters and were buried with them.

[10] Reports of the Commissioner of Indian Affairs, 1854, 202.

[11] Ibid., 202.

but the chiefs said "they could not speak for those of their tribes who were not present." Before the council broke up, the Governor distributed $600 worth of presents, with which the Indians "were greatly pleased."[12]

The next day Governor Stevens continued his railroad explorations westward. He was greatly pleased with his friendly reception by the warlike Blackfeet, as his diary entry clearly indicates. "As we left the fort . . . we felt that we had made warm and fast friends of all the inhabitants of that region—voyageurs, Indians, and gentlemen of the Fur Company." In his report to the Commissioner of Indian Affairs, he wrote of the Blackfeet: "Their present disposition towards the whites is unquestionably friendly. Undoubtedly a party of white men may travel through this country in perfect safety."[13]

Governor Stevens sent Alexander Culbertson to Washington to urge upon the Indian Department the importance of holding a formal treaty council with the Blackfoot tribes. He left his energetic and intelligent assistant, James Doty, with three men, to pass the winter at Fort Benton. They were to make meteorological observations and examinations of the country which would be of value to the railroad survey. Doty also was to collect information about and take a census of the Blackfoot Indians. And he was to "improve every opportunity to impress upon them the benefits of the proposed council and peace with the western Indians."[14]

For nearly a year James Doty remained in the Blackfoot country. His varied research added much to white men's knowledge of these Indians and the country in which they lived. He visited their winter camps on the Marias and Milk rivers, and made the first known physical measurements of these Indians. His sampling of several hundred adult males yielded an average height of about five feet, eleven inches.[15]

[12] Ibid., 202–203.
[13] Stevens, "Narrative," PRR, XII, 117; Reports of the Commissioner of Indian Affairs, 1854, 195.
[14] Hazard Stevens, The Life of Isaac Ingalls Stevens, I, 371.
[15] Isaac I. Stevens, "Narrative," PRR, XII, 183–87.

On the basis of both observation and inquiry, he compiled an estimate of Blackfoot population. Like the fur traders before him, he first determined the number of lodges, then computed the number of warriors and total population by formula. Doty allowed three warriors and nine persons per lodge. He distinguished between the North Piegans, who spent the summer season in the British possessions and traded with the Hudson's Bay Company on the Saskatchewan at that time of year, and the South Piegans, who summered south of the international border and traded only with the Americans on the Missouri. Doty's estimates were:

	Lodges	Souls	Warriors
The Blood Indians	270	2,430	810
The Blackfeet Indians	290	2,600	870
The South Piegan	200	1,800	600
The North Piegan	90	800	270
	——	——	——
Totals	850	7,630	2,550[16]

In the spring of 1854, Doty explored the Blackfoot country, following the eastern base of the Rockies northward from Sun River past the Teton to the upper tributaries of the Marias, Milk, and Belly rivers. Although he located the Marias Pass and followed it for several miles, he failed to reach the summit of this important crossing of the continental divide.[17] He also collected and preserved 320 varieties of flowers found in and near the Blackfoot country. His collection would have been of great value to botanists had it not become moldy and useless because of failure to carry out his instructions to forward the specimens down the Missouri.

Doty's presence among the Blackfeet and his frequent reminders of the proposed peace council may have deterred some of the chiefs from making war on their enemies, but other chiefs and many young warriors said, "This is the last winter we can

[16] James Doty to Isaac I. Stevens, December 20, 1854, Indian Office Records.
[17] Stevens, "Narrative," PRR, XII, 183–87.

go to war; next summer the white soldiers will stop us; let us steal this winter all the horses we can." Doty learned of more than five hundred warriors, mostly Piegans, who passed Fort Benton bound for enemy camps. He believed even larger war parties of Bloods, Northern Blackfeet, and Gros Ventres passed above and below the fort on their way to the Flathead, Shoshoni, and Crow camps that winter.[18]

After the council planned for the summer of 1854 had to be postponed, on account of Governor Stevens' preoccupation with his many other duties west of the Rockies, Blackfoot war parties continued to be very active. Entries in the Fort Benton Journal covering the period from October 4, 1854, to September 27, 1855, listed no fewer than forty-eight outward bound or returning war parties which stopped by that fort. Some comprised as many as thirteen men; others were considerably smaller.[19] There must have been many other war expeditions during that period which did not come near Fort Benton.

While he was en route eastward to the great Blackfoot council in the summer of 1855, Governor Stevens negotiated a treaty with the little Flathead and Pend d'Oreille tribes west of the Rockies. The chiefs assembled at that council complained bitterly of frequent Blackfoot attacks upon their camps during the two winters since Stevens had been among them urging that they make peace with their Blackfoot enemies. Father Hoecken, their priest, also reported that the Blackfeet had "committed more depredations than ever" during the spring of 1855.[20]

When Governor Stevens returned to the Blackfoot country, he knew that his northern route had no chance of being selected as the most practical and economical one for a Pacific railroad. Secretary of War Jefferson Davis, an ardent southerner and later president of the Confederacy, favored a southern railroad route so strongly that he had ordered the northern survey discontinued and opposed any further appropriations for work upon it. Un-

---

[18] James Doty to Isaac I. Stevens, December 28, 1853, Indian Office Records.
[19] McDonnell, "Fort Benton Journal," *MHSC*, Vol. X, 2–48.
[20] De Smet, *Life, Letters and Travels*, IV, 1235.

dismayed, Governor Stevens enthusiastically set about organizing the Blackfoot treaty council, for which he had obtained an appropriation of $10,000.[21]

During his travels westward through the Blackfoot country two years before, Governor Stevens had been impressed with the agricultural and stock-raising potentialities of the Indian lands near the Missouri. He had instructed James Doty to investigate the matter further while Doty remained in the Blackfoot country the following year. Doty's opinion "that a treaty with these Indians, and the establishment of an agency and farm in their country, will do much towards changing them from a warlike and nomadic to a peaceable and agricultural nation" strengthened Stevens' own belief that agriculture offered a rosy future for the nomadic Blackfeet.[22] Nor was his enthusiasm dampened by the contrary advice of Alexander Culbertson, who probably knew these Indians better than any other white man of the period. Culbertson wrote: .

As to Agricultural operations they are not to be thought of as long as Game is abundant. Indians will not work unless their necessities compel them—it is beneath their dignity—and it is evident the day is far off when the Blackfeet will turn the Sword into the Ploughshare and make the wilderness bud and blossom like the Rose.[23]

George Manypenny, commissioner of Indian Affairs, in his detailed instructions to the treaty commissioners issued that spring, did mention the government's plan to "gradually reclaim the Indians from a nomadic life" and to "encourage them to settle in permanent homes and obtain their sustenance by agriculture and other pursuits of civilized life." But he stressed that the major objective of the treaty should be the establishment of permanent peace "with all the most numerous and warlike tribes in that remote region of country."[24]

[21] Hazard Stevens, *Life of I. I. Stevens*, I, 430–31.
[22] Reports of the Commissioner of Indian Affairs, 1854, 207.
[23] Culbertson to Isaac I. Stevens, *ca.* 1853, Indian Office Records.

Governor Stevens, who had made all the field arrangements for the council, was irked that Alfred Cumming, superintendent of Indian Affairs from St. Louis, had been named senior commissioner for the United States at this important meeting. Cumming had had no firsthand experience with the Blackfoot tribes. But he thought he knew Indians. He took a dim view of the Blackfoot future in farming. He looked upon farms among these wild Indians as "opportunities for speculating under the disguise of philanthropy." The two commissioners disagreed repeatedly in drafting the treaty, yet the philosophy of Stevens prevailed.[25]

The commissioners originally planned to hold the council at Fort Benton, but the boats bringing the presents upriver from St. Louis were delayed. Since the presents were to be given to the Indians immediately after the conclusion of the council, they shifted the council site to a location one hundred miles down the Missouri, on its north bank a little below the mouth of the Judith. There, in a grove of large cottonwood trees, the council was formally opened at 1:00 P.M. on October 16. The Indians sat in semicircular rows, with twenty-six principal chiefs in the front row, the lesser chiefs behind them, and the other Indians in the rear. They faced a canvas-covered arbor, under which the commissioners, the seven interpreters, and James Doty, the secretary, took their stations. This scene was simply portrayed in an on-the-spot drawing by Gustavus Sohon, one of the interpreters for the Flathead Indians who were present.

In addition to the representatives of the four tribes of "The Blackfoot Nation," the Indians present included delegations from the Flathead, Pend d'Oreille, and Nez Percé tribes from west of the Rockies, and a single Cree chief, The Broken Arm, who two decades earlier had made the long journey to Washington to visit the Great White Father. He brought tobacco, which was distributed among the principal chiefs as a token of friendship from the Assiniboin and Cree tribes. No Crow Indian dele-

[24] Manypenny to Alfred Cumming, Isaac I. Stevens, and Joel Palmer, May 3, 1855, Indian Office Records.
[25] Hazard Stevens, *Life of I. I. Stevens*, I, 103.

gates were on hand. But Governor Stevens urged the assembled chiefs to send tobacco to the Crow Indians through their Nez Percé friends at the council.

In their opening speeches both commissioners stressed the theme of peace among all the tribes of the region and between Indians and whites. Governor Stevens branded as a lie the disturbing rumor that had been circulating among the Indians that their lands were to be taken from them and that they would be driven north to the Saskatchewan. He concluded his opening remarks with a simple statement of his plan for the civilization of the Blackfeet:

> We want to establish you in your country on farms. We want you to have cattle and raise crops. We want your children to be taught, and we want you to send word to your Great Father, through us where you want your farms to be, and what schools and mills and shops you want.
>
> This country is your home. It will remain your home. And as I told the Western Indians we hoped through the long winters, bye and bye, the Blackfeet would not be obliged to live on poor Buffalo Meat but would have domestic Cattle for food. We want them to have Cattle.
>
> You know the Buffalo will not continue forever. Get farms and cattle in time.[26]

Unfortunately, there is no record of what the wise old Blackfoot chiefs thought of this talk. Any of them who had ever tasted beef must have considered Stevens a strange man indeed if he preferred it to buffalo meat. His talk of raising crops must have brought to their minds the "Dirt Lodge People," the Mandans and Hidatsas down the Missouri, who owned few horses and lived at the mercy of the nomadic Sioux. It is doubtful that they comprehended at all Stevens' mention of schools, mills, and shops.

Then, article by article, the treaty written by the commission-

[26] Albert J. Partoll (ed.), *The Blackfoot Indian Peace Council*, Montana State University, *Sources of Northwest History No. 3,* 6.

ers was read and explained to the Indians. The first two articles, declaring perpetual peace between the United States and the Indians party to the treaty, as well as intertribal peace among those tribes and with all neighboring tribes, roused no discussion recorded in the official proceedings.

The third article declared that all of the country south of a line running from the Hell Gate or Medicine Rock passes in the Rockies eastward to the nearest source of the Musselshell River, recognized and defined as the territory of "The Blackfoot Nation" in the Fort Laramie treaty, "shall be a common hunting-ground, for ninety-nine years, where all the nations, tribes and bands of Indians, parties to this treaty, may enjoy equal and uninterrupted privileges of hunting, fishing and gathering fruit, grazing animals, curing meat and dressing robes." But no tribe would be permitted to establish permanent villages or exercise exclusive rights within ten miles of the northern line of this common hunting ground.

Articles IV and V described the exclusive territory of the Blackfoot Nation: bounded on the south by a line drawn eastward from the Hell Gate or Medicine Rock passes to the nearest source of the Musselshell River, down that river to its mouth, and down the Missouri to the mouth of Milk River; on the east by a line due north from the mouth of Milk River to the forty-ninth parallel (the Canadian border); on the north by this parallel; and on the west by the Rocky Mountains. Tribes from west of the Rockies were prohibited from hunting within this area, but the Assiniboins were given the right to hunt in the easternmost portion of the Blackfoot territory.

These boundaries were drawn on a map which was shown to the chiefs. Alexander, the Pend d'Oreille chief, objected to the provision prohibiting his tribe from hunting on the plains north of the Musselshell River. He asserted his ancestral right to hunt in that region, saying, "A long time ago our people used to hunt about the Three Buttes [Sweetgrass Hills] and the Blackfeet lived far north." Little Dog, the Piegan chief, was inclined to let Alexander have his wish. But the commissioners reminded the western tribes of their small numbers in comparison with those of the Blackfeet (one-fourth the latter's population) and of their right to use the common hunting ground farther south.

Alexander reiterated his desire to hunt on the plains in the territory assigned to the Blackfoot tribes. His fellow chief, Big Canoe, a courageous war leader, even questioned the basic concept of tribal boundaries, saying, "I thought our roads would be all over this country. Now you tell us different. Supposing that we *do* stick together and *do* make a peace . . . Now you tell me not to step over that way. I have a mind to go there."

Then, for the first time, Lame Bull, the venerable head chief of the Piegans, rose to speak for his people. He reminded the reluctant western Indians, professed friends of the whites, that his people did not write this treaty.

> It is not our plan that these things are going on. I understood that what the White Chiefs told us to do, we were to do both sides. It is not we who speak. It is the White Chiefs. Look at those tribes (pointing to the Western Indians), they are the first to speak, making objections this morning. We intend to do whatever the Government tells us; we shall take care to try to do it. We shall consider what the White Chiefs wish us to do, and I think we shall do it. They have done much and intend much more for us. Let us listen. We shall abide by what the White Chiefs say. I hope these Indians will make friends with us and that it may be shown by a friendly exchange of property.

Alexander remained silent, but the commissioners knew his silence did not indicate his acceptance of their definition of tribal hunting grounds. Commissioner Stevens, realizing that the council had reached an impasse, recessed the proceedings, saying,

> We will try this treaty again tomorrow. Think over the matter in your lodges tonight. I will say to the Western Indians that the proposition made to them I believe to be just and good. Let them council together and see tomorrow if it will not suit their hearts.

When you separate talk in friendship with the Blackfeet and see if your hearts cannot be one.[27]

What magic words were uttered, what arguments were used in lodges of the many chiefs who attended the council that evening, we shall never know. But when the great council was reconvened at noon the next day and the tribal boundaries proposed in the treaty were again explained to the Indians with the aid of a map and a rough sketch of the country drawn on a buffalo skin, no objections were raised.

The commissioners proceeded to read and explain the remaining articles of the treaty. Under the terms of Article VII, the Indians agreed to permit United States citizens to live in and pass unmolested through their territories, and the United States agreed to protect the Indians against depredations and other unlawful acts by white men. Article VIII contained the Indians' consent to the construction of roads of every description, the establishment of telegraph lines and military posts, and the building of houses for agencies, missions, schools, farms, shops, mills, and stations by the United States in their territory. They also agreed that the navigation of all lakes and streams in their country should be "forever free to citizens of the United States."

In return for these concessions the United States agreed to expend $20,000 annually upon useful goods and provisions for the four tribes of "The Blackfoot Nation" for a period of ten years, and to expend an additional sum of $15,000 annually during the same period in establishing and instructing these Indians in agricultural and mechanical pursuits, in educating their children, and "in any other respect promoting their civilization and Christianization." (Articles IX and X.)

Articles XI through XV provided compensation for Indian depredations upon whites or other Indians, either by return of stolen property or withholding of annuities, provided for the exclusion of intoxicating liquor from the Indians' country, and promised that annuities would not be withheld to pay individual

[27] *Ibid.*, 7–8.

debts. Finally, Article XVI stated, "This treaty shall be obligatory upon the aforesaid nations and tribes, parties hereto from the date hereof, and upon the United States as soon as the same shall be ratified by the President and Senate."[28]

The great chiefs of the warlike Blackfeet appeared to have been less concerned with the concessions granted the whites under this treaty than with its effect upon their traditional intertribal warfare. During the second and final day of the council only two of them spoke. Lame Bull wanted to know what they should do in case their Assiniboin, Cree, or Crow enemies, not parties to the treaty, should steal their horses. The commissioners advised the Indians to follow the thieves, retake their property if they could, and report the action to their agent.

Seen-From-Afar, the Blood head chief, realistically expressed his doubts of the effectiveness of the treaty as an instrument for assuring intertribal peace:

> I wish to say that as far as we old men are concerned we want peace and to cease going to war; but I am afraid that we cannot stop our young men. The Crows are not here to smoke the pipe with us and I am afraid our young men will not be persuaded that they ought not to war against the Crows. We, however, will try our best to keep our young men at home.

In their concluding remarks to the Indians, both commissioners attempted to answer Seen-From-Afar by re-emphasizing the importance of intertribal peace. Cumming's closing plea was eloquently direct and simple.

> Tell your young men that your Great Father wishes all his children to live in Peace; if you do not live in peace, and continue to go to war, he will be mad with his children. He will be ashamed of his children, and will not send you Blankets and provisions, coffee, and tobacco. Tell your young men to take wives and live

[28] Kappler, *Indian Affairs, Laws and Treaties*, II, 552–55. Contains the complete text of this treaty. The original treaty and the map used in explaining the tribal boundaries proposed by the commissioners are in the National Archives.

happily in their own lodges, then the old men will see their sons. Your sons will see their children, and you will all be happy. Remember my words.[29]

On this idealistic note the discussions ended. Satisfied that the Indians understood and agreed to the terms of the treaty, the commissioners proceeded to sign it. Then, in turn, the chiefs, headmen, and delegates of all of the tribes present came forward. Secretary Doty wrote the name of each, followed by the widely spaced words, "His Mark," and the Indian placed a neat X in the blank area between them.

The gifts which had been purchased for the Indians and freighted up the Missouri were piled high on the council ground, where they served as a constant reminder to the Indian negotiators of the happy prospects ahead. After the last Indian appended his mark to the treaty, these gifts were distributed. They included blankets, cotton prints, sugar, coffee, rice, flour, and tobacco. Many of the Blackfeet had no idea how to use the strange white men's foods. They threw the flour into the air and were amused to see it fall to the ground and cover the grass with its fine powder. They emptied quantities of sugar into a stream and eagerly drank the sweetened water. They cooked huge batches of rice until their kettles overflowed with the odd, sticky foodstuff. They did not care for the taste of the coffee and eventually bartered much of it to the white traders.[30]

Commissioner Cumming started down the Missouri for his headquarters in St. Louis six days after the treaty signing. The next morning Governor Stevens set out in the opposite direction, bound for Fort Benton and the west. Optimistically, he confided to his journal, "We got through the Blackfeet treaty, everything having succeeded to our entire satisfaction, and indeed, beyond our most sanguine expectations."[31]

Neither of the commissioners ever returned to the Blackfoot country. The treaty signed in the field October 17, 1855, was

[29] Partoll (ed.), *Blackfoot Indian Peace Council,* 10–11.
[30] Bradley, "Manuscript," *MHSC,* Vol. III, 271–74.
[31] Isaac I. Stevens, "Narrative," *PRR,* XII, 222.

Blackfoot Treaty Council at the mouth of the Judith River, 1855.
From a drawing by Gustavus Sohon (*Courtesy Smithsonian Institution*).

forwarded to Washington, ratified by the Senate on April 15, 1856, and proclaimed by the president of the United States ten days later. Although known to the white man's official records as the Treaty with The Blackfoot Nation, this first official negotiation with the United States has been remembered among the illiterate Blackfoot Indians as "Lame Bull's Treaty."

Lame Bull, also known as Lone Chief, was head chief of the Piegan tribe and first Indian signer of the treaty. He was chief of the Hard Top Knots Band which Stanley estimated at one hundred lodges in 1853.[32] Lame Bull was both a distinguished warrior and a skillful diplomat. He was the leader of the small Piegan trading party encamped near Fort McKenzie which was attacked by a large Assiniboin and Cree war party in the summer of 1833.[33] Twenty-one years later (in March, 1854) he led a large Piegan war party against the Crow Indians.[34] Yet Governor Stevens found him to be sincere in his desire to live at peace with other tribes.

In mid-September, 1856, Rev. Mackey met Lame Bull at the mouth of the Judith River, where the Blackfeet were awaiting the arrival of annuities due them under the terms of the 1855 treaty. When the Presbyterian missionary asked this chief if he would permit white men and women to establish a mission among his people, Lame Bull expressed his personal willingness, but wished to consult the other chiefs before making a decision in a matter of such importance. The next day he told Mackey he had brought the matter before all the chiefs in council and that they were agreeable to the proposal. With dignity the philosophical old chief explained,

> We are satisfied that white men are our friends, if they were not they would not go to the trouble of sending us so many valuable presents each year. We desire them to come and teach us about the Great Spirit & tell us plenty of good things. When we catch

[32] *Pacific Railroad Reports of Explorations and Surveys,* I, 449.
[33] See the description of that battle on pp. 62–63 of this book.
[34] James Doty to Isaac I. Stevens, December 20, 1854, Indian Office Records.

a wild animal on the prairie & attempt to tame him we sometimes find it very hard. It may take a long time & a great deal of patience. But almost any animal can be tamed by kindness & perseverance. We have been running wild on the prairie and now we want the white sons and daughters of our Great Father to come to our country and tame us. . . . We have a fine country & we are not ashamed to have white men come & see it.[35]

The following year Lame Bull's band was hunting buffalo near the Sweetgrass Hills. Amid the dust of the chase Lame Bull's horse was attacked by an enraged buffalo bull. The horse fell. Lame Bull's ribs were crushed and his neck broken. According to one Indian account, Lame Bull was buried on a platform inside his lodge and twenty of his horses were killed for his use in the afterworld. According to another story, the body of this great chief was taken to Fort Benton and buried there by the whites.

My older Piegan informants said that Lame Bull was about sixty years of age when he was killed. Although physically small, this courageous veteran of many intertribal wars and staunch advocate of peace with the whites had great influence among his people. Had he lived, his example and wise counsel might have helped to minimize interracial tensions in the Blackfoot country during the difficult decade that followed.[36]

Many of the other Piegan band chiefs who placed their marks on the 1855 treaty died equally violent deaths. Big Snake (rattlesnake), chief of the Small Brittle Fat Band, loud-mouthed announcer in the tribal summer encampment and prominent war leader, was killed in a battle with the Cree Indians near the Cypress Hills in 1858. Little Dog, Governor Stevens' favorite, chief of the Black Patched Moccasins Band and successor to Lame Bull as head chief of his tribe, was murdered by his own

---

[35] Klett, *Missionary Endeavors of the Presbyterian Church Among the Blackfeet Indians in the 1850s*, Presbyterian Historical Society, 343–44.

[36] When President Franklin D. Roosevelt was inducted into the Blackfoot tribe during his visit to the Glacier National Park in 1934, he was given the name "Lone Chief," in honor of this great leader, the first signer of the first treaty between "The Blackfoot Nation" and the United States.

223

people in 1866. Middle Sitter (also known as Many Horses), chief of the Never Laughs Band and owner of more horses than any other Blackfoot Indian, was killed by the Gros Ventres that same year. Mountain Chief, second in rank among the Piegan chiefs in 1858 and successor to Little Dog as head chief of the tribe, was shot and killed (possibly by mistake) by another Blackfoot Indian in 1872.[37]

At least two of the most prominent Blood chiefs who signed the treaty also met untimely deaths. Seen-From-Afar, their principal chief, brother-in-law of Alexander Culbertson and the wealthiest man in his tribe, died in the smallpox epidemic of 1869. He was chief of the powerful Fish Eaters' Band, and the head chieftaincy of the Blood tribe has descended in his family to the present day. Calf Shirt, chief of the Quarrelers Band, was murdered by whisky traders a few years after the smallpox epidemic.[38]

The Northern Blackfeet were represented at the council by only four band chiefs—Three Bulls, Old Kootenai, Pow-ah-que, and Rabbit Runner. Among the treaty signers there were also eight Gros Ventre chiefs and twenty-seven chiefs of tribes from west of the Rockies, including among them Victor, head chief of the Flatheads, Alexander, the Pend d'Oreille head chief, and the two great Nez Percé chiefs, Looking Glass and Eagle from the Light.[39]

This convocation of fifty-nine prominent leaders of eight different tribes at the Blackfoot treaty council in mid-October, 1855, was undoubtedly the most important intertribal gathering ever

[37] Other Piegan signers of this treaty were Low Horn, Little Gray Head, The Skunk, The Bad Head, Spotted Calf (Kitch-eepone-istah), and four minor leaders.
[38] Other Blood Indian signers were The Father of All Children, Bull's Back Fat, Heavy Shield, Sun Calf (Nahtose-onistah), The Feather, and White Eagle.
[39] Hazard Stevens, *Life of Isaac I. Stevens,* reproduces a number of pencil portraits by Gustavus Sohon of Blackfoot Indian chiefs who signed this treaty. The original drawings have been loaned to the Washington State Historical Society by the descendants of Isaac I. Stevens. Sohon's portraits of Flathead and Pend d'Oreille chiefs who signed this treaty are in the U. S. National Museum. These portraits have been reproduced in Ewers, *Gustavus Sohon's Portraits of Flathead and Pend d'Oreille Indians, 1854.* Smithsonian Institution *Miscellaneous Collections,* CX, No. 7.

held on the northwestern plains. Although the tribes which these chiefs led had a combined population of only about 12,000, they occupied a vast area in present Montana and the Canadian provinces of Alberta and Saskatchewan which was more than twice the size of New England. Furthermore, a century after that treaty was negotiated in the cottonwood grove near the mouth of the Judith River, Indian claims resulting from later cessions of land within the boundaries described in that treaty still remained unsettled.

13: Life with Our Father

A̲ᴛ ᴛʜᴇ ɢʀᴇᴀᴛ treaty council in the fall of 1855, Governor Stevens told the Blackfoot tribes, "The Great Father has sent an agent to live at the Forts above who will be your Father. When you have any trouble, go to him as you would go to your Father."[1] His Indian listeners took him at his word. To this day elderly Blackfoot men and women who speak little or no English call their agent *ninnàna,* "Our Father." They refer to his place of business as "Our Father's House."

Among the fur traders and other whites the early agents commonly were addressed by the honorary title of "Major." The first Blackfoot agent, Major Edwin A. C. Hatch from Minnesota, was presented to the Indians at the treaty council in mid-October, 1855. Shortly thereafter he established the first agency for his "children" at the fur trading post of Fort Benton.

Major Hatch's two most noteworthy achievements appear to have been the giving of a large ball for the traders at the fort on New Year's Eve, which was so successful that it lasted through the next day and night, and the management of the distribution of the first annuities paid the four tribes under the terms of the treaty eight months later. During most of the intervening period he could not discuss the Indians' troubles with them for the simple reason that he was not in the Blackfoot country. On February 6, 1856, Hatch started downriver to Fort Union to await the arrival of annuities from St. Louis. He did not return

[1]Partoll (ed.), *Blackfoot Indian Peace Council,* 9.

to Fort Benton until mid-August. In his diary he laconically described the most important actio.. of his administration, the payment of annuities to the Indians at the mouth of the Judith in late September.

Sept. 22. Beautiful morning.—Recd. the goods and distributed nearly all of them—shall finish in the morning—every thing went off quickly—about 8000 Indians present.

Sept. 23. Fine morning—closed with the Indians—said good bye—and we were off at five minutes of 11 o'clock.[2]

Major Hatch's first and only annual report was written from Fort Union, July 12, 1856. He had been father to the Blackfoot tribes for nine months, but he had not seen his children for five of them. As a result his report contained no recent information on either the condition or disposition of his charges. Nevertheless, it did substantiate the fears of the Blood head chief, Seen-From-Afar, which he had expressed at the treaty council, that he could not prevent his young warriors from going to war against the Crow Indians. Hatch reported that less than ten days after the treaty was signed a war party of Blood Indians departed for the Crow camps. Many others followed. In early February the Blood chiefs told the Major that their young men had supposed the Crows were not included in the peace treaty. Yet Hatch learned that Blood warriors passed through the Gros Ventre and Piegan camps on their way to the enemy, and "when they found the young men of those tribes did not join them, ridiculed them for listening to the advice of the whites." The agent reported that the Blood warriors "stole a few horses, destroyed one lodge of Crows, and killed five Assiniboines." He urged that every individual who had led a war party be arrested and punished by United States troops.[3]

Major Hatch's superior, Colonel Cumming, the superintendent of Indian Affairs in St. Louis, must have regarded this proposal

[2] E. A. C. Hatch, Diary, June 7–October 15, 1856, typescript copy in Montana State Historical Society Library.

[3] Reports of the Commissioner of Indian Affairs, 1856, 75–76.

of a green Indian agent to send troops hundreds of miles into the wilderness to punish a handful of Indian horse raiders as ridiculous. He had much more important worries on his mind. Cumming knew that hostile Sioux parties were roaming the Oregon Trail and that a full-scale Indian war was raging in Washington Territory. In his report to the Commissioner of Indian Affairs on September 25, Cumming expressed gratification that the tribes party to the Blackfoot treaty had been at peace, and he was relieved that these warlike people had refused all participation in the hostilities of the tribes of Oregon and Washington.[4]

The following year the Blackfoot tribes gained a new father, Major Alfred J. Vaughan. The fur trader Charles Larpenteur described Vaughan thusly:

A jovial old fellow, who had a very fine paunch for brandy, and, when he could not get brandy, would take almost anything which would make him drunk. He was one who remained most of his time with his Indians, but what accounts for that is the fact that he had a pretty young squaw for a wife; and as he received many favors from the [American Fur] Company, his reports must have been in their favor.[5]

Larpenteur's characterization should be taken with more than one grain of salt. It was his habit to damn virtually all Indian agents and some very able fur traders as drunkards. As for Vaughan's favoring the fur traders—it simply was not true. On the contrary, in his annual report of 1858 he went so far as to recommend the prohibition of trade in buffalo robes to prevent the ruthless slaughtering of more buffalo than the Indians needed for their subsistence.[6] Had such a prohibition been put into effect, it would have ruined the American Fur Company's business in the entire Upper Missouri region.

Actually, Major Vaughan was an experienced and able agent who conscientiously tried to implement the government's policies

[4] *Ibid.*, 66.
[5] *Forty Years a Fur Trader*, II, 417–18.
[6] Reports of the Commissioner of Indian Affairs, 1858, 83.

for the civilization of his Indian charges. Vaughan had served for fifteen years in the Indian Service. He had been agent to the Upper Missouri tribes since 1852 and knew a great deal about the Assiniboins, Crows, and Western Sioux from intimate contacts with them during that period. Ten days before his departure from St. Louis to become father to the Blackfoot tribes, on May 30, 1857, Vaughan wrote Father De Smet urging him to establish a mission among the Blackfeet which would advance the interests of the government and those of the Indians at the same time. Although Vaughan was a Protestant, he expressed the belief that "Catholic missionaries have always succeeded in gaining the Indians' hearts, in controlling their brutal outbreaks and ameliorating their condition in every respect."[7]

Although Vaughan by no means limited his activity to the distribution of the government's bounty among the Indians, he paid strict attention to the practical problems of distributing the annuities equitably and of suggesting substitutions in annuity goods to eliminate useless items and provide ones which would be more appreciated by the Indians. Shortly after he reached the Blackfoot country, he consulted with the Gros Ventre and Blood tribes and found that they cared little about the coffee furnished them and would prefer corn to rice.

When the annuities arrived in 1858, Vaughan employed a simple but ingenious method of assuring their fair distribution among the multitude of Indians who assembled to receive them:

> Having first ascertained the exact number of lodges by a bundle of sticks given me at my own request by the head men of the band, each stick indicating a lodge or family, I placed the representatives of the various lodges in a large circle, the presents to be distributed forming its centre. To each individual in this circle or ring was given in turn his just and due proportion, as nearly as the nature of the goods would permit, of every article of merchandise sent to the agency.[8]

[7] De Smet, *Life, Letters and Travels*, IV, 1317.
[8] Reports of the Commissioner of Indian Affairs, 1858, 77.

To simplify distribution of the goods in the future, Major Vaughan recommended that the contractors divide the whole quantity of each and every article into four parts—40 per cent for the Piegans, 25 per cent for the Bloods, 22 per cent for the Gros Ventres, and 13 per cent for the Northern Blackfeet. These proportions were based upon his count of the number of lodges in each of the four tribes.

Of what did these annuities consist? The list of annuities for the year 1858, distributed to the Piegan tribe (with a population of 460 lodges), reveals a considerable quantity and wide variety of goods. Of foodstuffs it included 10,000 pounds of flour, 57,000 pounds of rice, 7,600 pounds of sugar, 7,400 pounds of pilot bread, and 2,500 pounds of coffee. Among the many articles of cloth were 401 pairs of blankets, 2,280 yards of calico, 2,967 yards of checked, striped, and plaid material, 500 yards of flannel, and 152 flannel shirts. For the craftworkers there were 128 pounds of black and white beads, 84 pounds of ruby and blue beads, 4 gross squaw awls, and 25 pounds of linen thread. Household utensils included 9 dozen tin cups, 119 pounds of brass kettles, 26 dozen two-quart pans, 36 dozen butcher knives, 138 dozen frying pans, and 7 dozen fire steels. Toilet articles and cosmetics included 37 dozen combs, 10 dozen zinc mirrors, and 201 pounds of vermilion for face painting. Of tools there were 8 dozen files and 7 dozen half-axes. The quantity of weapons alone was impressive—108 Northwest guns (each valued at $6.50), 1,300 gun flints, 16 kegs of powder, 29 bags of bullets, more than 7 dozen powder horns, and 400 pounds of hoop iron for making arrowheads. In addition, the annuities included such odd items as 13 gross fish hooks and 23 dozen fish lines. And last, but not least appreciated, there were 2,660 pounds of tobacco.[9]

Major Vaughan found some of the items included in the Indians annuities very impractical. He recommended that flour be substituted for the pilot bread, which had become quite stale during its two months' journey up the Missouri, and that the amount of coffee, a drink little desired by the Blackfeet at that

[9] Annuities paid to the Piegans, August 28, 1858, Indian Office Records.

time, be reduced by one-half. He found the calico too flimsy to be useful, the American vermilion so inferior to Chinese vermilion that a far smaller quantity of the latter would be preferred. As for the fish hooks, combs, mirrors, and thread—the Blackfeet had no use for them whatever. He requested that the government send in their stead shirts, bed ticking, more powder and ball, one-point blankets, and about three dozen plain substantial saddles for the chiefs.[10] Probably in answer to his last request, "Eight Spanish Saddles" were included in the annuities for the Blackfoot tribes in 1860.[11]

Impractical as were the foods, sleazy as were the fabrics, cheap as was the hardware, and useless as were the fish hooks, most of the Indians looked forward each year to receiving their presents from the Great White Father with as keen anticipation as children awaiting the arrival of Christmas. Thousands of Indians were on hand to greet the arrival of the keelboats bearing their annuities upriver from Fort Union. They knew they could turn over the strange foods and other articles for which they had no real need to their "white brothers-in-law" (white men married to Indian women) at Fort Benton, and ride off to hunt buffalo— their traditional source of good meat and of basic materials for making scores of useful objects.

During his first year among the Blackfeet, Major Vaughan examined the valley of the Missouri and its tributaries, searching for the most promising site for the farm which was guaranteed the Indians by the 1855 treaty. With the advice of Father Hoecken and Major John Owen, whose years of experience among the Flathead Indian farmers west of the Rockies qualified them as the best agricultural experts in the region, he selected a site on Sun River some fifteen miles above its mouth. There the valley was a half-mile wide and the alluvial soil was rich and deep. Vaughan was "determined to spare neither labor nor expense to test fully its adaptation for farming." Yet he recognized that "the

[10] Reports of the Commissioner of Indian Affairs, 1858, 82.
[11] Annuities for the use of the Indians of the Blackfoot Agency, received in St. Louis, May 3, 1860. Indian Office Records.

climate and the shortness of the season" might prove a "drawback to at least partial success in our undertaking."[12]

The 1859 crop was a keen disappointment, damaged by a prolonged drought. But the next year the Major became lyrical over the success of his farming experiment. Wheat "as fine as ever was raised in any State," and "the best Indian corn and vegetables of all kinds and varieties in profusion" proved "the fertility and productiveness of the soil beyond all cavil and doubt forever."[13] To guard against future crop failures because of drought, Vaughan requested $2,500 to enable him to irrigate the farm. He also asked for $10,000 worth of cattle, believing that "the Sun River valley [was] unsurpassed as a grazing country."[14]

It was one thing to demonstrate that farming was possible in the Blackfoot country and quite another to induce the nomadic Indians to take a hand at it. However, Little Dog, the Piegan head chief, appeared interested in Vaughan's experiment. Believing that Little Dog's example would have a powerful influence upon his people, Vaughan decided to open and cultivate a small farm for him a few miles distant from the government one.[15]

In his enthusiasm for reporting the progress of his children toward civilization, Major Vaughan claimed that the dread Blackfeet had "become the most peaceful nation on the Missouri." This was hardly true. Small parties of Blackfoot warriors raided as far south as the Sioux, Arapaho, and Cheyenne camps on the Platte in 1857. The next year a large force of Northern Blackfeet fought a series of engagements with the Kutenais both east and west of the Rockies.[16]

Nevertheless, Little Dog, who had succeeded Lame Bull as head chief of the Piegans, tried conscientiously to live up to his promise of peace with neighboring tribes made at "Lame Bull's Treaty." In the spring or summer of 1856 he and members of

[12] Reports of the Commissioner of Indian Affairs, 1858, 78–79.
[13] Ibid., 1860, 83–84.
[14] Ibid., 83.
[15] Ibid., 83.
[16] Ibid., 1858, 95; William T. Hamilton, "A Trading Expedition Among the Indians in 1858," Montana Historical Society Contributions, Vol. III, 77–112.

his family paid a friendly visit to the Flatheads beyond the
Rockies. As they approached the Flathead camp, they unfurled
an American flag to show their peaceful intentions. Two years
later he made peace with the River Crows, and that fall two
chiefs of the Crow Indians led a group of their people to Little
Dog's camp to trade and hunt buffalo with their Piegan friends.[17]

It was much easier for Indian chiefs to negotiate a peace than
it was for them to get their ambitious young warriors to keep it.
In 1858 a group of "Blackfeet" met the Plains Crees on the North
Saskatchewan to arrange a peace. Soon after negotiations were
satisfactorily completed and the tribes went their separate ways,
some young Cree braves could not resist the temptation to steal
Blackfoot horses. The Blackfeet pursued them, killed one Cree,
and captured two others. They stripped their captives, tied their
hands behind their backs, bored holes in their wrists, and inserted sticks so tightly into the holes that they could not separate
their arms. Then they turned the captives loose. Only one of
these mutilated men reached his own camp.[18]

In the Indian country where the white population was limited
to a few fur traders, the Indian agent, his interpreter, and the
government farmers, Vaughan found it very difficult to impress
upon his children the power and the character of the white man's
civilization. It was not surprising that the Blackfeet regarded
themselves as numerous and strong and the whites as few and
feeble, or that they said to the Major, "If the whites are so numerous, why is it the same ones come back to this country year
after year, with rarely an exception?" To remedy this situation,
Vaughan recommended that parties of fifteen or twenty headmen and chiefs be taken on a visit to the East each year for five
years, "to impress the Indian with a proper view of the strength
and importance of the white man, and create in him a desire to
cultivate the pacific arts and sciences."[19] Indian junkets to Wash-

[17] *Ibid.*, 6–64; De Smet, *Life, Letters and Travels*, IV, 1247.

[18] Henry Youle Hind, *Narrative of the Canadian Red River Exploring Expedition of 1857 and the Assiniboine and Saskatchewan Exploring Expedition of
1858*, II, 126.

[19] Reports of the Commissioner of Indian Affairs, 1858, 119–20.

ington had been common policy for many years, but never before had Indians from so great a distance made the long trek east to see the Great White Father, nor on so great a scale as Vaughan suggested. This recommendation, like his request for cattle, died in the office of the commissioner of Indian Affairs.

Vaughan was pleased when, in 1859, the Jesuits accepted his long-standing invitation to establish a mission among the Blackfeet. That summer Father Hoecken and Brother Magri traveled with the Indians. Then they built three log cabins on the Teton River near present Choteau, where they spent the winter studying the Blackfoot language and catechizing some Indian children from the winter camps near by.[20]

The Major was pleased also when the first steamboat ever to reach Fort Benton, in the summer of 1860, carried three hundred uniformed soldiers of the United States. This first large body of soldiers to reach the Blackfoot country merely passed through it. From Fort Benton they proceeded westward over the Rockies, following the newly located Mullen Wagon Road. Nevertheless, Vaughan believed the sight of so many troopers would cause the Indians to "respect and fear the government accordingly."[21]

When the Civil War broke out during the next year, Major Vaughan had to be replaced. Vaughan was a Virginian, and there was no place in the government service for a potential southern sympathizer. It was a long time before the Blackfoot Indians received another "father" who was as sincere, able, and experienced as Major Vaughan, who, at the age of sixty, left the Blackfoot country. Eight years later he returned to help the government make treaties with the Blackfeet, Gros Ventres, and Crows.

Under the "fatherhood" of Major Vaughan (1857–61), the Blackfeet made no great strides toward the civilization which Governor Stevens had so glibly prophesied for them. Vaughan had seen to it that they received the annuities promised them under the terms of the treaty, had shown them that crops could be grown in their country, and had encouraged them to try farm-

[20] William N. Bischoff, *The Jesuits in Old Oregon,* 86–87.
[21] Reports of the Commissioner of Indian Affairs, 1860, 83.

ing. But the Blackfeet were in no hurry to forsake the excitement of the buffalo hunt for the monotony of tilling the soil. He had counseled peace with neighboring tribes, but ambitious young men continued to organize frequent small raiding parties. No attempt had been made to establish schools for the Blackfeet. Nevertheless, this agent's conscientious efforts to implement the government's policy and to show the Indians the white man's way were not in vain. He had won one important convert. Little Dog, head chief of the Piegans, had employed his influence as a peacemaker and had become the first Blackfoot Indian to try the farmer's life. However, converts to the cause of intertribal peace and the farming life were proving as difficult to obtain as were the missionaries' converts to Christianity—and for precisely the same reason. The Blackfoot Indians felt no real need for the government's program. They were happy with their traditional way of life.

14: Massacre on the Marias

MANY FACTORS contributed to the unrest that prevailed in the Blackfoot country during the 1860's. Certainly a major underlying cause was the Civil War. Of necessity, the problems involved in the pacification and civilization of western Indian tribes were of secondary importance to the complicated problems of prosecuting and winning a bloody war that divided the nation. During the war period the most able government administrators were absorbed in the war effort. Although the Blackfoot Indians were not entirely neglected by the Great White Father, his field representatives among them were weak, inept men who had little experience in Indian affairs. During a period of eighteen months they had no agent at all. Of Gad E. Upson, whom the Blackfeet called "Our Father" for two years after October, 1863, the outspoken old Indian trader William T. Hamilton scornfully wrote, "He knew as much about an Indian as I did about the inhabitants of Jupiter."[1]

It was another misfortune for the Indians that gold was discovered at Bannack during this period of national crisis and weakness in Indian administration. In the summer of 1862 the call of gold was attracting white men westward, through the Blackfoot country to the newly discovered mining area along the eastern base of the Rockies. Blackfoot chiefs, who only a few years before had doubted the numbers of the whites, began to complain to Agent Henry Reed of so many white men moving

[1] "The Council at Fort Benton," *Forest and Stream*, Vol. LXVIII, No. 17, 649.

through their country "lest there might be some design of getting their lands from them, which they could not consent to, as this had been their home as well as that of their fathers, and they hoped to make it the place of their graves and the home of their children." Reed tried to calm their fears by assuring them that "there was no such intention on the part of the Great White Father; that the whites now had by far more land than they could cultivate or knew what to do with."[2]

In his report to Washington, Reed expressed surprise that there had as yet been no troubles between the Indians and the large numbers of whites who were passing through their country from Fort Benton to the diggings, especially since there were "not a few" white men who would not "be tolerated in any civilized society." To keep the peace and to prevent the trade of intoxicating liquor to the Indians, Reed recommended that at least one or two companies of United States soldiers be stationed at Fort Benton.[3]

As for Major Vaughan's pride and joy, the Blackfoot farm, Reed considered it of no practical value to the Indians whatever. He noted that even Little Dog, feeling insecure on his eight- or ten-acre farm several miles from the agency farm, had returned to the nomadic camps of his people.[4]

In the year 1863 neither agent nor annuities reached the Blackfoot country. Low water prevented the steamboat carrying the Blackfoot annuities from moving upriver beyond Fort Union. The Sioux were on the warpath. Faint-hearted Major Reed left the annuities at Fort Union, sent letters to his Indian children by some more courageous men who were traveling to Fort Benton on horseback, boarded the steamboat bound down the Missouri, and wrote his annual report from the safety of his home in Epworth, Iowa, more than one thousand miles from his field station.[5]

Needless to say, Henry Reed's days as Blackfoot agent were

[2] Reports of the Commissioner of Indian Affairs, 1863, 179.
[3] Ibid., 180.
[4] Ibid., 180.
[5] Ibid., 172.

over. When his successor, Gad E. Upson, reached Fort Benton on December 21, 1863, the Indians told him they thought their Great White Father had forgotten them. Not only had they received no annuities, but they had had no agent in their country for eighteen months. Upson put it very mildly when he reported that he found "the affairs of the agency in a deplorable condition." The farm buildings were run down, many of the farming implements were missing, and there was no seed on hand for the spring planting. Whisky was being traded to the Indians. The Piegans were at war with their traditional allies, the Gros Ventres. And the Blackfoot warriors were stealing white men's horses.[6]

Perhaps even a strong, sympathetic "father" could not have prevented Blackfoot alarm at the increasing numbers of emigrants crossing their hunting grounds from ripening into open hostility. But certainly Upson's conception of the Indians as "degraded savages" whose potentialities for improvement appeared almost hopeless did not help matters. Under his unsympathetic care the aroused young warriors turned from stealing white men's horses to killing whites. Their actions were not unprovoked. "Sneaking drink givers," as they aptly termed the traders in illegal whisky, were inflaming the minds of restless, ambitious, red-skinned warriors with their low-grade liquor. Indian-hating whites were killing Indians in the town of Fort Benton as well as on the plains.

On April 23, 1865, some Blood Indians stole about forty horses from whites at Fort Benton. A month later a group of whites attacked a party of Blood visitors to Fort Benton and killed three of them. Two days after that, a large Blood Indian war party led by Calf Shirt, one of the chiefs who had signed the 1855 treaty of peace, discovered a party of ten woodcutters at the mouth of the Marias, twelve miles from Fort Benton, and killed all of them.

When the bloody corpses of the ten whites were found and word of their murder reached the capital of the new territory

[6] *Ibid.,* 1864, 293–98.

MASSACRE ON THE MARIAS

of Montana, Governor Edgerton, fearing war with the Blackfeet was imminent, called upon James Stuart to organize a volunteer force to chastise the Indians. But when it was discovered that the red warriors had withdrawn northward beyond the international boundary, the proposed campaign against the Indians was called off.[7]

Governor Edgerton's eagerness to call out the troops—volunteers though they might be—against the Indians was in sharp contrast to the fair and impartial Indian policy he had proclaimed to the first Montana legislature the previous December. "While I shall endeavor to punish with promptness and severity any Indian aggression upon our settlements, I shall at the same time, hold to strict accountability any who trespass upon the rights of the Indian."[8]

In the same speech Governor Edgerton had voiced a very popular hope among the white settlers of the new territory, that "the Government will, at an early date, take steps for the extinguishment of Indian title in this territory, in order that our lands may be brought into market."[9]

When Agent Upson returned to the Blackfoot country from the East in the summer of 1865, he was armed with detailed instructions from the Commissioner of Indian Affairs for the negotiation of a treaty with the Blackfoot tribes and the Gros Ventres which would push their southern boundary northward to the Teton River and so open the region south of that line to white settlement. In mid-November he met the principal chiefs of the Piegans and Gros Ventres, some of the Blood chiefs, and a single Northern Blackfoot chief in council. As an inducement to these chiefs to sign the proposed treaty, Upson promised that the government would pay each of them a sum not to exceed $250 annually in money or supplies "so long as they and their respective tribes remain faithful to their treaty obligations." Annuity payments to the value of $50,000 over a period of twenty

[7] *Ibid.*, 1865, 695; Bradley, "Manuscript," *MHSC*, Vol. VIII, 144–45.

[8] "Governor Edgerton's First Message to the First Legislature," Montana Historical Society *Contributions*, III, 344.

[9] *Ibid.*

years were promised the Indians in exchange for their cession of lands south of the Teton.[10]

At the conclusion of the treaty, Little Dog, head chief of the Piegans, was reported to have said, "We are pleased with what we have heard today. . . . The land here belongs to us, we were raised upon it; we are glad to give a portion to the United States; for we get something for it."

The special correspondent for *The Montana Post* who covered the treaty proceedings at Fort Benton hailed the treaty as a great victory for the whites, saying that Upson had made the "concessions on our part as few and light as possible." He exulted in the thought that the treaty "gives over to us all that vast extent of country [embracing between two and three hundred thousand square miles] in which are situated our largest towns—Helena, Virginia City, Bannack etc.—and containing all the rich mines, our best agricultural lands, some of our largest rivers and, in fact, all those portions of our Territory that have proved to be of any worth."[11]

Thomas F. Meagher, acting governor of Montana Territory, who had assisted Major Upson in negotiating the treaty, doubted that the Indians would keep the peace. He well knew that horse stealing was "accounted rather an heroic exploit by the best of these Indians."[12] But the Indians were not content with stealing horses. In less than two months after the treaty council Piegan and Blood war parties killed several miners and traders. When the Commissioner of Indian Affairs in Washington heard of these murders, he refused to recommend ratification of the treaty.[13]

During the following winter a reported gold discovery in the Sun River Valley drew more than five hundred prospectors to that region. Some of the die-hards who refused to believe the

[10] Treaty Between the United States and Blackfoot Nation of Indians, November 16, 1865 (unratified). Manuscript, with signatures, Indian Office Records.

[11] *The Montana Post,* December 9, 1865.

[12] Reports of the Commissioner of Indian Affairs, 1866, 196.

[13] D. N. Cooley, commissioner of indian affairs, to James Harlan, Secretary of the Interior, April 12, 1866, Indian Office Records.

report was false remained in the valley until they were over-taken by a severe snowstorm. They might have starved had not Little Dog, faithful friend of the whites, volunteered to hunt for them. In spite of the severe weather Little Dog managed to kill antelope and bring in the meat to feed the stricken miners.

His kindness contrasted sharply with the actions of an Indian-hating white man, John Morgan, who lived in a house on Sun River that winter. When four Piegan warriors paid a friendly visit to his home, Morgan enlisted the aid of a party of near-by prospectors to help him get rid of his Indian visitors. One of the red men was shot attempting to escape. The other three were hung from a convenient tree. Unknown to the executioners their cold-blooded actions were seen by a passing group of Piegans, who reported the murders to their people.[14]

In April a large revenge party, believed to have been North Piegans led by their chief, Bull's Head, attacked the Sun River farm, burned the buildings, and killed one of the two attendants. When George Wright, the new Blackfoot agent, visited the farm the following September, he found "the general appearance is that of desolation." The buildings were destroyed, the farming implements were gone, and the fields were overgrown with weeds. Emigrants passing along a near-by road had taken most of the rail fencing.[15] Thus the first noble experiment in demon-strating the advantages of the farmer's life to the buffalo-hunting Blackfeet ended in utter failure.

Nor was the agency farm the only symbol of civilization to fall before the vengeful Piegans. The Jesuit missionaries, then established on Sun River, had unwittingly given shelter to the wretched Morgan. The Indians shot several cattle belonging to the mission and killed the herder. On April 27 the priests aban-doned their mission and moved to safety west of the Rockies. Father De Smet, at Fort Benton in June, wrote, "A fresh and furious war has broken out between the whites and the Black-

[14] Bradley, "Manuscript," *MHSC*, Vol. IX, 251–54.
[15] George Wright to Commissioner of Indian Affairs, September 14, 1866, Indian Office Records.

feet, in which again the whites have given the first provocation, and our Fathers have been obliged to withdraw for the moment."[16]

Meanwhile, Little Dog, the only Blackfoot Indian who had shown any real interest in farming, continued to try to live up to his promise of peace with the whites professed at two treaty councils. In the month of May, not long after he had brought twelve horses stolen from the whites by the Piegans in to Fort Benton and turned them over to Acting Agent Upham, Little Dog and his family left the fort to return to the camp of their people. About three miles from the town he was overtaken by a party of drunken Piegans, who murdered both the old man and his son. Not satisfied with having killed their head chief, the murderers proceeded to mutilate his body with butcher knives. In reporting this incident to Washington, the agent stated his belief that Little Dog and his son were killed "because they were suspected of being too friendly with the whites."[17] So strong was Piegan animosity toward the whites that some of them regarded their peacemaking head chief as a traitor and removed him from his influential position with finality.

In spite of their new troubles with the whites, the warlike Blackfeet did not forget their long-standing quarrels with neighboring tribes. Indeed, since the 1855 treaty, the Piegans had added another tribe to their long list of enemies—their longtime allies, the Gros Ventres on Milk River. In 1861 a Pend d'Oreille raiding party from west of the Rockies had stolen horses from the Gros Ventres. In an effort to throw their pursuers off the track, they abandoned some of the stolen animals in the vicinity of a Piegan camp on the Marias. When the Gros Ventres found these horses they did not wait for an explanation, but attacked the Piegan camp.[18] The Piegans did not retaliate in force, but were content to raid the Gros Ventre camps in small

[16] Bischoff, *Jesuits in Old Oregon*, 89–90; De Smet, *Life, Letters and Travels*, III, 858.

[17] Reports of the Commissioner of Indian Affairs, 1866, 203; *The Montana Post*, June 9, 1866.

[18] Bradley, "Manuscript," *MHSC*, Vol. IX, 313–15.

parties, stealing horses and killing a few stragglers. Meanwhile, the Gros Ventres made peace with the River Crow Indians.

Late in the summer of 1866 the majority of the Piegan bands, under the leadership of Many Horses, wealthiest of the Piegan chiefs, who was beloved for his generosity in lending horses to the poor, were encamped near the Cypress Hills. Early one morning Many Horses and his wife left camp to hunt buffalo. While they were gone, the Gros Ventres and their Crow allies attacked the Piegan camp. Warned of the enemy approach, the Piegans fought back. While the opposing forces were engaged in a fire fight at a distance from one another, a young Piegan who had been out on the plains brought word that their enemies had murdered Many Horses.

When the news of the loss of their popular chief was announced to the Piegan force, these angry warriors, throwing caution to the winds, charged the Gros Ventres and Crows with such ferocity that the enemy broke and ran. The Piegans drove the disorganized and confused enemy like buffalo. They killed all the footmen and rode after the fleeing horsemen. The enraged Piegans followed their opponents for miles, overtaking and killing them with guns, bows and arrows, lances, war clubs, knives, and even stones, until the remaining enemy reached the shelter of timber. Then, looking back upon the field strewn with the bodies of Gros Ventres and Crows, the Piegans decided they had killed enough. In this most disastrous defeat within the memory of both the Gros Ventre and Crow tribesmen, more than three hundred of them were killed. A number of women and children were taken prisoner. The Piegans claimed to have lost less than twenty men in this, their most decisive victory. Their warriors counted many war honors by killing their enemies and capturing many horses, guns, shields, bows and arrows, and sacred articles.[19]

Compared with this all-out effort of the Piegans against their Indian enemies, the so-called "Blackfeet War" with the whites

[19] George Bird Grinnell, *The Story of the Indian*, 134–42. Piegan informants have described this battle to me.

was a sporadic, disorganized affair. At no time during the years 1865–70 did the Indians attempt any general operations against the white intruders. It was guerrilla warfare, comprising frequent small-scale attacks by a few warriors over a very wide theater of war. These actions resembled traditional Blackfoot horse-raiding operations rather than their large-scale revenge raids of earlier times.

Augustus Chapman, Flathead agent who passed through the Blackfoot country en route east in the spring of 1867, termed "Acting Governor Meagher's Indian war in Montana . . . the biggest humbug of the age, got up to advance his political interest, and to enable a lot of bummers who surround and hang on to him to make a big raid on the United States treasury." Chapman observed that hundreds of small parties of whites were traveling between Helena and Fort Benton and did not appear to "apprehend any more danger from hostile Indians than they would in Washington city."[20]

Nevertheless, the white settlers' repeated requests for protection from Indian raids brought a portion of the United States Army to the Blackfoot country as soon as soldiers could be spared for frontier duty after the close of the Civil War. In the fall of 1866 a battalion of the Thirteenth Infantry established Camp Cooke at the mouth of the Judith, near the site of Lame Bull's Treaty of eleven years earlier. The following summer Fort Shaw was built in the Sun River Valley, about twenty miles from the Missouri, and garrisoned with four hundred blue-coated infantrymen.

However, the mere garrisoning of soldiers in their country did not halt Blackfoot depredations. In April, 1867, a small war party killed John Bozeman, prominent trail blazer and pioneer settler in the Yellowstone Valley. The Blackfeet murdered several other ranchers in that region during the following winter. The establishment of military posts on their hunting grounds proved one more cause of Blackfoot resentment against the

[20] Reports of the Commissioner of Indian Affairs, 1867, 259.

whites. Another was the failure of the Indians to receive annuities promised them under the terms of the unratified treaty of 1865. The legal technicality of ratification meant nothing to the Indians. They knew their chiefs had signed a treaty which the commissioners had carefully explained to them would provide the Indians with sizable annuities. They expected to receive them just as they had after Lame Bull's Treaty a decade earlier. When they failed to get their annuities, the Indians concluded that the whites had lied.

To remedy this misunderstanding and to clear up the confusion in the minds of both Indians and whites regarding the status of Indian land ceded by the 1865 treaty, William J. Cullen was commissioned to make another treaty with the Blackfoot tribes and the Gros Ventres. At Fort Benton on September 1, 1868, he negotiated a treaty with the Piegan, Blood, and Northern Blackfoot tribes. Although the last-named tribe was again represented by a single chief, Three Bulls, the treaty was signed by Mountain Chief as head chief of the Piegans and by Calf Shirt as Blood head chief, as well as by a considerable number of lesser chiefs of both tribes. The terms of this treaty were largely repetitions of those of the unratified treaty of three years earlier. The most noteworthy omission was the promise of special payments to individual chiefs. The reservation boundaries were the same. And the fate of this treaty was the same—it was never ratified. The Gros Ventres were treated with separately, with the view that they should be separated from their Blackfoot enemies on the eastern portion of the reservation, along with their more recent allies, the River Crow Indians.[21]

In 1869 the Indian agency was moved from Fort Benton, where the municipal officials and many of the townspeople were unfriendly toward Indians, to a new location on the Teton River, a few miles north of present Choteau and about seventy-five miles northwest of Fort Benton. There the agent hoped he could

[21] Treaty Between the United States and the Blackfoot Nation, September 1, 1868 (unratified). Manuscript, with signatures, Indian Office Records.

"be his own master in controlling the affairs of his agency, without being dictated to . . . by merchants, thieves and blackguards," as he termed the Fort Benton townsfolk.[22]

During the years the agency had been at Fort Benton, a number of Blackfoot Indians had been killed in its streets and bars. Shortly after signing the ill-fated treaty of 1868, Mountain Chief, head chief of the Piegans, had been insulted and abused by some of the white men at Fort Benton because he had requested the treaty commissioner to put certain troublesome whites out of the Indian country.[23] The following summer Alexander Culbertson sent an old man who was the brother of Mountain Chief, and an Indian boy on an errand to Fort Benton. They were shot down in the streets of the town in broad daylight in revenge for the Indian killing of two white cattle herders near Fort Benton a few days earlier. General Alfred Sully, newly appointed superintendent of Indian Affairs for Montana, reported:

> I think I can arrest the murderers but I doubt very much if I can convict them in any court. Nothing can be done to insure peace and order till there is a military force here strong enough to clear out the roughs and whisky-sellers in the country.[24]

Without waiting for the white man's justice to take its tedious course, the enraged Indians took matters into their own hands. By August 18, Sully was reporting to Washington, "I fear we will have to consider the Blackfeet in a state of war."[25]

Employing the hit-and-run tactics familiar to Blackfoot horse raiders, small Piegan war parties attacked freighters on the Fort Benton–Helena road and descended upon outlying ranches, running off horses and killing whites. On the night of August 17, some twenty-five young Piegan warriors visited Malcolm Clark on his ranch near the mouth of the Prickly Pear Canyon, within twenty-five miles of Helena. Clark had known the Blackfeet well

[22] Reports of the Commissioner of Indian Affairs, 1868, 206–207.
[23] *Ibid.,* 215.
[24] *Piegan Indians,* 41 Cong., 2 sess., *House Executive Document 269,* 3.
[25] *Ibid.,* 4.

for more than a quarter of a century. He was married to a Piegan woman. But he was shot and killed by these Indians. News of the death of Malcolm Clark, one of the most prominent men in the territory, roused the white citizens of Montana to urge prompt and effective military and civil action against the Indians. Yet Alexander Culbertson, a former colleague of Clark in the Blackfoot trade, found no "general hostile feeling" among the Piegans on a visit to the agency in early September. He attributed their depredations to "a portion of the young rabble over whom the chiefs have no control, and nothing but the strong arm of the government can control."[26]

The depredations continued into the fall. When United States Marshal William F. Wheeler went before a grand jury in October, he listed fifty-six whites who had been murdered and more than one thousand horses stolen by the Blackfeet in the year 1869. Malcolm Clark's children had recognized five of the young Piegan warriors who were members of the party that had killed their father. Wheeler named them and asked that they be indicted for the willful murder of Malcolm Clark. The grand jury proceeded to indict them. Warrants for their arrest were given to General Sully.[27]

When he was informed of conditions in Montana, General Philip H. Sheridan, the Civil War hero and champion of aggressive action against hostile Indians, then in charge of the Military Division of the Missouri, expressed regret that the expiration of enlistments left too few troops in Montana "to do much against these Indian marauders." However, the ranks of the regiments were soon to be filled, and Sheridan proposed a plan of action he had followed with devastating effectiveness against hostile red men on the Southern Plains. "Let me find out exactly where these Indians are going to spend the winter, and about the time of a good heavy snow I will send out a party and try and strike them." General of the Army William T. Sherman in

---

[26] *Ibid.*, 6.
[27] William F. Wheeler, "The Piegan War of 1870," *Helena Daily Herald*, January 1, 1880.

Washington approved Sheridan's plan of action on November 4.[28]

In spite of his superior's plan and the persistent clamors of Montana citizens for military action, General Philip de Trobriand, in command of Fort Shaw, kept a cool head. On November 26, he reported:

> I do not see so far an opportunity for striking a successful blow. The only Indians within reach are friendly, and nothing could be worse, I think, than to chastise them for offenses of which they are not guilty. I speak not only with a view to justice and humanity, but for the best interests of the Territory.

De Trobriand was aware that the known hostiles were near the Canadian border. They would cross the international line to safety as soon as troops started after them.[29]

On New Year's Day, 1870, General Sully visited the Indian agency on the Teton to demand that the murderers of Malcolm Clark be turned over to the authorities. There he met four peaceful chiefs, Heavy Runner, Little Wolf, and Big Lake of the Piegans, and the Blood chief Gray Eyes. Sully told them that the government was "tired out with the repeated aggressions of their people" and "was determined to make war against them as the only way to protect the lives and property of the whites." He told them that the hostile Indians would be pursued across the international boundary. Sully believed his bluff of carrying the war into the area north of the line greatly impressed the chiefs. These friendly chiefs agreed to try to kill the murderers and to bring in their bodies and all the stolen stock they could find.

Sully himself had little faith in the success of his mission. He recommended that the army "be ready to strike if necessary, should it prove that these chiefs cannot carry out their good intentions with their own people."[30]

[28] *Piegan Indians*, 8.
[29] *Ibid.*, 21.
[30] *Ibid.*, 24.

Meanwhile, General de Trobriand learned from his scouts that Mountain Chief's band of the Piegans, which was believed to be harboring Malcolm Clark's murderers, had moved south to the Marias to winter near the Northwest Company's trading post about five miles below Medicine Creek. De Trobriand proposed a surprise attack on Mountain Chief's camp.

But as the two-week period he had given the friendly chiefs to bring in Clark's murderers drew to a close without word from the Indians, Sully advised that "no blood should be shed." He recommended a police action to seize old Mountain Chief and about half a dozen of the principal men of his band.[31]

Col. E. M. Baker had already moved from Fort Ellis to Fort Shaw with four companies of cavalry. He was prepared to march against the Indians and attack them. When the failure of the Indians to bring in the bodies of the murderers was reported to General Sheridan, he was in no mood for merely taking hostages. His terse telegraphic reply of January 15 read:

> If the lives and property of the citizens of Montana can best be protected by striking Mountain Chief's band, I want them struck. Tell Baker to strike them hard.

General de Trobriand's marching orders to Colonel Baker told him "to chastise that portion of the Indian tribe of Piegans, which, under Mountain Chief, or his sons, committed the greater part of the murders and depredations of last summer and last month in this district." These orders stated clearly that the friendly band of Heavy Runner should not be molested.[32]

On January 19, Colonel Baker led his four cavalry companies, augmented by fifty-five mounted infantrymen and a company of infantry, northward from Fort Shaw. To prevent whisky traders from warning the Indians, this troop movement was kept secret. Joe Kipp, mixed-blood son of the trader who had established the first American trading post among the warlike Piegans thirty-

[31] *Ibid.*, 25–28.
[32] *Ibid.*, 15.

nine years before, guided this first military expedition against those Indians. He had been among the Piegans near the Big Bend of the Marias only ten days before, and he thought he could distinguish Mountain Chief's camp from those of friendly chiefs.

The march was made in some of the worst winter weather Montana had seen in years. The temperature hovered around twenty degrees below zero, and howling winds swept the plains. Blackfoot Indians huddled close around their campfires in such weather. It was an ideal time to catch them by surprise.

At daybreak on January 23, Baker ordered his men to attack an Indian village of some thirty-seven lodges on the Marias. The soldiers killed 173 Indians and captured 140 women and children and more than 300 horses. But this was not Mountain Chief's village. It was the camp of friendly chief Heavy Runner. Many of its people were victims of a smallpox epidemic. The troops burned the lodges and camp equipment and turned loose the homeless captives.

Army and Indian accounts of what happened in this brief but disastrous action are irreconcilable. Baker's reports profess that he did not know he was attacking the camp of the friendly chief, Heavy Runner. The Indians have claimed that as soon as Heavy Runner learned troops were approaching, he walked out alone to meet them, and that he was holding up his hands and waving his identification paper when a soldier shot him dead. A later apologist for the army claimed that the Indians fired first and that casualties to their noncombatant women and children resulted from the fact that the red-skinned warriors fought from inside their tipis, forcing the soldiers to shoot into the tipis until all resistance ceased. Not until two months after the action did Baker submit his report, which stated that in the judgment of the officers of his command, all of the Indians killed were able men except for fifty-three women and children who were killed accidentally. He admitted the figures were estimates. Baker's estimate was submitted at the request of his superiors, after the Indian agent, W. A. Pease, himself an army lieutenant, had reported that only fifteen of the dead Indians had been fighting men between the ages of twelve and thirty-seven, while ninety were women and fifty were children under twelve years of age. Of the soldiers' losses, there was no question. One man was killed. Another suffered a broken leg when he fell from his horse.[33]

When Vincent Colyer, secretary of the Board of Indian Commissioners, made Pease's figures available to the newspapers in a letter calling attention to "the sickening details of Colonel Baker's attack on the village of Piegans," the action was promptly termed a massacre—which it was. *The New York Times* of February 24, 1870, commented editorially, "The question is whether a wholesale slaughter of women and children was needed for the vindication of our arms."

The massacre on the Marias not only roused a storm of protest in the East against the army's ruthless treatment of the Indians, but it had political repercussions on a national scale. A movement to transfer the Indian Bureau to the War Department, which was then before Congress, was nipped in the bud. When the Army Appropriation Bill was discussed in the House of Representatives on March 10, 1870, Congressman John A. Logan from Illinois, who, as a volunteer officer, had risen to the rank of major general during the Civil War, vehemently declared:

I have always believed the War Department to be the proper place for the Indian Bureau; but I went the other day and heard the history of the Piegan massacre, as reported by an Army officer, and I say now to you Mr. Speaker, and to the country, that it made my blood run cold in my veins. It satisfied me; and I shall therefore move to strike out this section at the proper time and let the Indian Bureau remain where it is.[34]

Not only did the Indian Bureau remain in the Department of the Interior, but the prevailing practice of employing army offi-

[33] *Ibid.*, 16–17, 73; Lieutenant W. A. Pease to General Sully, February 8, 1870, in Reports of the Board of Indian Commissioners, 1870, 89; Wheeler, "The Piegan War of 1870," *Helena Daily Herald*, January 1, 1880.
[34] *The Congressional Globe*, March 10, 1870, 150.

cers as Indian agents was abandoned.

But the white settlers in Montana, who had called repeatedly for military aid to put an end to Blackfoot depredations, vigorously approved the army's action. The generals firmly supported the accomplishments of their officers in the field. Tough-minded Sheridan explained, "If a village is attacked, and women and children killed, the responsibility is not with the soldier, but with the people whose crimes necessitate the attack." His philosophy of warfare differed little from the primitive Blackfoot one—that losses suffered from enemy raiders should be vigorously avenged by attacking any members of the enemy tribe.

The massacre on the Marias had an immediate pacifying effect upon the warlike Blackfeet. They were suffering terribly from the smallpox plague and were not in any position to mount a full-scale offensive against the army. Yet when their band chiefs met in council not long after the massacre, a few of them wanted revenge in the traditional blood-for-blood fashion. However, the majority were strongly impressed by this demonstration of the terrific striking power of the United States Army, even in the worst possible weather. They saw that the power of the whites to wipe them out had been demonstrated, and they believed "that to attempt to provoke further war would only result in their total extermination."[35] The advice of the majority prevailed. Less than two months after the massacre, Father Imoda met Mountain Chief and seven other Piegan chiefs in a council on the Belly River north of the international boundary. He informed General Sully that they were unanimous in their desire for a good and lasting peace.[36] Never again did the Blackfoot Indians face the United States Army in battle.

Ten years after the massacre Marshal Wheeler wrote:

Ever since January 1870, the Blackfeet tribes . . . have been peaceable and quiet, and it has been safe to travel in their country. Very few white men have been murdered by them, and they

[35] Reports of the Commissioner of Indian Affairs, 1878, 82.
[36] Father John Imoda to General Sully, March 17, 1870, Indian Office Records.

were generally whisky traders and characters dangerous in any community and caused their own calamities.[37]

[37] Wheeler, "The Piegan Indian War of 1870," *Helena Daily Journal,* January 1, 1880.

15: Whisky Traders, Redcoats, and the Law

During the sixties the international boundary between Montana Territory and the British possessions was marked only on white men's maps. For generations the Blackfoot tribes had crossed and recrossed the forty-ninth parallel on their hunting and war excursions. They were equally at home on both sides of the boundary. As the decade of the sixties wore on, this "medicine line," as the Indians called it, became very useful to Blackfoot raiding parties. It afforded a handy escape hatch to Northern Blackfoot, Blood, and North Piegan warriors, who rode south, stole horses from Montana settlers, and hurriedly drove them northward across the boundary. Many of the occasional murders as well as thefts of horses committed by Blackfoot Indians in the years preceding the massacre on the Marias were the work of these elusive northerners. Neither civil nor military authorities from Montana were permitted to cross this "medicine line" to arrest the murderers or horse thieves.

Montanans commonly blamed the Hudson's Bay Company for encouraging these Indian marauders. Testimony of a few whites who had traveled north to the fur posts on the Saskatchewan appeared to support these suspicions. At Fort Benton in January, 1870, three of the travelers swore they saw horses bearing the brands of United States citizens traded by Blackfoot Indians at Rocky Mountain House, and that Hudson's Bay traders were giving these hostiles powder and ball in exchange.[1]

[1] *Piegan Indians*, 66–69.

When these allegations were brought to the attention of the Hudson's Bay Company through diplomatic channels, W. T. Christie, its chief trader for the Saskatchewan district, would not deny that some of the horses brought to his posts might have been stolen from United States citizens. But he pointed out that the Indians did not tell the traders where they got the horses, and that Indians commonly passed the stolen horses to others so that the sellers were not the thieves. Besides, his company bought few horses, preferring to save its trade goods to exchange for furs. As for the trade in ammunition, the men of the Hudson's Bay Company fort at Rocky Mountain House, for their own protection, never traded percussion caps, but only limited amounts of powder and ball for flintlocks. On the other hand, he claimed that American traders were crossing the border to trade revolvers, rifles, and ammunition to the Indians. "Every othei Blackfoot who trades at Rocky Mountain House now has a Revolver in his belt; and in our trade with them our lives are in great danger."[2]

It was during the winter of 1869 that American traders began crossing the "medicine line." Since 1834 the trade of intoxicating liquor to Indians had been prohibited in the United States. But this law had been virtually unenforceable in the vast Blackfoot country, where the Indians' craving for "white man's water" was great and law enforcement officers were few. Repeatedly, Blackfoot agents had blamed the liquor traffic for inciting Indian depredations, but they did little about it until 1868. Then Agent George Wright managed to have a few whisky traders arrested, taken to Helena, tried, convicted, and imprisoned.[3] It began to look like hard times were ahead for the "sneaking drink givers" in Montana.

That summer, in a further effort to control the whisky trade, the government restricted the Blackfoot trade to two licensed Fort Benton firms. One was the Northwest Fur Company, located

2 Christie to W. G. Smith, secretary of the Hudson's Bay Company, June 29, 1870. Copy in Indian Office Records.
3 Reports of the Commissioner of Indian Affairs, 1868, 204.

on the Teton near present Choteau for trade with the Piegans. The other, I. G. Baker and Brother, built a post at Willow Round on the Marias. During their first winter's trade with the Northern Blackfeet, Bloods, and North Piegans, Baker's traders cleared $40,000.[4]

After the Hudson's Bay Company ceded its vast territory north of the "medicine line" to Canada in 1869, there was no law to prevent the invasion of their land by traders from south of the border. The first Americans to take advantage of this situation were John J. Healy and Alfred B. Hamilton, nephew of I. G. Baker. They left Fort Benton armed with a permit to travel through the Indian country north of the Marias to the Canadian line for the purpose of prospecting and exploring in Canada. Their real objective, of course, was trade, and part of their $25,-000 worth of trade goods included fifty gallons of alcohol to use as an inducement to the Indian trade. Late in 1869, they crossed the line and built a log fort at the junction of Oldman and St. Mary rivers, less than forty miles north of the border. In their first winter's trade with the Blackfeet, they netted $50,000, which the editor of the *Helena Daily Herald* observed was "not very bad for six months' cruise among the Lo Family across the border."[5]

News of their success soon brought a host of American competitors to that lawless land. During the next four years more than a dozen stockaded forts, large and small, flew the American flag on Canadian soil in the river valleys of what is now southern Alberta. The most important ones were on Oldman River and its southern tributaries, conveniently located for trade with Piegan bands from the United States as well as with the Blackfoot tribes of Canada.

The largest and best known of these "whisky forts," as they became known, was the daddy of them all, Healy and Hamilton's Fort Whoop-Up. Of the many stories purporting to explain the

[4] S. C. Ashby, Reminiscences on the Indian Trade of the 1860's. (Manuscript in Montana Historical Society Library.)

[5] June 15, 1870.

origin of its picturesque name, the most likely is the one to the effect that as Healy and Hamilton left Fort Benton for the north, I. G. Baker shouted to them, "Don't let the Indians whoop you up." When they returned to the site of their first post in 1870, they found that the Indians had burned it during their absence. They rebuilt it on a grander scale. When completed, Fort Whoop-Up was a stockade of heavy squared logs about 130 feet square, with stout corner bastions and loopholes at intervals along the walls for musketry. The chimneys were barred to prevent Indians from getting into them. Only a small opening was left in the heavy oak gate, through which the Indian trade was conducted. Within the stockade were the employees' quarters, a kitchen, shop, blacksmith shop, stables, and storerooms for trade goods and for robes and furs received from the Indians.[6]

Whoop-Up's two principal rivals bore equally colorful names. Fort Standoff, built by Joe Kipp and partners at the confluence of the Belly and Waterton rivers, was named in memory of an encounter between U. S. Marshal Charles D. Hard and Joe Kipp's whisky traders a short distance south of the unmarked boundary. Nervy Kipp managed to stand off the law by claiming he had just crossed the Milk River into Canada, where Hard had no jurisdiction. Outnumbered by the traders, Hard did not argue the point.[7] Fort Slide-Out, operated by Mose Solomon farther down the Belly River, was named when a Dutchman at that post suggested the traders had better "slide out" after the Blood Indians killed one of their men while he was hauling supplies.[8]

In spite of their colorful names, these American posts north of the "medicine line" were responsible for one of the darkest chapters in Blackfoot Indian history. At a time when these Indians were disturbed by the steadily growing influx of white settlers upon their Montana hunting grounds and by the United States government's refusal to honor treaties made with them, when another smallpox epidemic was carrying away large num-

6 MacInnes, *In the Shadow of the Rockies*, 64–65.
7 James Willard Schultz, *My Life as an Indian*, 291–92.
8 Dempsey, *Historic Sites of the Province of Alberta*. Includes a map locating the "whisky forts" of the period 1869–74.

bers of their sturdy young people, and when they were thoroughly shaken by the massacre on the Marias, it took but little more to demoralize the Blackfeet completely. That little was a ready supply of "white men's water" with which to drown their sorrows.

Exploiting the Indians' well-known weakness for liquor, the American traders used it as their primary lure to bring the red men flocking to their posts with buffalo robes, furs, horses, and women. To make their beverage even more attractive, the Americans mixed their alcohol not only with the usual branch water, but also with black chewing tobacco, red peppers, Jamaica ginger, black molasses, and other strong substances. Twenty cupfuls of this hot Indian whisky sometimes was given for a fine head and tail robe, three gallons for a good lively horse, and still more for an attractive Indian girl whose charms appealed to one of the traders. The Indians were warned not to drink the stuff near the fort. Some of them froze to death before they reached their lodges. In their camps drunken Indians quarreled and killed one another. Eighty-eight Northern Blackfeet were said to have been killed in drunken brawls in 1871.[9] In a brief period two years later, thirty-two of the Piegans, including two prominent chiefs, were killed.[10] Rev. John McDougall, a missionary, claimed that forty-two able-bodied Northern Blackfoot men lost their lives in shootings, stabbings, or by freezing to death following drunken rows in the winter of 1873–74.[11] Sometimes the Indians played a macabre joke on the traders by propping the frozen body of a dead comrade against the fort gate so that when the whites opened it in the morning, the stiffened corpse would fall on them.

There are no complete records of the number of Indian deaths caused by "white men's water" in the period 1869–74. But the Blackfoot agent in Montana estimated that six hundred barrels of liquor were used in the Blackfoot trade in 1873, and that in

[9] MacInnes, *In the Shadow of the Rockies,* 75.
[10] Reports of the Commissioner of Indian Affairs, 1873, 252.
[11] John McDougall, *On Western Trails in the Early Seventies,* 129.

the six years prior to that time, 25 per cent of the members of these tribes died from the effects of liquor alone.[12]

Memories of these lawless days have survived in the often exaggerated tales of both whites and Indians. None of these yarns is more symbolic of the demoralization of the Indians and the cold-bloodedness of the traders than the story of the murder of the Blood chief Calf Shirt, which is vividly recounted by members of his tribe.

Calf Shirt was one of the signers of Lame Bull's Treaty in 1855. His name appears on the unratified treaty of 1868 as head chief of his tribe. He was well remembered by the traders as the leader of the Blood war party that wiped out ten white settlers on the Missouri in 1865. Calf Shirt was a powerful, muscular man who became very mean after he had had a few drinks. The traders were afraid of him. They gave him more liquor for his robes than they did anyone else, even more than his robes were worth. Sometimes Calf Shirt visited the traders with nothing to trade, and they gave him a gallon of whisky to take home. He came to the posts so often to beg for whisky that the traders tired of him. So they made plans to get rid of him.

The next time Calf Shirt appeared at Joe Kipp's fort asking for liquor, the traders gave him some poisoned whisky. As soon as he tasted it Calf Shirt said, "Now, my children, you are giving me a bad drink." But he drank it all and returned to camp. Later that night he came back to the fort and begged the traders for "some more drink." They gave him a stronger dose of poison. Still it didn't affect him.

Then, seeing that their attempts to poison the Indian were of no avail, the traders told him to go home. But Calf Shirt said, "No, I want some more drink." Whereupon the angry traders seized their guns from behind the counter, where they always kept them loaded, and fired at him. But Calf Shirt's power came from the bear. Bullets could not hurt him. They just made little black marks on his skin.

Furious at their repeated failures to kill this irritating Indian,

[12] Reports of the Commissioner of Indian Affairs, 1873, 252.

the traders jumped on him and tried to tie him up. But Calf Shirt was too strong for them. He shook them off and walked out of the traders' store. In the darkness outside the fort, Calf Shirt fell into a hole. The traders ran after him, shot at him, hit him with an axe, and tied a rope around his neck. But still they could not kill him.

It was winter. The river was frozen over. The traders dragged Calf Shirt down to their water hole in the river ice by the rope around his neck and threw him into the water. Once, twice, Calf Shirt rose to the surface. With long sticks the traders pushed him back down. The third time he stayed down. Then the white men placed sticks across the hole and tied the end of the rope to it. Next morning they returned to their water hole and cut the rope. They saw no more of troublesome Calf Shirt.[13]

Older Indians of my acquaintance credited Healy and Hamilton with introducing another deadly item among the Blackfeet—the first "many shots" (repeating rifles). Whether these were Spencer '65 repeaters, Henry rifles, or the more famous Winchester '66 carbines is not clear. There may have been some of all three makes. We do know that they were traded to the Indians in the first year of Whoop-Up's existence and that the Indian recipients had very good reason to be grateful for these new wonder weapons soon thereafter.

In October, 1870, large camps of Blood and Piegan Indians were pitched on Oldman and St. Mary rivers while their occupants traded at the near-by whisky forts. They knew nothing of the plan of a large party of several hundred Cree and Assiniboin warriors to fall upon them while they were occupied in the drunken carousals that usually followed Blackfoot visits to the forts. At daybreak the enemy attacked the Blood camp. When the Piegans heard gunfire and yelping dogs in the Blood village, their men quickly seized their weapons, mounted their horses, and rode to the aid of their allies. With their few repeating rifles,

[13] This story was told to me by Frank Red Crow in 1951. Other versions of this well-known Blood tale are given in Hugh A. Dempsey, "The Amazing Death of Calf Shirt," *Montana Magazine of History*, Vol. III, No. 1.

augmented by old muzzle-loading flintlocks and bows and arrows, the Blackfoot allies forced the Crees and Assiniboins to retreat. The Blackfeet, in hot pursuit, drove the enemy into the river. Their repeating rifles "dropped the Crees like ducks." In the ensuing slaughter, few of the enemy escaped. Their losses were reckoned (perhaps too generously) at from two hundred to four hundred. Big Brave, son of the old Piegan chief, Mountain Chief, claimed to have taken nine scalps in this great victory. It was the last sizable intertribal battle the Blackfoot tribes ever fought.[14]

Soon Whoop-Up's competitors were also trading repeating arms to the Blackfeet for ten or more head-and-tail robes each. The new weapons revolutionized buffalo hunting. This gun that could easily be reloaded on a running horse rendered the bow and arrow obsolete for both hunting and warfare. With these improved arms the Indians could kill more buffalo and have more robes to trade with the Americans for more whisky and ammunition. It was about as vicious as any circle could be.

Yet the whisky traders' luck was fast running out in the Whoop-Up country. The Hudson's Bay Company, whose trade suffered from the American competition in their own country, and Rev. John McDougall, a Methodist missionary who was shocked by the drunken orgies he had seen among the traders at Whoop-Up, notified the Canadian government of the Americans' invasion of Canada and their debauching of Canadian Indians. In 1870, Captain W. F. Butler, commissioned to investigate conditions in the field, recommended the organization of a well-equipped force of 100 to 150 men to bring law and order to the region. Two years later Colonel Robertson Ross reported nearly 100 Indians murdered in drunken brawls, and called for effective Canadian action to rid their land of the American desperados.[15]

[14] Dixon, *The Vanishing Race*, 112–15. Includes Frank Mountain Chief's account of his participation in this battle.

[15] William F. Butler, *The Great Lone Land*, 380; John Peter Turner, *The North-West Mounted Police*, I, 81.

Corruption of Indians by whisky traders was not the only problem of the West that disturbed Canadian lawmakers. They anticipated white settlement of their prairie provinces, and wanted to avoid the bloody and costly Indian wars that had followed white penetration of Indian hunting grounds in the United States. In an effort to find a solution to both problems, the Canadian Parliament, on May 20, 1873, authorized the establishment of a civil police force in uniform, patterned after the Royal Irish Constabulary, to bring law and order to the West. By the summer of 1874 this North-West Mounted Police force had been selectively recruited and trained and was on the march westward over the plains.

Warned of the approach of the Mounties, the most intelligent American traders either cleaned up their posts or cleared out. When the police reached notorious Fort Whoop-Up in October, not a drop of whisky was found. On Oldman River they established a divisional headquarters, naming it Fort Macleod after their assistant commissioner, James F. Macleod. It was garrisoned with 150 men. Methodically they set about the task of routing out the die-hard whisky traders who persisted in their nefarious business. Several small parties were arrested, their whisky spilled on the ground, their buffalo robes, wagons, and teams confiscated; the traders themselves were fined or imprisoned.[16]

Most of the American traders needed no such experience to be convinced that the palmy days of the whisky trade north of the line had ended abruptly. A few of them dropped south of the "medicine line" and became "sneaking drink givers" in Montana. Some of the most able ones attained considerable success in legitimate business and in politics. Alfred Hamilton became manager of his uncle's licensed trading post on the Teton River and later was elected to the Montana legislature. His partner in the Whoop-Up trade, Johnny Healy, became sheriff of Choteau County. D. W. Davis, another of the old Whoop-Up group, became Alberta's first representative in the Canadian Parliament.

[16] Sir Cecil Denny, *The Law Marches West*, 38–48.

The Mounties were extremely fortunate in their selection of a Blackfoot interpreter. Jerry Potts, mixed-blood son of a Scottish trader and a Piegan woman, was well liked by the Indians. He had played a prominent role in the great Blood and Piegan victory over the Crees and Assiniboins in the fall of 1870. His efforts to explain the policies of the "Red Coats," as the Indians quite naturally referred to the scarlet-clad Mounties, coupled with the effective action of the police in stamping out the whisky trade, did much to convince the Indians that these men were their friends. Assistant Commissioner Macleod, in top-level conferences with the principal chiefs, won their personal friendship and respect.

The police officials wisely realized that the primitive Indians' customs could not be changed overnight to conform to the strange laws of civilized men. They consulted with the chiefs to determine what penalties should be imposed upon Indians who had committed offenses which among white men would have been punished by imprisonment. Even in cases of murder, they sometimes adopted traditional punishment in preference to the more severe death penalty common among whites. In 1881 a ticklish intertribal situation arose when a Blackfoot Indian killed a Cree. Inspector Denny averted warfare and solved the problem to the satisfaction of both sides by arranging for a Blackfoot payment of horses to the family of the murdered Cree.[17]

On July 8, 1876, scarcely two weeks after Custer's decisive defeat on the Little Big Horn in Montana, Inspector Denny was shown a piece of tobacco which the fighting Sioux had sent to the Northern Blackfoot camp along with an invitation to join them in their war against the Americans. In return for Blackfoot help, the Sioux promised plenty of horses and mules and several white women they had captured. They also offered to come north and aid the Blackfeet in killing off the whites in Canada after they had rid the Sioux country of palefaces.

The Blackfoot messenger to the Sioux carried word of their

[17] *Ibid.*, 60, 152–55.

Piegan Indians hunting buffalo near the Sweet Grass Hills. From a painting by John Mix Stanley in 1853 (*Courtesy the National Archives*).

refusal to accept the proffered tobacco. He brought back the Sioux leaders' angry threat to make war on the Blackfeet after they had exterminated the American soldiers and taken their forts. Denny found Crowfoot, head chief of the Northern Blackfeet, very uneasy. He wanted to know if his people could call upon the "Red Coats" if they were attacked by the Sioux. Denny assured the chief that Blackfoot Indians had the same right to protection as any other subjects of "The Great Mother" (Queen Victoria).[18]

Another disturbing influence was the arrival of white settlers in the Blackfoot country north of the line. In 1876 they had established farms and ranches near Fort Macleod and Fort Calgary farther north. To avoid bloody conflicts between Indians and settlers such as had occurred far too frequently in Montana in the sixties, the Canadian government moved quickly to treat with the Indians. In the broad river bottom on the south side of the Bow River, near an old Indian fording place known as Blackfoot Crossing, David Laird, lieutenant governor of the North-West Territories, and Lieutenant Colonel James F. Macleod of the Mounties met the Northern Blackfoot, Blood, North Piegan, Sarsi, and Stony (Assiniboin) tribes in the early fall of 1877. In his speech at the council, Chief Crowfoot paid a glowing tribute to the "Red Coats":

> If the police had not come to this country, where would we be now? Bad men and whiskey were killing us so fast that very few of us would have been left today. The police have protected us as the feathers of the bird protect it from the frosts of winter.[19]

At this council on Bow River on September 22, 1877, the Canadian government negotiated its only treaty with the Blackfoot Indians. Treaty No. 7, as it is known, spelled out its conditions in simple, direct language. The Northern Blackfeet,

[18] *Ibid.*, 97–100.

[19] Alexander Morris, *The Treaties of Canada with the Indians of Manitoba and the North-West Territories*, 272.

Bloods, and North Piegans agreed to conduct and behave themselves as good and loyal subjects of Her Majesty the Queen. They surrendered to the crown all their lands, comprising some fifty thousand square miles lying west of the Cypress Hills, north of the international boundary, and east of the Rockies. In return, the government agreed to permit the Indians to continue to hunt throughout this vast tract, and assigned reserves to each tribe within the area large enough to allow one square mile for each family of five. The government further agreed to pay $12.00 to each Indian man, woman and child after the treaty signing, as well as an annuity of $5.00; to furnish $2,000 worth of ammunition annually, as well as a stipulated number of cattle, agricultural tools, hand tools, and seeds; and to maintain schools for Indians on each reserve. Each head chief was to receive an annual salary of $25.00 and each minor chief, $15.00. Furthermore, these chiefs were to receive a suit of clothes every three years, a medal and a flag upon signing the treaty, and "next year or as soon as convenient . . . a Winchester rifle."[20]

After the head chiefs—Crowfoot, Old Sun, and Heavy Shield of the Northern Blackfeet; Red Crow and Rainy Chief of the Blood tribe; Sitting-on-an-Eagle-Tail of the North Piegans—as well as the minor chiefs of each tribe, had affixed their marks to the treaty, Commissioner Laird called each of them by name and gave him his uniform, flag, and medal, while the Mounted Police band played "God Save the Queen."

Three days were required to pay the twelve dollars a head promised in the treaty. It was difficult for the Mounties to ascertain the exact number in each family, especially when some Indians argued that they should receive payments for babies which were expected soon. The ubiquitous white traders were on hand to get as much of the Indians' money as they could. These Indians were not used to money, so the sharp traders tried to pass off labels from fruit jars as change. But they soon found that the "Red Coats" were on hand to keep them honest.[21]

[20] *Ibid.* The full text of Treaty No. 7 appears on pages 368–75.
[21] Denny, *The Law Marches West,* 116–19.

The Blackfoot, Blood, and Sarsi tribes were assigned a common reserve on the north side of the Bow and South Saskatchewan rivers. But the three tribes did not get on well together. In the next year the Blood Indians were transferred to a new reserve on Belly River. This Blood Reserve remains the largest Indian reservation in the Dominion of Canada. The North Piegans were placed on a smaller reserve near the Porcupine Hills on Oldman River, west of Fort Macleod.

So long as there were wandering herds of buffalo to be followed, the boundaries of their reserves meant little to these Indians. The Canadian Blackfoot tribes continued to hunt on their ceded land and to cross the "medicine line" both to hunt and to trade. Despite the vigilance of the "Red Coats," their wild and ambitious young men continued to capture horses from enemy camps and cleverly to evade the Mounties in bringing them home safely.

South of the "medicine line" in Montana Territory, the movement toward law and order proceeded more fitfully. Our government was experimenting with a new Indian policy. President Grant's administration, after the movement to place the Indian Bureau under the army had been defeated in Congress in 1870, decided upon a policy of feeding the warlike tribes of the West instead of fighting them. Under this new "Peace Policy," as it was commonly known, Indian agents were to be appointed upon the recommendation of organized church groups. It was expected that this restriction would insure the appointment of honest, dedicated agents. In the division of tribes among the Christian denominations, the Blackfeet fell to the Methodist Episcopal church, even though there never had been a Methodist missionary among these Indians in the United States.

During the early years of this idealistic arrangement the character and ability of Blackfoot agents showed no improvement. Few able, honest men cared to play the role of "father" to a people reputed to be the most bloodthirsty Indians of the northwestern plains for the petty salary of $1,500 a year. But there was no dearth of incompetent applicants for the post. Between

September, 1870, when Lieutenant Pease was relieved of duty by army orders, and late January, 1875, the Blackfeet had four "fathers." The first served less than three months before he was under fire from the Republicans of the territory. Governor Potts declared, "His character is such that he ought not to hold the office even if a Republican." His successor was removed because he drank to excess. The next agent resigned under suspicion of having diverted Indian supplies to the store of a private trader, and the fourth was discharged for incompetence. When John McDougall, himself a Methodist missionary from Canada, visited the agency on the Teton in the spring of 1874, he was shocked by what he found. "It is no wonder that Uncle Sam was constantly having trouble with his native wards. The Government and the Indians were, both of them, looked upon by the ordinary Government employee as legitimate prey."[22]

McDougall also paid a short visit to the wide-open town of Fort Benton. He observed that "the wildest thing in this big country . . . was the ordinary white man."[23] Two years earlier another Methodist missionary had reached a similar conclusion. In 1872, William Wesley Van Orsdel, a young, vigorous lay preacher from Gettysburg, Pennsylvania, had gone west to the agency on the Teton to found a mission among the Blackfeet. This robust, intelligent, and sympathetic Pennsylvania Dutchman had no difficulty at all in making friends with the Blackfeet, who came to call him "Big Heart." Together, he and the Blackfeet sang songs and discussed religion. The Indians told him their origin legends, and "Big Heart" told them the equally dramatic Old Testament stories, which he believed were particularly well suited to the understanding of the nomadic Indians. He and the Indians agreed that there was no real conflict between Napi, the traditional Blackfoot creator, and the white man's God. But this open-minded missionary soon realized that little could be done for the Indians until the moral ideals and practices of their white neighbors improved. So "Brother Van," as he was affection-

[22] McDougall, *On Western Trails*, 143.
[23] *Ibid.*, 145.

267

ately known throughout Montana, devoted the rest of his very active life to founding churches and preaching a message of tolerance and interracial understanding among the whites. Not until twenty-one years later was a permanent Methodist mission founded among the Blackfeet in Montana.[24]

At Lame Bull's Treaty in 1855, Governor Stevens had talked of schools for the Blackfeet, but it was not until the fall of 1872 that the first school was opened at their Teton River agency. Then curious children flocked into the brand-new schoolhouse, sat down, looked around, and walked out. None of them attended with any regularity until some white children from the families of agency employees started school.[25] Still the number of Indian pupils remained pitifully small. Regular attendance was impossible because their parents spent most of the year hunting buffalo far from the agency. The average daily attendance during the first quarter of 1874 was twenty—four whites, six half-bloods, and ten Indian children.[26] Progress of the Indian children was painfully slow. As their teacher could not speak their language, she used pictorial charts which were first explained to the white children and the half-bloods in English. Then the bilingual half-blood children explained them to the full-bloods. A Blackfoot agent, interested in showing the effectiveness of his school's teaching methods, reported, "I held up my hat and the school as with one voice said 'hat.' So with slate, pencil, book, pen and the pictures of dog, cat, horse, cow, etc. It was a very satisfactory evidence of progress."[27]

In 1875 the agent enthusiastically reported that he had succeeded in getting the children to wash and comb their hair before entering school. The pupils were singing hymns "with great taste and correctness." Girls were receiving instruction in cutting and sewing, and they appeared to be making rapid progress in their studies. Boys, however, were very irregular in at-

[24] Stella W. Brummitt, *Brother Van*.
[25] Reports of the Commissioner of Indian Affairs, 1873, 252.
[26] School Report, Blackfeet Agency, First Quarter 1874, Indian Office Records.
[27] John Young to Commissioner of Indian Affairs, May 1, 1878, Indian Office Records.

tendance. Children whose parents took them out of school to accompany them on long buffalo hunts were likely to return "having forgotten everything previously learned." Although this agent claimed that twelve pupils had learned to read during the year, it is improbable that any of them were full-bloods.[28]

The agents had even less luck in encouraging Blackfoot adults to take a serious interest in farming. The government farmer annually planted crops on the agency farm, but he could get few Indians to follow his example. Seven families of half-blood men married to Piegan women had farms near the agency in 1872, and three houses had been built for the leading chiefs to encourage them to settle down. Two years later, some old Indians each planted an acre of potatoes and vegetables—but the grasshoppers harvested their crops. Discouraged, Agent May concluded, "The present generation of the tribes of this reservation will never take much interest in agricultural pursuits. The hunt is too attractive and game too plentiful."[29] With the exception of a few old or blind Indians and their families who lived near the agency, for whom one beef steer a week was killed, the Piegans were depending entirely upon the hunt for their subsistence. Not more than half of the Blackfoot, Blood, or Piegan Indians had been fed at the agency at any time during the preceding two or three years.[30]

In 1870 the government, in keeping with the new "Peace Policy," had resumed distribution of annuities to the Blackfeet. The annual expenditures of $50,000 were the same as the amount promised in the unratified treaties of the sixties. The Indians were acquiring a taste for the white man's coffee, and made ready use of the blankets, cloth, and hardware furnished them by the government. The agency blacksmith helped them by mending their frying pans and kettles. In the month of April, 1874, he put handles on about 200 frying pans and made about 500 fire steels

---

[28] Reports of the Commissioner of Indian Affairs, 1875, 300–301.

[29] Ibid., 1874, 276.

[30] R. F. May to Commissioner of Indian Affairs, May 27, 1874, Indian Office Records.

and 555 sharp iron blades for the Indian women's use in dressing buffalo hides.[31]

Agent May's indignation was aroused by the number of white men who were living with Indian women on the Indian lands. He proposed that they should marry these women or leave the reservation, saying, "I will not, if left to act upon my own judgment allow so many bastard families to flourish under my eye."

When, in the year 1871, the United States government discontinued the policy of making treaties with Indian tribes as if they were foreign nations, the status of Blackfoot lands still was confused. The Indians supposed they had relinquished their lands south of the Teton River by the treaties of 1865 and 1868, but those treaties had never been ratified. Legally the Blackfeet had ceded none of their land. Yet there were thousands of white settlers living on ranches and farms, in mining camps, and in several flourishing towns on land formerly occupied by the Blackfoot Indians.

To legalize white settlement of this Indian land, President Grant, on July 5, 1873, issued an executive order establishing a large reservation, including all of Montana east of the Rockies and north of the Missouri and Sun rivers, for the Blackfoot tribes, the Gros Ventres, Assiniboins, and River Crow Indians. But the new order was obsolete before it was issued. White ranchers were running thousands of cattle on the Indian lands north of Sun River. Dissatisfied with the new boundary, Montana settlers put pressure upon their territorial delegate in Washington, Martin Maginnis, to get the line moved farther north. On February 7, 1874, a letter from Maginnis read before the Montana legislature told of his progress in getting this boundary redrawn.

> After a hard struggle I succeeded in obtaining from the Indian Department an agreement to change the boundaries of the reservation for the Blackfoot and other Indians. They agree to recede to the line of the Marias, from its mouth to the mountains.[32]

[31] May to Commissioner of Indian Affairs, May 1, 1874, Indian Office Records.
[32] *Weekly Independent* (Deer Lodge City, Montana Territory), February 14, 1874.

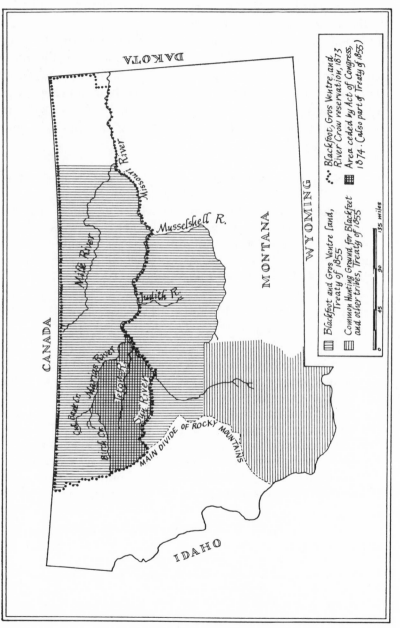

Blackfoot Lands in Montana, 1855–74.

When word of this intended boundary change reached the Indians, a delegation under the Piegan chief, Little Plume, visited their "father" at the agency. Little Plume said that his people never would consent voluntarily to the change in the line. It would confine them to too narrow a strip of territory and deprive them of a large and desirable portion of their hunting ground. Agent May's letter to Washington roused the wrath of Maginnis. In a letter to the *Helena Daily Independent*, on May 8, Maginnis gloatingly wrote:

> The bill which I introduced to move the Blackfoot Reservation back to the line of the Marias and Birch Creek, has become a law. The present Agency will be moved back on the Reservation and the Teton Valley thrown open to settlement. The remonstrances of the present Agent against this bill were received at the Department before its passage, but it was passed and signed notwithstanding, and that too with the approval of the Department.[33]

In reply to the letter published in the newspaper, the spunky agent wrote Maginnis:

> I am sure I do not overstate the case when I say the Indians residing upon this reservation are unanimous in their opposition to the change of line—that is the removal beyond the Teton— South of the Teton they do not care for . . . I could have sent to you for presentation to Congress a "remonstrance" bearing more than two thousand Indian signatures, but I contented myself by sending to the Hon. Commissioner the substance of the words spoken by the Chief Little Plume, and I know now, and knew then that he spoke the sentiments of his Tribe.[34]

Four months later, in his annual report to the commissioner of Indian Affairs, Agent May again showed his indignation at

[33] May to Commissioner of Indian Affairs, March 24, 1874, Indian Office Records; *Helena Daily Independent*, May 22, 1874.

[34] May to Martin Maginnis, May 25, 1874. Maginnis Papers, Montana Historical Society Library.

the treatment of his "children." "To take from peaceable, friendly Indians a very large portion of their best hunting and pasture land without consultation or remuneration, is a violation of the wise and Christian policy of the Government."[35]

By an act of Congress of April 15, 1874, the reservation boundary was officially moved northward to the Birch Creek–Marias River line. But Agent May made no effort to remove his agency from the Teton northward to some locality on the reservation. His stubborn championing of the rights of the Indians ended with his removal from office the following January.

May's successor, John Wood, fresh from a period of service as city marshal of Ottumwa, Iowa, brought to his new job an enthusiasm for law and order that soon was reflected in his relations with the Blackfeet. Wood found the Indians leaderless and demoralized. During the preceding year, fifteen to twenty men, including five chiefs, had been killed near the agency as the result of quarrels induced by too liberal use of whisky. The success of the Mounted Police in Canada had driven the whisky traders southward to Montana, where they operated in apparent collaboration with the licensed Blackfoot traders. Among the Indians killed had been the head chief of the Piegans. Agent May had appointed a successor to this chief, but the majority of the Indians refused to recognize him. They wanted to choose their own chief.[36]

One of Wood's first acts was to call in the scattered hunting bands. When more than five thousand Indians had gathered around the agency, he began to urge them to organize, elect head chiefs, and adopt laws for their tribal government. He warned them that unless they changed their habits, they would become extinct in a few years. After five days of talks with the Indians, Wood convened a council on April 20, 1875, to elect chiefs and to make laws. He called upon the Indians to elect a head chief who did not drink and who would care for and control his

[35] Reports of the Commissioner of Indian Affairs, 1874, 260.
[36] John Wood to Commissioner of Indian Affairs, February 2 and February 11, 1875, Indian Office Records.

people. Unanimously the band chiefs selected Little Plume as their head chief and Generous Woman and White Calf as subordinate chiefs.

Agent Wood and the chiefs then proceeded to draft a code of laws for their people. The new code, as recorded by the agent, provided for a tribunal consisting of the head chief, the two subordinate chiefs, and the agent. Any Indian charged with a breach of the law was guaranteed a trial before this tribunal, which had the power to inflict a punishment which must be neither barbarous nor cruel. Nine crimes and their punishments were spelled out in the code. An Indian found guilty of murdering another Indian was to be hanged by the neck until dead. If an Indian killed a white man, he was to be turned over to the civil authorities. The other and lesser crimes, which were punishable by fines of horses, robes, or peltries, were listed in order—threat to kill, theft, assault, wife beating, polygamy, rape, sale of a female relative to a white man, and the buying, selling, or keeping of intoxicating liquor. On April 23 the new code was signed by the three newly elected principal chiefs and seventeen chiefs of bands.[37]

This was a revolutionary document for the primitive Blackfoot Indians. Undoubtedly, its conception and many of its provisions originated with the former city marshal of Ottumwa, Iowa. The substitution of the death penalty for the traditional Blackfoot punishment by retaliatory action against the killer by members of the murdered man's family must have been Wood's idea. The recognition of polygamy, wife beating, and the sale of a female relative to a white man as crimes represented an acceptance of moral values which were quite new to these Indians. Nevertheless, Wood got the chiefs to agree to these provisions of the code. Some months later Inspector Watkins of the Indian Bureau expressed the opinion that no law existed under which the new Blackfoot tribunal could act legally. Nevertheless,

[37] Code of Laws Adopted by the Blackfeet, Blood and Piegan Indians in Council, April 23, 1875, Indian Office Records.

he thought the new code of laws was "eminently just and the practical working of the system very beneficial."[38]

Agent Wood found the Indians' bitterness over the loss of the southernmost portion of their reservation had been aggravated by his predecessor's promises to get the land back for them. He was not unsympathetic to the Indians' feelings in the matter; nevertheless, as a good law officer he recognized his duty to persuade the Indians that the new boundary line had to be respected. Meanwhile, the old agency within the ceded land on the Teton was becoming more and more untenable. White men had filed claims on the farm and even on the stockade of the very agency itself. Whites stole so many horses from Indians visiting their "father" at the agency that the red men preferred not to go back.[39]

Quietly, the agent won the consent of the majority of the Blackfeet to go north to the new reservation, where buffalo still were plentiful. When Chief White Calf complained to him of the whites' having taken "the fairest portion of their reservation," Wood replied with the common sense argument "that they had more land than they wanted; that if he or any other Indian would take ten acres and cultivate it, the same as white men do, it would yield enough food to feed over ten persons during the entire year."[40]

In the month of May, Wood traveled northward and selected a site for a new agency on Badger Creek, some fifty miles north of the old site on the Teton and fourteen miles beyond the southern boundary of the new reservation. He found there "about 100 acres of well watered, arable land and timber sufficient to last the Indians for 10 years for firewood."[41] On June 4, 1875, the commissioner of Indian Affairs authorized Wood to proceed with the construction of a new agency on Badger Creek. This was the

[38] Reports of the Commissioner of Indian Affairs, 1875, 47.

[39] John Wood to Commissioner of Indian Affairs, February 2 and May 14, 1875, Indian Office Records.

[40] Reports of the Commissioner of Indian Affairs, 1875, 300.

[41] John Wood to Commissioner of Indian Affairs, May 14, 1875, Indian Office Records.

first agency to be established within the boundaries of the present Blackfeet Reservation. It is interesting to note that its location was within a few miles of the place where Meriwether Lewis first met the Piegans sixty-nine years before.

So it was in the middle of the decade of the 1870's that law came to the Blackfoot tribes on both sides of the "medicine line." On both sides of the line the same period witnessed the cession of large areas of Blackfoot Indian hunting grounds and the nominal confinement of these people to reservations. The line itself came to have new meaning, for it divided the Blackfoot tribes into two groups—the Northern Blackfeet, Bloods, and Piegans on the north, who had become loyal subjects of "The Great Mother" (Queen Victoria), and the majority of the Piegan bands on the south, who remained "The Great White Father's children."

Albert Mad Plume, Piegan Indian, wearing "the Lord's shirt" mentioned on page 193 (*Courtesy Bureau of Indian Affairs*).

Curly Bear, a noted Piegan warrior, 1903 (*Courtesy Smithson-ian Institution*).

Two Guns White Calf, son of White Calf and a successful
rancher, 1923 (*Courtesy Smithsonian Institution*).

White Calf, last head chief of the Piegans in Montana (*Courtesy Montana Historical Society*).

Bird Rattler, Blood Indian, wearing traditional straight-up feather bonnet (*Courtesy Smithsonian Institution*).

Weasel Tail, Blood Indian veteran of the intertribal wars (*Courtesy Glacier Studio, Browning, Montana*).

16: The Tail of the Last Buffalo

For two decades prior to the middle seventies, Blackfoot agents had been telling their "children" that the buffalo, their staff of life, were decreasing in numbers and would soon disappear. But the testimony of the Indians' own eyes contradicted these gloomy prophecies. Their plains were black with buffalo. Why should they plant seeds and grub in the earth for a living when they could kill enough buffalo to feed themselves well and to supply the white traders who encouraged them to continue the chase?

Unknown to the Blackfeet, the range of the buffalo was indeed contracting. On the Great Plains to the east only sun-bleached buffalo bones were found where countless herds had roamed only a few years before. But in the Blackfoot country there was no apparent diminution of the herds. When the party of whites surveying the boundary between the United States and Canada moved westward along the forty-ninth parallel in the summer of 1874, they saw no buffalo at all until they were within about fifty miles of the Sweet Grass Hills. The North-West Mounted Police, who marched westward less than fifty miles farther north that same summer did not kill their first buffalo until they reached the Cypress Hills. The farther westward both parties traveled, the more plentiful buffalo became. When the survey party returned eastward through the Blackfoot country from the Rocky Mountains to the Sweet Grass Hills, they observed that "the plains and the eastern slopes of the hills were literally black with the creatures."[1] Standing at an elevation of eighteen hundred feet above the plains on one of the three Sweet Grass Hills, in the month of August, 1874, Captain W. J. Twining, chief astronomer and surveyor of the American party, saw the front of a great herd moving south, and was unable to see the end of it in either direction. He considered the Sweet Grass Hills in the Blackfoot country to be the center of the feeding ground of the great northern buffalo herd which ranged from the Missouri River northward to the Saskatchewan and which was so large that the Red River half-bloods, Sioux, Assiniboins, Gros Ventres, and Blackfeet, "with all their wasteful slaughter made but little impression upon it." He found that the traders at Fort Benton believed that the buffalo were increasing in late years because of the destruction of wolves, the natural enemies of the buffalo.[2]

In that same year of 1874, Lieutenant G. C. Doane, traveling eastward from the vicinity of Bozeman to the Judith Basin south of the Missouri, encountered large herds of buffalo. He estimated the great northern buffalo herd at four million head.[3]

Such common reports of the vast herds of buffalo on the plains of Montana and present Alberta certainly did not suggest any urgent need for government action to conserve this most important natural resource of the Blackfeet. On the other hand, the fur traders continued to urge the Indians to bring in more and more robes. They were reaping a golden harvest. In 1876 Baker and Brothers of Fort Benton shipped 75,000 buffalo robes. The next year 30,000 robes were shipped from Fort Macleod. In 1877 the Council of the North-West Territories began to be alarmed at the diminution of the buffalo in Canada. It prohibited the use of buffalo pounds and the killing of animals under two years of age, and prescribed certain closed seasons.

But it was too late to save the buffalo on the Canadian plains.

[1] W. J. Twining, "Report of Capt. W. J. Twining, Chief Astronomer and Surveyor," *Reports Upon the Survey of the Boundary between the United States and the Possessions of Great Britain*, 282.

[2] *Ibid.*, 63–64.

[3] Merrill G. Burlingame, *The Montana Frontier*, 71.

By the following year they had become so scarce that the restrictions were repealed. In the summer of 1878 prairie fires swept a wide area of grassland west of the Cypress Hills. The buffalo, seeking pasturage, moved southward, and the Canadian Blackfoot tribes followed them across the line. The main herd remained south of Milk River, extending southward to the Judith Basin. The great buffalo herds never returned to the land of "The Great Mother."[4]

In 1879 hunger stalked the camps of the Canadian Blackfeet. By summer some of the Northern Blackfeet had died of starvation. Others were eating dogs, horses, soup made from old buffalo bones gathered on the plains, and even grass, to keep themselves alive. Inspector Denny, at the Mounted Police post of Fort Calgary, reported that twenty-one Indians starved to death by July 5. He was then buying cattle to feed the Indians. When a steer was shot, Denny saw the famished Indians "rush on the animal with their knives before it had ceased kicking, cut away the flesh and maddened by hunger, devour it raw."[5]

More than three thousand destitute Indians, primarily Bloods and North Piegans, camped around Fort Macleod that fall. Pathetically, Indian parents called upon the police for help, saying, "We have had nothing to eat for two, three, or four days, and our children are crying with the hunger; we do not care so much for ourselves but we do not like to see our children die."[6] Unable to feed this multitude, Indian Commissioner Edgar B. Dewdney gave the Indians some provisions and advised them to cross "the medicine line" into Montana. He later claimed that this action had saved the Canadian government "at least $100,000."[7] It also gave the Canadian officials valuable time to set up a feeding program for the destitute Blackfoot Indians, who only the year before had been haughty, happy, self-sufficient people.

South of the boundary, the Piegans in Montana still relied primarily upon buffalo for their subsistence. When their new

[4] MacInnes, *In the Shadow of the Rockies*, 145.
[5] Denny, *The Law Marches West*, 130, 143–44.
[6] *The Saskatchewan Herald* (Regina), November 3, 1879.
[7] Paul F. Sharp, *Whoop-Up Country*, 155.

"father," John Young, arrived from Brooklyn, New York, in December, 1876, he found only the old, infirm, and blind Indians, with some children, encamped in the valley of Badger Creek near the new agency. The able-bodied Indians were away hunting buffalo.[8]

The agency had been moved north from the Teton River only the month before, to a site less than five miles west of the present Browning–Great Falls highway crossing of Badger Creek. Although it did not have a stockade or bastions as did the old trading posts, it resembled them in its hollow, rectangular plan. Built of squared logs, with the doorways to the buildings on the interior sides of the rectangle, it could serve as a fortress in case of an attack by hostile Indians.

Throughout the remainder of the seventies, Young's children continued to hunt buffalo both summer and winter at considerable distances from the agency. Although these hunts were not uniformly successful, they provided the Indians not only with the greater part of their food, but also with skins for lodges and a considerable number of hides for trade. On the winter hunt of 1877–78 some of the families got as many as seventy robes. During the next winter a large hunting camp of four hundred lodges, led by Chief White Calf, found "robes and meat plenty" near the Bear Paw Mountains. But a smaller party under Fast Buffalo Horse, hunting farther south took few buffalo. It was a severe winter. A woman and child of Fast Buffalo Horse's party froze to death, and the horses grew so weak they could barely travel. When this camp returned to the agency, their leaders were convinced that the time was fast approaching when failure of the buffalo would force them to make a change in their way of life. One of the men told John Young, "The time is close when the tail of the last buffalo will be seen disappearing from the prairie."[9]

So long as there were fat buffalo to be killed, most of these

[8] John Young to Commissioner of Indian Affairs, December 22, 1876, Indian Office Records.

[9] Reports of the Commissioner of Indian Affairs, 1879, 90; Young to Commissioner of Indian Affairs, March 1, 1878, Indian Office Records.

Indians had little desire for the beef and bacon issued in their annuities or for the potatoes and turnips they might raise themselves. They missed the non-food items when their annuities failed to arrive in 1876. In October of the next year, Young distributed the goods for both 1876 and 1877, commenting that "in no previous distribution had the old, infirm and children been so comfortably clothed and provided for against the winter." These annuity goods included such useful items as woolen blankets, red flannel shirts, calico prints, linen and cotton thread, iron kettles, short-handled frying pans, tin pans, plates and cups, tinned iron table spoons, knives, and forks, six-inch hunting knives, and tapered saw files.[10]

Agent Young's official reports on the progress of his "children" revealed a tendency, not uncommon among Indian agents, to couple current discouragement with an unwarranted optimism toward the future. In 1877 he wrote:

> I find it difficult to prevail upon even the more sensible and reflecting portion to give up their nomadic life and settle down to farm or raise cattle. They admit the time approaches fast when buffalo will disappear, but until then the excitement of the chase and the notion that labor is only for women will prevent the change to a more certain and civilized life.

On the other hand, he found some encouragement in the fact that some of the chiefs had "requested to be allowed, with their own hands, to put some of the seeds in the ground that they might watch their progress with more interest," and also in the fact that they were "talking of selecting locations and asking help to build cabins." The agent parlayed these faint glimmers of hope into a prophecy that "with proper management they can soon be made self-supporting."[11]

During the next year the first concrete evidences of settling down appeared. That winter two Indians, Gambler and Spotted

[10] Reports of the Commissioner of Indian Affairs, 1878, 83; Blackfeet Agency Annuity Estimate for 1877, September 22, 1875, Indian Office Records.

[11] Reports of the Commissioner of Indian Affairs, 1877, 132.

Eagle, with the help of white men, built two log cabins on Birch Creek, and White Calf, the head chief, followed their example. By summer there were ten Indian cabins on the reservation and these cabin-dwellers had planted forty acres of potatoes and turnips. My older informants said that most of these pioneer Piegan farmers were members of Running Crane's band, whose garden plots were on Badger Creek very near the agency. Although Young was proud of these achievements, he managed to temper his report of these humble beginnings with a realistic appraisal of the future.

> To extend these improved matters and make them permanent will require time, patience, and discretion. Many difficulties lie in the way. The Indians have no correct notion of continuous labor. It is rare for the same Indian to work for more than a few days at a time, and he is apt to stop as the whim or notion moves him.[12]

Agent Young dealt with many other problems involving his "children" which were not directly related to the major one of getting them to settle down and try to make a living at civilized pursuits. These problems involved their spiritual welfare, their physical health, their education, their tribal government, their relations with the traders, and even the relocation of the agency.

Young felt strongly that the lack of missionaries handicapped his efforts to civilize "these savages." He complained bitterly that the large Methodist missionary societies, which "do so much for India and China," had totally neglected the Blackfeet, even though this reservation had been assigned to their denomination. He organized a Sunday school and was delighted to hear the women in the brush cutting firewood "enliven their toil by singing our Sabbath-school tunes." But he felt the need of a full-time missionary to help eliminate the Indians' "superstitious practices" in such practical ways as by inducing them to see the physician at the agency when they became sick rather than to call upon the traditional medicine man.[13]

[12] *Ibid.*, 1878, 84.

Meanwhile, Roman Catholic missionaries, denied access to the reservation by the fact that it had been officially designated Methodist territory, traveled with the Blackfoot hunting bands and performed baptisms and marriages among them. In 1881, Father Prando built a small chapel on the south side of Birch Creek. The Indians could go to him, but he was forbidden to cross the river to pursue his work on the reservation. By that time some of the Piegan bands had settled on Birch Creek near this mission station and had become ardent followers of this priest. When, in the fall of 1883, a senatorial investigating committee visited the reservation, it found that head chief White Calf's principal complaint against Agent Young was his refusal to allow the Jesuits on the reservation.[14]

By 1878 top-level Indian Bureau administrators were convinced that the civilization of the Indians could be brought about more speedily through the education of their children than by any other means. On the Blackfeet Reservation in the late seventies they had little opportunity to prove their theory. The great majority of the Indian families spent too little time near the agency. When they were near by, the school was crowded. When they folded their lodges and went on a buffalo hunt, the children went with them, even though a few ran away from their families and returned to school. Of the twelve hundred Indian children of school age in 1878, only twenty boys and thirty girls attended school for more than one month, and only two children learned to read and write during the year.[15]

Both children and adults were reluctant to speak the English words they knew, fearing that they would be laughed at if they mispronounced any of them. At the same time, the Indians laughed loudly at the crude and halting efforts of the whites employed at the agency to speak Blackfoot.[16]

The investigating committee in 1883 found that the school teachers, the Misses Young, daughters of the agent, were "most

13 *Ibid.*, 1877, 132; 1879, 91.
14 Bischoff, *Jesuits in Old Oregon*, 90–91, 100.
15 Reports of the Commissioner of Indian Affairs, 1878, *xxiv*, 83, 288–89.
16 *Ibid.*, 1877, 131.

estimable and energetic young ladies, but the school is doing very little in the education of the Indian children." On ration days as many as two hundred children attended; on other days, no more than fifty. Chief White Calf also complained that this school "amounted to nothing."[17]

Following the decision in 1877 of the Northern Blackfeet, Bloods, and North Piegans to swear allegiance to The Great Mother and to receive land in Canada under the terms of Treaty No. 7, only eleven bands among all the Indians known by the general designation of Blackfeet remained as wards of the United States. It was not surprising that Agent Young observed that the Indians on his reservation were "now calling themselves by the general name Piegan" in 1878. They were members of Piegan bands. Yet the official estimate of seventy-five hundred Indians on the Montana reservation at that time was excessively high. It must have included a large number of Canadian Indians who had crossed the "medicine line" to get in on the distribution of annuities from "The Great White Father." For nearly two decades thereafter the problem of determining on which side of the line some of these Indians belonged was a perplexing one for both governments, and especially for their agents in the field. Meanwhile, many clever Indians managed to move back and forth across the line to get in on rations and payments issued by both the United States and Canada. My elderly Piegan informants told me they had no trouble getting a share of the Canadians' bounty prior to the middle eighties. The problem was complicated by the common practice of intermarriage between the several Blackfoot tribes. It was not until the middle nineties that definite reservation assignments were made for some individuals by agreement between their agents in the United States and Canada. In the meantime, the population figures for the Blackfoot tribes in both Canada and the United States were

[17] *Report of the Subcommittee of the Special Committee of the United States Senate Appointed to Visit the Indian Tribes of Northern Montana, 48 Cong., 1 sess., Senate Report No. 283, 233–34.* (Hereafter referred to as *Subcommittee Report, 48 Cong., 1 sess., Senate Report 283.*)

inaccurate in that they included some Indians who were counted twice.

Since their removal to the new reservation, the Piegan Indians had remained at peace with the whites, although their young men continued their occasional horse raids against alien tribes. Fearing that they would be prevented from going if their objectives were known, these war parties left secretly, usually at night. The code of laws adopted in 1875 continued in operation. Little Plume, the popular head chief, died on August 22, 1877. He was buried in the ground on a hill overlooking the agency, and his favorite horse was shot beside his grave in accordance with traditional custom. Two months later the leading Indians in council elected White Calf head chief and Generous Woman second chief of the tribe.[18]

A year later (October 21, 1878) Generous Woman died and was buried beside Little Plume. He was succeeded in the chieftaincy of the Grease Melters, the most populous of all Piegan bands, by Three Suns (also known as Big Nose), a famous warrior who was very popular among the people of his tribe. Whether or not Three Suns also succeeded to Generous Woman's title of second chief of the tribe, it is certain that both the Indians and the agent regarded him as more than a mere band chief. The following May it was Three Suns' band that was the first to receive annuities, and it was Three Suns who supervised the division of annuities among the remaining ten bands, including the Skunks, the band of White Calf.[19]

As leader of the conservative, heathen faction on the reservation, Three Suns became a powerful rival of White Calf, leader of the Christian, progressive faction. Many of my elderly informants regarded Three Suns as the real head of the tribe and claimed that he had the larger following among the Indians. On the other hand, they blamed White Calf for being a tool of the whites, who had too readily agreed to the white men's wishes

[18] John Young, Monthly Reports to Commissioner of Indian Affairs, September and November, 1877, Indian Office Records.
[19] Young to Commissioner of Indian Affairs, May 8, 1879, Indian Office Records.

in accepting the Birch Creek boundary and the land sales of the eighties and nineties, which further reduced the size of the reservation. One old Indian complained bitterly, "White Calf would sell anything to keep his position as principal chief." Another stated, "If White Calf was still living we would probably all be living on top of Chief Mountain."

It is only fair to say that however much Three Suns may have "bucked the government" in other matters, his name also appears on the land agreements. Three Suns died in the late winter of 1896. White Calf, the last head chief of the South Piegan Indians, died on January 29, 1903, while on a visit to "the Great White Father" in Washington. His body was returned to the reservation and buried on top of a hill overlooking his home on Cut Bank Creek. Undoubtedly, both White Calf and Three Suns were intelligent and able men. They symbolized the conflict in the minds and hearts of all the Indians during that difficult period of readjustment to a new way of life which began before the buffalo were gone and has continued for some to the present day. Co-operative White Calf could see things as the whites presented them to him. He was willing to accept new conditions and try new ways. Conservative Three Suns was skeptical, suspicious of white men's motives. He would have preferred the traditional ways. To impatient administrators, he was an obstructionist because he questioned their plans for his people. In most writings on the Blackfoot Indians of this period, White Calf is pictured as the heroic and wise chief. Three Suns is virtually ignored.

The rivalry between these two leaders survived their deaths in the form of jealousy and a certain amount of ill feeling between those Piegans living on the north side of the reservation, White Calf's section, and those dwelling on the south side, where Three Suns lived.

Both the agent and the chiefs received helpful assistance in preserving law and order when an Indian police force was organized on October 1, 1878. This new force was composed of Indians selected on the basis of their courage and reliability. They were clothed in plain, inexpensive uniforms which distinguished them from other Indians. Each private received five dollars a month, each officer eight dollars. They operated under a simple set of rules. Although there was some doubt at first whether these Indians would hesitate to bring charges against their friends and members of their own bands, they proved to be impartial agents of the law. Young found that they performed their duties well, and that their authority was respected by the other Indians. Perhaps this police force was less of an innovation than he realized. Certainly these Indians long had known the strict regulation of the summer tribal hunt by members of their own men's societies.[20]

Relations with the traders remained a vexatious problem for the agent. Not only was there the perennial problem of the "sneaking drink givers," but there was the new problem of illegal trade in ammunition. After the Sioux wiped out Custer's command on the Little Big Horn, using some weapons that were more effective than those of the soldiers, steps were taken to deprive hostile or potentially hostile Indians of the use of repeating firearms. On November 23, 1876, President Grant issued an order prohibiting sales of metallic cartridges or fixed ammunition to hostile Indians. In vain, Agent Young protested that the Piegans were not hostile and that they needed metallic cartridges to feed their many Winchesters on their buffalo hunts.

The order proved impossible to enforce. Unlicensed traders peddled ammunition in the Indian camps when they were far from the agency hunting buffalo. Others operated from posts on the south side of the Marias at Willow Round and farther downstream. When Young ordered them to stop selling the forbidden ammunition to the Piegans, they figuratively if not literally thumbed their noses and reminded him that their side of the river was not reservation land and so they were not subject to any orders from the Indian Department. Two of the suspected traders were Bill Hart and Weatherwax, tough veterans of the

[20] Reports of the Commissioner of Indian Affairs, 1878, *xlii*; 1879, 91.

whisky trade that flourished in Canada before the coming of the Mounted Police.[21]

Meanwhile, the licensed trader, limited to the sale of antiquated powder and ball, lost business at his post near the agency. In the light of this background information it is understandable that the investigating committee in September, 1883, found the post trader's store "a very poor one, with indifferent stocks of goods."[22] He just had not been able to compete with those sharp fellows on the Marias.

Agent Young had never been happy about the location of the first agency on Badger Creek. The valley was too narrow and contained too little arable land. The hilly surroundings made cattle herding difficult, or would have if the Indians had owned any cattle. In the fall of 1878 he enlisted the aid of the Indians in moving the agency buildings a few miles downstream to a site east of the present Browning–Great Falls highway. Both men and women assisted him in digging cellars, hauling stone, mixing mortar, hauling poles for fences, and erecting the fences. The Indian women covered the outside of the buildings with lime hauled from a kiln near Heart Butte. Young was pleased to report that the removal was accomplished at very small cost and without any special appropriation because the Indians had pitched in and helped.[23] Although the buildings erected in this first Blackfoot Indian public works project have disappeared, the site of Young's bright new agency of 1879 is still known as "Old Agency."

The experience gained in moving the agency encouraged some of the Indian families to build cabins of their own on Badger Creek or Birch Creek in the southern part of their reservation. By the summer of 1881 there were eighty Indian-owned cabins, including ten built by Three Suns' band on Two Medicine River, the first attempted settlement on a stream north of the agency. But persistent Cree horse raids on this outlying settlement in

[21] John Young correspondence, December 27, 1876–September 11, 1877. Agents' Letter Book, The Blackfeet Archives, Museum of the Plains Indian.

[22] *Subcommittee Report*, 48 Cong., 1 sess., *Senate Report 283*, 234.

[23] Reports of the Commissioner of Indian Affairs, 1879, 90.

the spring of 1883 compelled Three Suns and his followers to abandon their homes and return to the vicinity of the agency for protection. By that time the number of Indian cabins had increased to two hundred. The agency carpenter was kept busy making doors, tables, and bedsteads for these new homes. Some of the Indians furnished their log cabins with clocks, stoves, and chairs and decorated the walls with pictures from illustrated papers. The greatest hindrance to permanent occupancy of these sturdy houses appeared to be the persistence of the Indian belief that a dwelling must be abandoned after a death occurred in it.[24]

Meanwhile, the Piegans continued to hunt buffalo where they could find them. In the winter of 1879–80, the Piegans journeyed south for a buffalo hunt in the Judith Basin. A number of the Canadian Blackfeet were there also, to escape the starvation that faced them in their barren land north of the border. White settlers, disturbed by the great influx of red men to land far south of their reservations, claimed that the Indians were killing cattle and called upon the army to compel the Indians to go back to their own lands. The Piegans were led home by a military escort. Chief White Calf protested vigorously that his people had not killed cattle, saying, "Why should we kill cattle when we had plenty of meat?" It was not until some time after his Indians had returned to their reservation that Agent Young learned directly from the North Piegan Chief Running Rabbit that his hungry young men had killed white men's cattle on land south of the Missouri. Young, however, believed the white cattlemen's claims that they had lost three thousand animals from Indian depredations were highly exaggerated.[25]

The following June a herd of five hundred cattle was received at the Blackfoot Agency. It was anticipated that this herd would increase sufficiently in five years to feed the tribe. Agent Young painstakingly explained to the chiefs the purpose of this first

[24] *Ibid.*, 1883, 96–97; Young to Commissioner of Indian Affairs, November 1, 1880, July 1, 1881, and July 31, 1881, Indian Office Records.

[25] *Ibid.*, January 6, 1882.

cattle herd on the reservation and told them the animals should not be killed for food until their numbers increased. By the next summer, this agency herd had increased to six hundred head. It looked as if the Blackfeet were building up a solid hedge against distress when the buffalo disappeared.[26]

The winter hunt in 1881 had been unsuccessful. But the following December the Indians discovered buffalo in considerable numbers on the reservation, between the Sweet Grass Hills and the Bear Paw Mountains. They returned from the winter hunt in March, 1882, to report "plenty to eat and no sickness among them."[27]

Nevertheless, each year a smaller number of Piegans were going on the winter buffalo hunt, while more of them remained encamped near the agency, depending primarily upon government rations for their food. At the end of January, 1881, there were only 605 Indians near the agency; at the same period a year later there were 1,955, and in 1883 there were about 3,000. Only a small portion of the tribe went on the winter hunt in 1883, and they brought back only a few robes. By February 1, 1883, the demands for rations had become so great that Agent Young was having to supplement his beef and flour issue by giving his "children" potatoes. He wrote the commissioner, "But for this there would be suffering for want of food." By April, shortened rations brought complaints of hunger from the Indians. And by May even the potato stock was reduced to the small quantity reserved for seed. The anxious agent reported, "As I cannot get cattle to buy I fear suffering and trouble." A week later he telegraphed Washington, "There will not be provisions enough to prevent suffering. Can anything be done?"[28]

Early in July two Piegan bands led by chiefs Little Dog and Bull Shoe rode to hunt in the neighborhood of the Sweet Grass Hills, where nine years before buffalo had been seen in countless numbers. They killed just six buffalo and a few antelope. The

[26] *Ibid.*, June 16, 1880.
[27] *Ibid.*, March 1, 1881, April 1, 1881, and April 1, 1882.
[28] *Ibid.*, February 1, April 2, May 1, 1883; telegram of May 8, 1883.

Canadian government was about to make its annual distribution to the Indians north of the line, yet Young conscientiously forbade his Indians to leave the reservation, even though he was well aware "that the larger the number that go, my issue of provisions has the fewer to feed."[29] Instead, he began killing cattle from the agency herd. Late that month delivery of fifty steers was received. It wasn't a drop in the bucket.

On September 14, Senator George Vest of Missouri and Montana's delegate Martin Maginnis visited the reservation on a tour of investigation of the condition of the Indians. Their principal objective appears to have been to talk with the chiefs regarding another land cession. However, they learned the Indians were eating their limited weekly rations in two days and starving the rest of the week. They were there on ration day and saw the pitiable "eagerness in the hungry eyes of the waiting crowd as the beef was being distributed." They heard Three Suns say in the council:

> Major Young has done a little, and would do more if he could. If a man asks for a horse and you have only a colt, that is all you can give him . . . but the winter is close. You see how poor we are; there is no buffalo; we are on the verge of starvation. I would like to know if anything will be done this winter. If not, it will be too late for many; they will starve.

Senator Vest replied that it would be three months before the Great Council (Congress) would meet, but he promised he "would immediately ask that something be done to keep them this winter."[30]

The summer's crops had been a complete failure as a result of late frosts in spring, drought, and early fall frosts. The few potatoes obtained had been frozen in the ground and would not keep. Late in September, Young received a letter from Commissioner Price in Washington, informing him that the total

29 *Ibid.*, August 1, 1883.
30 *Subcommittee Report*, 48 Cong., 1 sess., *Senate Report 283*, 233, 244.

appropriation for supplies for his agency was already exhausted, and "as it is not in the power of this department to make any further provision for their support than the appropriations of Congress allows, nothing further can be done." Young immediately penned his resignation, reminding the Commissioner that high officials of the department as well as members of the Senate Commission had given the Indians strong hopes that more food would be sent them, and adding, "It is a grave error not to keep even an implied promise, made to Indians. The Division of Supplies authorized will not prevent distress and loss of life, and in all probability [will] lead to outrage."[31]

Neither letters of explanation nor of resignation brought any relief to the starving Indians. Agent Young stuck to his post through the horrible winter until his relief came. By the end of October none of the food purchases of the fiscal year had been received except sugar. In mid-November Inspector C. H. Howard visited the agency. He had seen white men's cattle illegally grazing on the reservation, but he found the Indians starving for want of meat. Howard feared the desperate Indians might kill the white men's cattle, the cowboys defend their herds with firearms, and another Indian war break out. He reported that the Indians were receiving rations at the rate of one and one-half pounds of beef and two and one-fourth pounds of flour per person per week. No other food was available. He visited many houses and lodges on a Thursday, two days before the weekly ration issue, and in most of them found no food at all. With winter coming on, the road to Fort Benton might soon become impassable. Howard recommended that because of its light weight compared to beef, bacon should be purchased for the Indians.[32]

In December, Young received a shipment of enough beef to last until April at one-fourth rations. He also received a sizable supply of bacon. But when the agency doctor inspected the

[31] Commissioner Price to John Young, September 13, 1883; John Young to Price, September 24, 1883, Indian Office Records.

[32] C. H. Howard, Special Report on Condition of the Blackfeet Indians, November 16, 1883, Interior Department Archives.

bacon, he found it so filled with worms and pervaded by stench that it was unfit for human food.[33]

By mid-February the agency cattle herd was reduced to 117 animals. From his log mission south of Birch Creek, Father Prando reported that an epidemic of erysipelas had struck the weakened Indians and they were dying at a rate of from one to four a day. He noted that in spite of the uproar in the newspapers about the deplorable condition of these Indians, no help had come to them.[34]

When Reuben Allen relieved Young in April, he wrote to the commissioner in Washington, "I find here about twenty-five hundred Indians in almost a starving condition. I am credibly informed that many have died in the past few months for want of sufficient food."[35] Montana newspapers, which, without bothering to investigate the situation, had castigated his predecessor as the fiend who had caused the starvation among the Piegans, hailed Major Allen as the hero who would solve the problem. (Even as late as July 3, 1884, the *Sun River Sun* was claiming that Young had kept Washington ignorant of the condition of affairs at the agency.)

But Allen brought no food with him, and nothing else would save the Indians. By May 3 his meat supply was gone and he had little flour. "To prevent further suffering and loss of life by starvation," he went to the warehouse where the supply of condemned bacon was stored, sorted it, salvaged 2,112 pounds, and issued it to his "children." Agent Allen was desperate, and he justified his action on the grounds that it was the only thing he could do to alleviate the Indians' suffering.[36]

Spring had brought no relief. When Allen gave out five thousand pounds of seed potatoes to the Indians for planting, most of them were eaten. Those that were planted never had a chance

---

[33] Young to Commissioner of Indian Affairs, December 3, 1883, Indian Office Records.

[34] Bischoff, *Jesuits in Old Oregon*, 92.

[35] Reuben Allen to Commissioner of Indian Affairs, April 9, 1884, Indian Office Records.

[36] *Ibid.*, June 16, 1884.

to mature, as the Indians dug and ate them at the first opportunity. In June they stripped the cottonwood trees and ate the inner bark. In August they found some small game and berries in the mountains. Allen informed Washington that unless he obtained more supplies when the berries were gone, the carpenter would again be kept busy making burial boxes. He wrote that he could give the Indians less than five ounces of meat (one-fifth rations) and less than six ounces of flour a day. "On such an allowance, having nothing else, how could they avoid starving?"[37]

The Indian Bureau obtained authority to spend all of its inadequate appropriation for the Blackfoot Agency for the fiscal year 1885 by March 30, thus increasing the daily rations. And on January 8, 1885, Congress provided a special appropriation to feed these Indians during the remaining three months of that year. Thus the frightful epidemic of starvation finally was brought under control.

There is no adequate record of the number of Piegan deaths from starvation during those nightmarish years 1883–84. The agents' annual report for the year preceding July 1, 1884, listed only 247 deaths from all causes. But the Indian Rights Association, which investigated the disaster, found that "upward of four hundred were starved to death."[38] Almost-a-Dog, a Piegan Indian, is said to have kept a record of each death as it occurred by cutting a notch in a willow stick, and the number of those marks is said to have reached 555. Between one-fourth and one-sixth of the Piegans in Montana must have perished from starvation in the years 1883–84. So many of the victims were buried on the hill south of Badger Creek during that period that the Indians came to refer to it as "Ghost Ridge."

Some earlier writers seemed to feel that a disaster of such horror and magnitude demanded a scapegoat. Much of the blame for it was heaped upon resigned Agent John Young. J. Willard Schultz went so far as to picture him as a heartless wretch

---

[37] *Ibid.*, August 11, 1884.
[38] Indian Rights Association, *Second Annual Report for the Year Ending December, 1884*, 19.

who was content to sit by and see his Piegan "children" starve before his eyes while he fed his chickens corn.[39] But the official correspondence of the period, to which Schultz had no access, tells a different story. Agent Young was not popular among the Indians, but he did not fail in his duty to keep Washington informed of the sad condition of the Piegans resulting from the sudden disappearance of their major food resource, the buffalo.

The Indian Bureau, despite the warning lesson of the starvation among the Canadian Blackfeet which had followed the sudden extermination of the buffalo north of the boundary four years before, had instituted no program to regulate the slaughter of the northern herd by either Indians or whites in this country. Large numbers of white hide hunters, as well as Indians from Canada and the United States, had been allowed complete freedom to kill as many buffalo as they could. When "the tail of the last buffalo disappeared from the prairie," the Indian Bureau was caught unprepared to meet the immediate emergency. Its funds for the purchase of rations were estimated and tightly budgeted a year in advance of their expenditure. There was no margin to care for emergencies. The failure of crops in the summer of 1883, delays in the delivery of food purchased, and the fact that the bacon obtained in December was unfit for human consumption were contributory causes.

Yet had the Indian Bureau been able to obtain a special appropriation from Congress in the early months of 1884, some, if not much, of the starvation would have been avoided. The Indian Rights Association, which thoroughly investigated this disaster, pulled no punches in blaming Congressman John Ellis, chairman of the House Sub-committee on Indian Appropriations, for the failure of the Indian Bureau to obtain the special appropriation to care for this emergency which it had requested of Congress in 1884. Throughout the late months of that year, the Indian Rights Association worked hard and persistently to convince members of Congress of the urgency of action for the relief of the starving Indians. Yet it was not until after the Indian Rights

[39] Schultz, *My Life as an Indian,* 394–408.

Association offered an open letter to the newspapers pointing out that Ellis's delaying action placed in jeopardy the lives of many of the Montana Indians that he introduced a joint resolution calling for $50,000 to be made immediately available for the support and maintenance of the destitute Indians. Once introduced, the resolution passed both houses within two days.[40]

Actually this emergency did not affect the Piegans alone. It was a regional one. The Gros Ventres and Assiniboins farther east, who shared with the Blackfeet the great reservation covering all of northern Montana Territory east of the Rockies, also shared their suffering when "the tail of the last buffalo disappeared from the prairies." The suffering of the Indians on Milk River was somewhat relieved when their menfolk offered their wives and daughters to soldiers at near-by Fort Assiniboine in return for money with which to buy food from the post trader.[41]

It was remarkable that, in spite of the fears of Inspector Howard and of many white-skinned Montanans, the destitute Blackfoot Indians, whose ancestors bore such a reputation for "bloodthirstiness," did not in their desperation descend in force upon the great herds of settlers' cattle on the plains south of the reservation and take what food they needed. Perhaps Indian memory of the massacre on the Marias was still too fresh in their minds. The suffering Piegans remained remarkably orderly.

It was doubly tragic that many of these Indians starved to death almost in the midst of plenty, while no well-fed settlers living on former Blackfoot lands offered any effective aid. The Piegans had been starving for fully a year when, on August 29, 1884, Governor John Schuyler Crosby piously wrote the Secretary of the Interior in Washington: "As Governor of Montana, in the name of her people I protest against keeping the nation's wards within the limits of this Territory in such pitiable, starving condition. Humanity and justice demand their immediate relief."[42]

[40] Indian Rights Association, *The Action of Congress in Regard to the Piegan Indians of Montana*, 1-20.
[41] *Ibid.*, 4.
[42] *The Congressional Record*, January 6, 1885, 485.

17: Trading Land for a Living

THE EXTERMINATION of the buffalo quickly transformed the strong, mobile, independent Blackfoot Indians into a weak, sedentary, dependent people. They had land—lots of it. Together with the Gros Ventres, Assiniboins, and Sioux, the Piegans in Montana owned a vast tract almost as large as the state of Indiana, extending from the Rockies eastward to present North Dakota. But of what value was it to them? Hunters could not make a living in an almost gameless land.

When Senator Vest and Delegate Maginnis met the South Piegan chiefs in council at the Blackfoot Agency on September 25, 1883, they found these Indian leaders willing to exchange land for other things which would enable them to make a living now that the buffalo were gone. Chief Little Dog spoke:

> I want a reservation with the Birch Creek on the south, as now. We like the land near the mountains. On the east you can draw a line from the western end of the Sweet Grass Hills to the Marias River . . . From that line down to the Bear Paw we have no use for the country. There is no game there. We don't want to go there. We would rather stay here where there are streams and good land, and where our homes lie. The reason I put the line so far east is that I want the people to have a good living; plenty of range for horses and stock. We want the Government to help us.[1]

[1] *Subcommittee Report,* 48 Cong., 1 sess., *Senate Report 283,* 242–43.

The other prominent chiefs—White Calf, Three Suns, Little White Cow, and Running Crane—echoed Little Dog's sentiments. Yet nearly three and one-half years passed before a land sale was negotiated and these Indians began to receive the cattle and the equipment they sorely needed to help them make a living on their remaining land.

Meanwhile, the two thousand South Piegans who survived the starvation of 1883–84 settled down within a radius of fifteen miles of their agency and lived from week to week upon the rations given them by their agent. The majority of the old hunting bands settled on Badger Creek. The westernmost settlement, farthest upstream, was that of the Black Door Band, under Chief After Buffalo. It was just east of the present crossing of Badger Creek by the road from Browning to Heart Butte. Downstream, near the site of the first agency on Badger Creek, was the Lone Eater's Band, led by Chief Running Crane. On the north side of the stream, opposite present Mad Plume School, lived a mixed group composed of families from several of the old hunting bands, under Big Plume's leadership. Below this group was the large Grease Melters' Band, under the noted Chief Three Suns. And farther downstream was Chief Little Dog's Black-patched Moccasins Band.

Just west of Old Agency, on land now crossed by the highway from Great Falls to Browning lived the Indians' "white brothers-in-law," the white men who had taken Piegan wives. Below them was the agency, and near it stood about one hundred log cabins built to house the old people when Old Agency was erected in 1879. The little remnant of the once large and powerful Small Robes Band, led by Chief Lodge Pole, occupied cabins just east of the agency.

About one mile east of the agency, on a flat south of Badger Creek, was the trader's store. Below it were settled the members of the Buffalo Dung Band. Farther downstream were some of the older people of the Black-patched Moccasins Band, led by Shaggy Bear Chief. It was on the flat south of this band that the Piegans held their first sun dance after the buffalo were gone

—the first in which cattle tongues were the sacred food.

On downstream was a small, detached group from the Buffalo Dung Band who recognized White Grass as their chief. The easternmost band on Badger Creek consisted of a few families, all of the members of the Bugs Band who had survived the starvation.

The three remaining Piegan bands resided on Birch Creek along the southern boundary of the reservation. They were the Skunks Band of Head Chief White Calf, the Blood Band led by Fast Buffalo Horse, and the All Chiefs under Chief Horn.[2]

At that time the white men with Indian families, some of the aged Indians near the agency, and a few families elsewhere on Badger and Birch creeks lived in log cabins. But the majority of the fullbloods still resided in tipis the year round. Lacking buffalo cowskins, they covered their tipis with government-issue canvas.

Each Friday, cattle were butchered at the slaughterhouse, and each Saturday the Indians trekked toward the agency to receive their weekly rations. Each family head carried a cardboard ration ticket bearing his name and the number of persons in his family. One ration was considered a day's food for one person—man, woman, or child; therefore a man and wife with three children were entitled to thirty-five rations a week. The Indians were warned not to lose their precious ration tickets. Some men carried their tickets in little leather cases tied around their necks at the end of skin cords.

When the family head received his rations, a clerk punched his ticket and checked his name off the long, printed ration roll of the agency. Meat, always the main item in Blackfoot diet, was rationed at one and one-half pounds per person per day. A daily ration also included one-half pound of flour. Other foodstuffs were distributed in smaller quantities: a pound of bacon for every ten rations; a pound of coffee for every twenty-five rations;

---

[2] Adam White Man and Louis Bear Child, Piegan informants, pointed out to me in 1951 the locations of Piegan bands on Badger Creek in the period immediately following buffalo extermination.

and three pounds of beans, eight pounds of sugar, and one pound of soda and of salt for every one hundred rations. With every one hundred rations a half-pound of tobacco was issued.[3]

The hides of cattle killed to provide the Indians' meat were given to the Indian women on ration day. In some weeks as many as fifty hides were distributed, never more than half a hide to any woman. The women made rawhide rope and containers from these hides, just as they had made similar articles of buffalo hide in earlier days. They also cut moccasin soles from cattle rawhide to make a hard-soled moccasin which was becoming the most popular type of Blackfoot footgear. It wore much longer than the traditional soft-soled moccasin. On the other hand, commercial leather was replacing rawhide for saddle rigging, belts, cartridge cases, and ration ticket pouches.

Since the middle seventies, Blackfoot women's crafts had been undergoing marked changes. About the time the agency was moved northward from the Teton River (1876), some Piegan Indian women who were married to white men began to employ little glass beads, known as seed beads, in their beadwork. These beads were only about half the size of the beads women had been accustomed to use in their embroidery. But they were available in a much wider range of colors. They were sewn to the basic skin or cloth material by taking stitches between every second or third bead, giving the finished beadwork a neat, flat appearance. It wasn't long before other Piegan women were imitating this new style of beadwork. By the middle eighties the earlier "big beads" were rarely employed except in the decoration of women's dresses. The Indian wives of white men have also been credited with introducing new beadwork designs— fine-line curved motifs and floral patterns. These, too, were admired and copied by most other Blackfoot Indian beadworkers.

So popular had seed beads and the new designs become by the middle eighties that the younger generation of beaders began

[3] Data from Blackfeet Agency Ration Rolls of 1887, in the Blackfeet Archives, Museum of the Plains Indian.

to lose interest in porcupine quillwork. Very few girls bothered to learn the quillworker's craft.

Other traditional crafts were becoming decadent for other reasons. Government issue of cheap tin plates, cups, knives, and forks made it unnecessary for the Indians to fashion wooden bowls or horn cups and spoons. The issuance of strong, white men's stock saddles rendered the more picturesque but weaker Indian-made saddles obsolete. The solid-colored trade blanket replaced the buffalo robe both as an outer garment and as a bed covering. Not until collectors of ethnological specimens began to encourage veterans of the intertribal wars to record their war deeds on skins (in the 1890's) was there a slight revival of the decadent old art of robe painting. However, owners of painted lodges readily transferred their religious symbols from worn buffalo-skin tipi covers to new canvas ones.

For a few years after the buffalo were gone, restless young men continued to raise small war parties to raid enemy camps in quest of horses. In 1881–82 a serious mange epidemic killed many Piegan-owned horses. Agent Young estimated that "about half of the horses these Indians owned died."[4] Young men, set afoot as a result of this plague, redoubled their efforts to obtain mounts in traditional forays against the Crows, Crees, and Assiniboins. But times had changed for horse raiders also. They had to leave home secretly at night to avoid being caught and detained by their own Indian Police. On their outward journeys they could find little to eat. Sometimes they went without food for days. Sometimes they begged some food from the ranch houses of white cattlemen. They were lucky indeed if they could kill an antelope or a few rabbits. If they did reach an enemy camp and run off some horses, they risked being overtaken on their way home by troops from Fort Shaw or Fort Assiniboine and having their stolen horses taken from them. Even after they reached home, the horses might be confiscated by the Indian Police.

The "medicine line" continued to serve as a convenient escape

[4] Reports of the Commissioner of Indian Affairs, 1882, 100.

hatch for Canadian and American horse raiders, who crossed the line, stole a few Indian or white men's horses, and drove them home. A considerable part of the agent's time was spent in hearing complaints of settlers who had been robbed of their horses.

Nor were the Blackfoot tribes alone in continuing their old pastime of horse raiding. Their old enemies, the Crow Indians, remained very active. In the summer of 1886 they ran off some two to three hundred horses belonging to the Piegans in Montana. Again the following summer, ten Crow Indians stole forty-four Indian-owned horses and two agency-owned ones on the Blackfeet Reservation. But the Piegans had adopted a tribal horse brand by means of which the Crow Indian agent could identify and recover a number of the stolen animals.[5]

One of the last Piegan horse raids was also one of their most daring and spectacular ones. White Quiver, the cleverest of all Blackfoot horse thieves, took about fifty horses from the Crow Indians. On his way home he was apprehended by United States authorities, who confiscated the herd. Undismayed, White Quiver restole the horses from the whites and drove them north into Canada. There the Mounted Police took his horses from him. But White Quiver refused to give up. He recaptured most of the Crow horses from the vigilant "Red Coats" and drove them back across the border to his Montana home.

Horse raiding virtually ended in 1887. In his annual report that summer, Agent Baldwin stated that "not a single instance of horse stealing has occurred during the past year."[6] Nevertheless, as late as August 17, 1892, the notorious White Quiver stood trial before the Court of Indian Offenses on charges of horse stealing. The brief record of the proceedings noted: "White Quiver, having turned over to Little Dog, Capt. of Police, the 4 horses alleged to have been stolen from the Crow Indians, the Court released him for lack of sufficient evidence."[7]

[5] Agent Baldwin correspondence, July 1, 1886, to February 14, 1889, in Letter Book, the Blackfeet Archives.
[6] Reports of the Commissioner of Indian Affairs, 1888, 152.

Like many another war veteran, White Quiver had difficulty adjusting to the monotony of peacetime living. Police records show that he was repeatedly arrested and jailed for drunkenness until, in 1897, this very able man was given a sergeant's uniform and enrolled in the Indian Police.

For four long years the hapless Piegans remained huddled together in their little band camps on Badger and Birch creeks on the far southern portion of their huge reservation. Their economic progress was painfully slow, slower in fact than that of any other tribes in Montana. Drought, strong winds, and late spring and early fall frosts discouraged their meager efforts at tilling the soil. In 1886 their agent reported "quite a number of potato patches" cultivated by the Indians. But the total farming effort of more than two thousand Indians amounted to but twelve acres.[8] Obviously, these former big game hunters derived little satisfaction from grubbing in the dirt.

While the individual Indians owned no cattle, the agency herd of about five hundred head proved a tempting target for adventurous meat-loving Indians, who found they could kill a cow or steer and get away with both meat and hide before the herder discovered them. Agent Allen reported that "many cattle have been lost in that way."[9] Occasionally, young Indians killed a steer belonging to a white rancher south of the reservation. They justified their action by saying that the whites had killed a great many of their buffalo. Why shouldn't they kill a few of the white men's cattle?

Meanwhile, white cattlemen cast envious eyes on the great expanse of reservation grassland unused by the Indians. On February 25, 1884, Delegate Maginnis introduced into the House of Representatives a bill which was intended to reduce the area of the reservation and throw the ceded portion open to settlement. But the Commissioner of Indian Affairs objected to the

[7] Journal of Indian Police, 1890–1895, the Blackfeet Archives.
[8] Reports of the Commissioner of Indian Affairs, 1885, 118.
[9] *Ibid.*

bill on the ground that a land cession should be negotiated with the Indians in the field.[10]

On May 15, 1886, Congress authorized the appointment of the Northwest Commission to negotiate with the Sioux, Assiniboin, Gros Ventre, and Blackfoot Indians of Montana for the cession of "so much of their land as they do not require, in order to obtain the means to enable them to become self-supporting, as a pastoral and agricultural people, and to educate their children in the paths of civilization."[11]

After completing negotiations with the tribes farther east, the commissioners proceeded, under abominable weather conditions, toward the Blackfoot Agency. Traveling through snow as much as two feet deep, in temperatures as low as fifty degrees below zero, it took them sixteen days to make the last one hundred miles from Sun River northward to the agency. They arrived at the agency on February 8, 1887, to find that "the Indians had been tampered with by designing white men whom we found at the Agency—men who hoped to gain some advantage to themselves, in one way or another." Prompted by these men, the chiefs demanded $3,000,000 for their surplus lands. This was much more than the commissioners believed they were authorized to offer. Finally, "after long and patient reasoning with them," the Indians agreed to accept $150,000 per year for ten years.[12]

On February 11, an agreement was signed by the commissioners, by chiefs White Calf and Three Suns (Big Nose), and by 220 other adult males of the Piegan tribe. Elderly Indians who, as young men, affixed their marks to this paper, referred to it in their conversations with me as "when we sold the Sweet Grass Hills." Although the eastern boundary between the Piegans and their Gros Ventre neighbors had been indefinite, the Piegans considered the Sweet Grass Hills the most prominent landmark in

[10] Commissioner of Indian Affairs to Secretary of Interior, April 3, 1884, Indian Office Records.

[11] Kappler, *Indian Affairs, Laws and Treaties*, I, 261–62.

[12] Report of Negotiations of the Commissioners, February 11, 1887. Special Case No. 144, Indian Office Records.

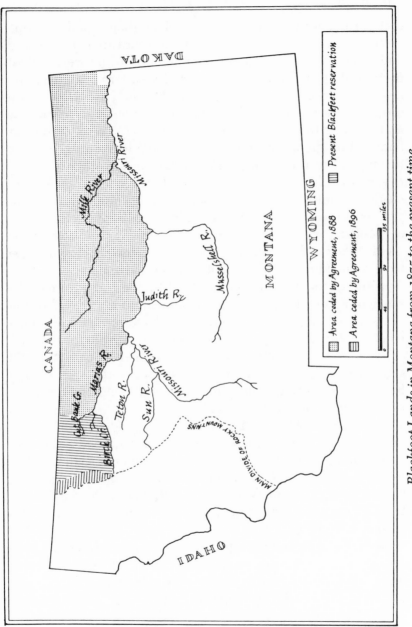

Blackfoot Lands in Montana from 1875 to the present time.

that portion of the ceded area over which their buffalo hunting parties used to roam. The Blackfeet Reservation established under the terms of this agreement comprised the westernmost portion of their former reservation. Its eastern boundary followed the main channel of Cut Bank Creek, from its mouth upstream for a distance of twenty miles, thence in a line due northward to the Canadian boundary. The new reservation was bounded on the north by the international line, on the west by the summit of the Rockies, and on the south by Birch Creek. It was still a large area in proportion to the number of Indians residing upon it. Its 1,760,000 acres provided an equivalent of 775 acres for each man, woman, and child among the Piegans of Montana. When their agent stated that "this reservation gives them sufficient land for all their wants," his conclusion must have sounded reasonable to both whites and Indians.[13]

In return for the land relinquished by the Indians, the government agreed to spent $150,000 annually for a period of ten years to purchase livestock, agricultural and mechanical implements, goods, clothing, and subsistence, to provide for the education of the Indian children, to furnish medical care, to build a new agency, schools, and shops, to assist the Indians in building homes and enclosing their farms, and "to promote their civilization, comfort and improvement."

As an incentive to Indian industry, the agreement further provided that in the distribution of livestock, goods, clothing, agricultural implements, and the like, "preference shall be given to Indians who endeavor by honest labor to support themselves, and especially to those who in good faith undertake the cultivation of the soil or engage in pastoral pursuits as a means of obtaining a livelihood."[14]

Congress approved the agreement on May 1, 1888. That very spring some of the Piegan bands, encouraged by the government's promise to reward industry, moved northward from Badger Creek. They broke 150 acres of land on Two Medicine River

[13] Reports of the Commissioner of Indian Affairs, 1888, 150.
[14] Ibid., 1888, 302–19. Contains full text of this agreement.

and about 70 acres on Cut Bank Creek, and planted oats, potatoes, and barley.[15] The old Indian pattern of residence in bands began to give way to the rural white man's practice of individual family residence. The Indian families built their homes along the streams near water and timber.

A delegation of Piegan leaders traveled to Washington and asked the Great White Father to spend a goodly portion of their new annuities for cattle and large horses. In 1890 some one thousand heifers and twenty-five bulls were issued, and the Piegans got their start as cattlemen. Many of them who had shown no interest in farming found herding cattle enjoyable work. It wasn't unlike caring for horses. More cattle were distributed in subsequent years. By 1896 there were more than five hundred different brands on the reservation stock book. The Great Northern Railway, which was built across the center of the reservation in the early nineties, offered a ready outlet to market for the Indians' cattle. In 1895 they shipped $30,000 worth of prime beef steers to Chicago. By 1896 the Indians were operating two hundred mowing machines to cut wild hay for winter cattle feed.[16]

During the late eighties and early nineties large stallions were given owners of Indian ponies to breed with their small mares in order to obtain stronger farm animals capable of pulling a plow or a wagon. The fullbloods could not forget that their people used to measure a man's wealth in horses. They counted their colts sired by big Morgan stallions as they were born to their Indian pony mares. The little Indian pony was disappearing, but the Indians' horse herds were increasing rapidly. Some men specialized in horses of particular colors and bragged of their hundreds of whites, browns, or pintos. Owl Child, one of the most successful Piegan stockmen of this period, was very proud of his large horse herd. He owned nearly five hundred head of cattle, worth much more than his horses, but he never mentioned them in his bragging.

Five hundred wagons were issued to the Piegans in the early

15 *Ibid.*, 1888, 151.
16 *Ibid.*, 1896, 176–77.

nineties. They were light, thin-spoked vehicles, poorly suited to rough usage over rock-strewn plains and deeply rutted wagon trails. They seemed always to be breaking down. So Indian women clung to the old horse travois in preference to the new-fangled four-wheeled box which they called "something that rolls."

During the late eighties and early nineties the Indian home rapidly evolved from the canvas-covered tipi to the small, round-log cabin with dirt floor and roof of pine poles covered with earth, to the hewn-log cabin, to the neat clapboard house with wood floor and shingled roof. By the late nineties the most prosperous Indian cattlemen were living in multiple-room frame houses, while poor families still occupied one-room dirt-floored cabins.

The everyday clothing of these Indians also changed during this period, particularly in men's wear. In the early eighties men had worn cloth shirts, breechclouts, and leggings. Even in 1887 the only men who wore coats and trousers were the Indian Police and some of the chiefs.[17] During the nineties most of the younger men discarded their leggings and breechclouts in favor of what the Indian Service called "citizen's dress"—coat and trousers. But many Indians found white men's shoes stiff, confining, and uncomfortable. Consequently, the moccasin survived as a common article of adult Blackfoot footgear long after these people adopted white men's body clothing.

While Washington authorities had talked glibly during the eighties of education as the primary civilizing agent for Indians, the Piegans continued to suffer from lack of school facilities. As late as 1889 their agent was trying to squeeze ten boys and twenty-two girls into a schoolroom intended for only sixteen pupils. Yet the school-age population of the reservation numbered 350. Thus, less than 10 per cent of the children could receive the advantages of schooling on their own reservation.[18] For several years some children had been sent across the Rockies

[17] Grinnell, *Blackfoot Lodge Tales*, 293.
[18] Reports of the Commissioner of Indian Affairs, 1889, 223.

to the Catholic school at St. Ignatius Mission. Some of them were among the forty-five children who comprised the first Blackfoot students to be sent to the famous Carlisle Indian School in Pennsylvania in 1889.

In the next three years opportunities for schooling increased rapidly. In September, 1890, the new Holy Family Mission School opened on Two Medicine River with accommodations for one hundred pupils. In 1892 a new government industrial school was opened at the former military post of Fort Shaw on Sun River and sixty Piegan children were enrolled. And that same year a new boarding school was opened on Willow Creek, west of present Browning. By 1894 three-quarters of the children of school age were in school.

The Indian boarding school took upon itself the difficult task of impressing upon the Indian child the superiority of the white man's values. Learning to be "civilized" meant learning a host of little things—to comb one's hair, to wear a coat, trousers, and shoes, to sit in a chair and sleep in a bed, to use a knife and fork, to tell time, and much more. In McGuffey's classic graded readers, the Indian child was exposed to the white man's strange code of ethics as he learned to read. As he progressed through the grades, he thrilled to *Robinson Crusoe* and *Swiss Family Robinson*. The Indian boy learned to milk a cow, to drive a team of horses, to build a fence, to care for livestock, and to plant, cultivate, and harvest crops. The girl learned to cook strange foods, to launder clothes, make dresses, and perform general housework according to the white housewife's standards. Both boys and girls learned to honor the American flag and to appreciate the symbolism of such great national holidays as the Fourth of July, George Washington's birthday, Christmas, and Easter. Thus, the work of civilizing Indian children required much more than constant drill in the three R's. It required painstaking indoctrination in the basic fundamentals of the white man's culture.

The task of civilizing adult men and women was much more difficult. Blackfoot agents had received very little assistance from Christian missionaries. In 1890 the census estimated that "5 per cent of these Indians are Roman Catholics and the others are sun worshipers."[19] Not until three years later was a permanent Protestant mission established on the reservation. Then Rev. and Mrs. Dutcher built a Methodist church on Willow Creek near the boarding school.

Meanwhile, some of the agents charged with the difficult task of reporting the Indians' progress toward civilization were not satisfied with the results they could obtain by example and persuasion alone. They offered bribes or threatened punishments in their efforts to destroy the symbols of the Indians' savage life which were distasteful to them. Disregarding the time-honored American principle of freedom of religion, they directed their attack primarily against the Indians' tribal ceremonial, the sun dance. In 1887 Agent Baldwin ordered members of the Indian Police not to participate in or to encourage this ceremony. He exacted a pledge of each Indian who received a brood mare from the government that he would take no part in the sun dance. Consequently, there was no sun dance the following summer.[20] Major Baldwin also pointed with pride to the fact that he had required all members of the Indian Police to cut their hair and to "abstain from the objectionable habit of painting their faces."[21] Friends of the Indians prevailed upon Washington officials to remove this hostile agent.

Yet, six years later, Captain Lorenzo Cook, another strict disciplinarian, ordered two sun dance lodges used in previous years to be torn down and the timbers used for erecting branding corrals. He prohibited not only the sun dance but "Indian mourning, beating the tom-tom, gambling, and wearing Indian costumes" as well. And he tried to discourage "less pernicious practices such as horse racing." Captain Cook even asked the traders not to stock the paints Indians used for painting their faces.[22] Short

[19] *Report of Indians Taxed and Not Taxed*, U. S. Bureau of Census, 360.

[20] Reports of the Commissioner of Indian Affairs, 1888, 151–52.

[21] Mark D. Baldwin to Commissioner of Indian Affairs, August 1, 1886, Indian Office Records.

[22] Reports of the Commissioner of Indian Affairs, 1894, 159.

Face, one of my elderly informants, recalled that this unsympathetic agent sentenced Indians who cut off their fingers in mourning or built a sweat lodge to thirty days in jail. He even threatened to jail women who did beadwork.

Such efforts to force the Indians to abandon their traditional ceremonies and customs served only to rouse the Indians' resentment. After the persecuting agents were replaced, the Piegans resumed the forbidden practices with even greater zeal. Under less hostile agents they revived and continued the sun dance, making only one concession to the interests of the whites. They moved the ceremony ahead several weeks so it would coincide with the white man's July 4 holiday season. In 1900 boys were playing hooky from Willow Creek School to visit the picturesque sun dance encampment near by.[23]

Often visitors from neighboring tribes formerly hostile to the Blackfeet visited the sun dance encampment. These visits were accompanied by exchanges of gifts between the visitors and their hosts. The Assiniboins from the east gave the Piegans shiny catlinite pipe bowls, beautifully made buckskin suits decorated with porcupine quillwork, and breastplates and necklaces of bone hairpipes. Piegan women admired the feather designs employed in Assiniboin quillwork and copied them in their own beadwork. The Assiniboins also gave some Piegan men flowing feather bonnets of the Sioux type, which became very popular with Blackfoot leaders for ceremonial wear and for dress-parade headgear. By the turn of the century, some Piegan men were making these bonnets as skillfully as the Sioux craftsmen. The traditional straight-up bonnet of the Blackfeet was becoming obsolete.

From the Assiniboins in the mid-nineties the Piegans also acquired the grass dance, a lively, young men's social dance with its associated paraphernalia of deer hair roaches and hawk bells which jingled merrily as the dancers cavorted.

Friendly Crow Indians gave the Piegans moccasins and pendants of human hair which could be worn by a short-haired In-

[23] *Ibid.*, 1900, 267.

dian on dress occasions to create the impression that his hair
was long. The Crows also transferred one of their sacred ceremonies, which the Piegans called the "Crow Water Beaver Ceremony." It became so popular that the Montana Piegans taught
it to their North Piegan relatives in Canada in 1905.[24]

From west of the Rockies, the formerly hostile Flatheads, Kutenais, and Nez Percés brought cornhusk-and-yarn flat pouches
and many well-dressed deerskins and elk hides. In return, the
Piegans gave their western friends beautifully beaded men's
suits and women's dresses. Piegan women readily acknowledged
the superior skill of the Flatheads and Kutenais in dressing skins.
By the turn of the century they were obtaining the great majority of the skins employed in their own craftwork in trade or
by gift from those overmountain tribes. Very few Piegan women
bothered to continue the arduous labor of fleshing, scraping, and
softening buckskin.

It was like old times for the Piegans to gather for a few weeks
in summer, set up their tipis, take off their white men's somber
garments and don their colorful Indian clothes, paint their faces,
gamble on horse races and in the stick game, enjoy social dances,
and, above all, to experience once again the religious stimulation
of the great tribal sun dance. Women made handsome costumes
for their menfolk and other fine craftwork for presents to visitors
from other tribes. Their rivalry as craftswomen was no less keen
than was that of their menfolk, who bragged of their fine herds
of horses and their success as cattlemen.

After the Indians spread out along the valleys of their reservation, many of them found it inconvenient to travel south to
Badger Creek for their weekly rations. The agent found his
headquarters poorly located for administering to the needs of
his far-flung Indians. His agency had become an obsolete stockade of rotting logs. So in 1894 the agent and chiefs selected a
new site nearer the center of the reservation, on Willow Creek,
some two miles from the new railroad. There twenty-two new

---

[24] McClintock, *The Old North Trail*, 407–10. Describes this ceremony at the
time of its transfer to the North Piegans.

buildings were erected, among them a hospital and a modern slaughterhouse. The new agency was occupied in the spring of 1895.

In the early nineties the Blackfoot agent was constantly bothered by white prospectors who were invading the westernmost portion of the reservation in search of precious minerals, and by Indians who complained that these whites were stealing their gold. This mountainous area was of little value to the Indians for grazing or farming. Agent George Steel, in 1893, recommended that the mountainous strip be sold and the proceeds placed to the credit of the Indians as an additional fund for their support and maintenance.[25]

During the month of September, 1895, three commissioners met with the Indians on the Blackfeet Reservation to negotiate an agreement for the sale of this western strip. They found the Indian leaders again asked $3,000,000 for the strip of land the whites wanted. They offered $1,250,000. A compromise was finally reached in which the Indians were allowed $1,500,000 in addition to the right to hunt, fish, and cut timber in the mountainous area as long as it remained public lands of the United States. The provisions of this agreement were very similar to those of the treaty negotiated in 1887. In effect, they provided a continuation of government expenditures at the rate of $150,-000 per year for another decade after the expiration of the payments under the terms of the previous agreement.

The agreement acknowledged that the Blackfeet Reservation was "wholly unfit for agriculture," but since the Indians demonstrated their ability to raise cattle, "and there is every probability that they will become self-supporting by attention to this industry," the whole reservation was to be held by these Indians as a communal grazing tract during the period of the agreement.[26]

When the ceded strip was opened to prospectors under the

[25] Reports of the Commissioner of Indian Affairs, 1893, 173.
[26] Kappler, *Indian Affairs, Laws and Treaties,* I, 604–609. Contains full text of this agreement.

mineral-land laws in mid-April, 1898, more than five hundred whites searched the valleys on the eastern slope of the Rockies, hoping to strike it rich. But they found no gold and very little other precious mineral. The gold rush to these former Blackfoot lands proved a dismal disappointment.[27] Today much of this land is included in Glacier National Park.

Between the years 1887 and 1900, the Blackfoot Indians in Montana made greater progress toward civilization than in any other period of equal duration in their history. A few comparisons of figures from the annual reports of the Commissioner of Indian Affairs for 1886 and 1900 clearly portray the extent of this progress:

	1886	1900
Number of Indians who can read	18	900
Number who wear citizens dress	40	2,085°
Horses and mules owned by Indians	1,205	22,004
Cattle owned by Indians	0	12,000
Acres cultivated by Indians	12	500
Bushels oats, barley, rye harvested	30	700
Bushels vegetables harvested	100	3,700
Tons of hay cut	170	6,000

° All.

In 1886 the primitive Blackfeet had not recovered from the double shock of the disappearance of their staff of life, the buffalo, and the prolonged period of starvation following the extermination of that animal. They had neither the knowledge nor the resources to make a living in the white man's world.

Even though their reservation area was twice reduced during this period, these Indians still owned a large area in proportion to their numbers. The 2,085 Indians on the Blackfeet Reservation still owned in common nearly 1,500,000 acres. Furthermore, this was good land—some of the finest grazing land in the United States. The Indians were demonstrating their willingness to work at a task which they enjoyed, the raising of cattle and horses.

[27] Reports of the Commissioner of Indian Affairs, 1898, 182.

At the turn of the century these Indians were still receiving weekly rations. But their valiant struggle and their solid accomplishments in the recent past caused competent officials to be very optimistic regarding their future. James H. Monteith, their agent, confidently predicted, "As to this particular tribe, it can with proper management be made self-supporting in a few years."[28]

[28] *Ibid.,* 1900, 265.

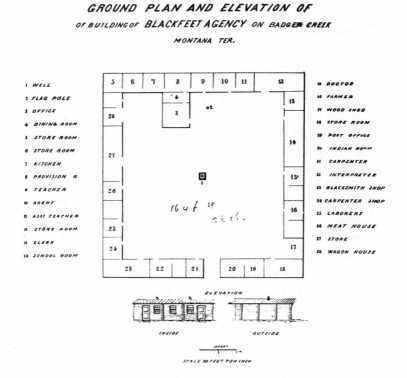

18: Learning to Walk Alone

Gᴇᴏʀɢᴇ ʙɪʀᴅ ɢʀɪɴɴᴇʟʟ, one of the Blackfoot Indians' staunchest friends, told them in council in the year 1895, "If you are helped for ten years . . . you will not then want any more help. You will learn to walk alone like the white man; the only difference will be the color of the skin."[1]

This philosophy dominated the thinking of white men who planned and administered government policies for the Blackfeet Reservation in the early years of the present century. Knowing that the Blackfeet had made remarkable economic progress since the late eighties, they assumed this progress would continue at an accelerated pace in the years ahead. The Indian population of the reservation appeared to be relatively static. In fact, the Bureau of the Census, in reporting its findings in 1910, took pains to point out that the 2,268 Indians then living on the Blackfeet Reservation in Montana little exceeded the number residing there a quarter of a century earlier.[2] The planners assumed that when the tribal lands were divided equally among these Indians, each would receive enough land to provide him a good living as a farmer or stockman. Then surely the Indian would "learn to walk alone like the white man."

In that paternalistic system of Indian administration, it was always assumed that the Great White Father knew what was

[1] Proceedings of the Commissioners, Blackfeet Land Agreement, Doc. No. 51 (1895), 494, Indian Office Records.

[2] *Indian Population in the United States and Alaska, 1910,* U. S. Bureau of Census, 75.

best for his children. The Indian agent, not the chiefs, would be the Moses who would lead his children out of the bondage of ignorance and poverty into the promised land of knowledge and prosperity. There was no place in that system for the traditional pattern of Indian leadership. Consequently, the position of head chief was abandoned after the death of White Calf in 1903. Indian achievement of a way of life like that of rural whites was the goal toward which the planners were striving. That many of the Indians, especially the fullbloods, cherished attitudes, beliefs, and customs which were quite unlike those of whites did not seem important to the policy makers of the time.

Many factors conspired to impede the Indians' progress toward the goal set for them. Elaborate and costly programs devised by whites failed to rouse the interest and co-operation of Indians who were supposed to benefit from them. Frequent changes in agents provided fitful and sometimes very weak local leadership, while white men covetous of the Indians' land exploited this weakness to gain possession of some of the best land on the reservation. Finally, the vagaries of the weather—prolonged summer droughts and harsh winter storms—nullified the best laid plans of men.

During the first decade of this century irrigation came to be regarded as the magic formula for the agricultural development of the low rainfall areas of the west. Oblivious to the fact that the Blackfoot Indians had shown little desire to make their living by growing crops, the planners embarked upon the construction of extensive irrigation projects on their Montana reservation in 1908. For several years hundreds of Indian men found employment on these construction projects. Even though much of the equipment was strange to them, they learned to use it and did well in their work. They enjoyed working for regular daily wages. But when the projects were completed, very few Indians could be induced to farm the irrigated lands. When Frank Knox, a member of the Board of Indian Commissioners, visited the Blackfeet Reservation in 1926, he found that Indians were farming only 306 acres, or a little over 1 per cent of the 21,341 acres that had been brought into these projects at a cost of more than $1,100,000. He termed the irrigation experiment on the Blackfeet Reservation "a monument to the unthinking enthusiasm with which this country 20 years ago embarked upon its reclamation projects."[3] It was no less of a monument to the futility of planning the economic future of the Indians without regard for the Indians' own habits and desires.

Prior to 1907 the Blackfoot Indians owned the land on their Montana reservation in common. Then, in keeping with the national policy of placing Indians upon individually owned lands, Congress ordered the reservation to be surveyed and land allotted to each member of the tribe. Allotment proceeded slowly. In the year 1912 it was completed. Each of the 2,623 Indians living on the reservation during the allotment period had received 320 acres, held in trust for him by the government. Each Indian was given the option of receiving 40 acres of irrigable land and 280 acres of grazing land, or of taking his entire 320 acres in grazing land. The persistent prejudice of many Indians against farming was again demonstrated by their avoidance of lands within the irrigated projects.[4]

By the middle-teens it was becoming clear to the planners, as it had been to their predecessors two decades earlier, that the Blackfeet Reservation was better adapted to the raising of livestock than for farming. A considerable number of the progressive mixed-bloods and some of the fullbloods were prospering as cattlemen. But the unprogressive and the shiftless, as well as the aged and physically handicapped, leased their allotted lands to white stockmen and tried to live on their meager returns in lease money. To encourage the able-bodied men of this latter group to raise cattle on their own land, the government purchased 1,888 head of cattle to form a tribal herd. But the fullbloods, who had always considered livestock in terms of individual possessions, showed little interest in the tribal herd. They acted as if it belonged to someone else. As an object lesson in

[3] Reports of the Board of Indian Commissioners, 1926, 30.
[4] Reports of the Commissioner of Indian Affairs, 1912, 59.

stock raising and as an incentive to cattle raising among the less ambitious fullbloods, this experiment was a failure, even during the few years that it was a financial success.[5]

For a brief period during World War I, when cattle prices were high, the reservation cattlemen prospered. In 1918 the Blackfoot Indians led those of most other western reservations in the purchase of Liberty Bonds. Then disaster struck. Two years of summer drought withered the crops in the fields. No hay could be cut for winter feed. The reservation range became overstocked. When the dry summer of 1919 was followed by one of the severest winters on record, thousands of weak, under-fed cattle and horses froze to death. White settlers on lands in northern Montana suffered along with the Indians. Many of them abandoned their homes and sought employment elsewhere. But the Indians had no other place to go. They were wiped out.

By 1920 most of the Blackfoot Indians had little left but their land. And some of them had lost even that. Two years before, authority had been granted to convert the trust patents of those Indians who were declared competent to fee patents, which would permit landholders to sell or otherwise dispose of their land. These patents were issued to debt-ridden, illiterate Indians, who became easy prey for white land-seekers, who acquired some of the best land on the reservation at a fraction of its value. When Walter W. Liggett investigated the affairs of the Blackfeet Reservation for the Committee on Indian Affairs of the United States Senate a decade later, he reported that "210,000 acres of land formerly owned by the Indians has passed into the possession of white men after the Indians were granted fee patents. . . . There is no doubt at all that scores of these patents were issued illegally to Indians incompetent in fact as well as in the eyes of the law. In nearly every case the issuance of the patent meant that the Indian was defrauded of his land."[6]

Liggett learned that these land frauds were but the culmina-

---

[5] Reports of the Board of Indian Commissioners, 1918, 28.
[6] *Survey of Conditions of Indians in the United States*, 70 Cong., 2 sess., *Senate Resolution No. 79*, 12747–48.

tion of a decade of weak and ineffective local administration of Indian affairs: "No less than seven different individuals acted as superintendents from 1910 to 1921 . . . and no less than three of these superintendents were dismissed from the Indian Service, one later landed in the penitentiary and another hurriedly left Browning to avoid indictment."[7]

When General Hugh L. Scott visited the Blackfoot Reservation in the fall of 1920, he was appalled by the rundown condition of the agency and the poverty of the Indians. The blind and helpless old people were given only twelve pounds of meat, together with a little flour, beans, and coffee for a month's rations.[8] During the winter of 1920–21, two-thirds of the Indians on this reservation were again dependent upon government rations for their daily bread. It was a humiliating experience for men who had prided themselves on their success as stockmen barely two years before. At no time since the starvation winter of 1883–84 had the future of the Blackfoot Indians looked so hopeless.

Then in the spring of 1921 an energetic, sympathetic superintendent took charge. It was no easy task to try to restore the pride and initiative of the discouraged Blackfoot people and to try to interest them in still another economic program. But Frank C. Campbell, accompanied by the agency doctor and farmer, visited every Indian family in its own home and discussed its economic and social problems. Then he inaugurated what became known as the Five-Year Industrial Program for the Blackfeet Reservation. Its beginnings were modest indeed. In the first year about 40 per cent of the Indians were induced to plant vegetable gardens and 25 per cent to plant small fields of grain. With the co-operation of the Indians, Campbell organized the Piegan Farming and Livestock Association, with twenty-nine chapters in the various reservation communities. Several district community houses were built as centers for social life, and an

[7] *Ibid.*, 12748.
[8] Reports of the Board of Indian Commissioners, 1921, 54–57.

annual fair was instituted to encourage improvement in the quality of farm products and of such women's work as home canning, needlework, and beadwork. As the program expanded, a flour mill was built, agricultural machinery purchased in limited quantities, and small numbers of pigs, chickens, and sheep were acquired by individual Indian families.

Prior to Campbell's superintendency, the tribal sun dance encampment had occupied a full month of the Indians' time at a crucial period in early summer when they should have been home tending to their crops or livestock. Campbell was sympathetic toward the Indians' religious traditions, but he was also a practical man. He and the Indians worked out a compromise. Instead of a single tribal sun dance there would be three of them in three districts of the reservation. Each family would attend the ceremony held nearest its home. The encampment would be of a single week's duration. Even then, Big Lodge Pole insisted on bringing his cow, chickens, and pigs to the 1923 encampment in his district, saying that he did not want to neglect his stock, but did not want to miss the sun dance either. Every evening he sent one of his sons on horseback to make sure that his crops were doing all right back home.

The Five-year Program achieved its greatest success among the older and middle-aged fullbloods who took pride in being able to feed themselves and their families through their own labors in small-scale farming operations. The modest accomplishments of some of them were widely publicized. Thus, by the fall of the second year of the Five-year Program, it could be said of Bull Calf, president of the Bull Calf Chapter:

This old man has a married son living on the place with him and they work together. They have three stacks of hay, wheat enough for their flour and for seed; also some oats. They have a good root-house full of potatoes, and other vegetables. They were laying in their winter's supply of wood and had a few loads already hauled.

Another report, on a member of the Bull Shoe Chapter, read:

Ed Running Crane, secretary of the Bull Shoe Chapter, produced 53 sacks of oats. He had a new chicken house and 19
chickens. He also had a small band of sheep and a milk heifer.
He had 37 sacks of potatoes, and some rutabagas, carrots, beets,
etc., in his root-house. He had recently constructed a new outside toilet.[9]

On his visit to the Blackfeet Reservation in August, 1922,
General Scott "was much pleased to find a complete reversal of
the bad conditions which were encountered there two years ago."
He concluded that "Supt. Campbell . . . has awakened the
spirit of the Blackfeet people."[10]

After his inspection of conditions on this reservation in 1925,
Frank Knox was enthusiastic about the results achieved in the
Five-year Program.

Nowhere else in the Indian Service have I encountered among
the Indians themselves a more hopeful, forward-looking spirit,
characterized by self-respect and self-reliance, than that which
I met on this reservation. The application of the same principles
adopted and pursued by Supt. Campbell throughout the Indian
Service would be a God-send, and speedily provide a solution
to most of the perplexities of the service.[11]

Nevertheless, the Five-year Program failed to hold the enthusiasm of the ambitious mixed-bloods on the Blackfeet Reservation itself. One of them told me that he had participated en-
ergetically in the program, but had become discouraged when a
well-meaning official patted him on the back and said, "You're
making fine progress. In ten more years you should be independent." The mixed-bloods were not satisfied just to feed themselves and their families. They wanted farming or livestock

[9] "The Five-Year Program on the Blackfeet Indian Reservation," *The Indian
Leader,* Vol. XXVI, No. 25.
[10] Reports of the Board of Indian Commissioners, 1923, 47.
[11] *Ibid.,* 1926, 29.

operations on a large enough scale to bring them a cash return. They were unhappy with the limited credit provisions of the program, which prevented its rapid expansion. They were impatient with the frequent and time-consuming chapter meetings, which were geared to the understanding of the less sophisticated fullbloods.

In the late twenties the Industrial Program foundered under the growing opposition of the discontented mixed-bloods, the less enthusiastic leadership of Campbell's successors, and the impact of nationwide depression. Many of the younger people preferred the small cash returns from work on federal relief projects to subsistence farming. Agricultural Extension Agent Earl Stinson's report for the year 1934 indicated the official abandonment of the objectives of the Campbell program. At that time only 138 Indians were self-supporting, while 747 families had to be assisted through distribution of rations and relief. The average family income amounted to but $150, exclusive of relief payments. Despairing of the possibility of the Indians' growing grain on a commercial basis, Stinson proclaimed, "Livestock in large enough numbers will be the only way the Blackfeet will ever be self-supporting."[12]

It was in that year of 1934 that Congress passed the Indian Reorganization Act, which provided a new national policy in Indian administration. This new legislation halted the piecemeal disposal of the Indians' land, such as had been taking place on the Blackfeet Reservation since fee patents were issued in 1918. It provided for the conservation of reservation resources in grass, soil, timber, and water. It extended credit to Indian individuals who sought to start or expand livestock or farming operations. And it gave to Indian tribes a voice in the management of their own affairs such as the Blackfeet had not enjoyed since the disappearance of the buffalo half a century earlier.

The Indians on the Blackfeet Reservation were among the first tribes to organize under the provisions of this act. Their

[12] Agricultural Extension Agent's Report, December 31, 1934. (Typescript on file in the Blackfeet Agency.)

new constitution declared that all persons of Indian blood whose names appeared on the official census roll of the tribe as of January 1, 1935, as well as all children born of any blood member of the tribe maintaining legal residence on the reservation at the time of such birth, were considered members of the Blackfeet Tribe. A Tribal Council of thirteen members, elected semi-annually by residents of the various districts or communities on the reservation, was empowered to manage tribal property and money, to regulate law and order on the reservation (except for certain major crimes), to supervise the preservation of reservation wildlife, and to encourage Indian arts and crafts, culture, and traditions.

In spite of continued national economic depression, the condition of the Blackfoot Indians improved under the new Indian policy. Revolving credit loans enabled Blackfoot stockmen to increase their cattle and sheep holdings nearly fourfold between the years 1933 and 1941. By 1943 the average family income among the Blackfeet had risen to $1,320. Seventy-five families had agricultural incomes in excess of $1,500. However, 112 households received direct relief in December of that year. Nearly three-fourths of those families were fullbloods.[13]

During World War II, hundreds of young men and women, descendants of generations of Blackfoot Indian warriors, answered their country's call to service in the armed forces. Before they left the reservation, many of those who enlisted or were drafted were feasted by their relatives while aged veterans of the intertribal wars sang their sacred war songs and prayed for the young men's success. Parents of full-blood servicemen were comforted by the age-old Blackfoot saying, "It is better for a man to be killed in battle than to die of old age or sickness." Those who remained at home purchased war bonds, formed an active War Mothers' Club, and performed the sacred sun dance in honor of their loved ones whose lives were in danger overseas.

Blackfoot Indians served with distinction beside non-Indian

[13] Freal H. McBride, Ten-Year Program for the Blackfeet Indian Agency, 1944. (Mimeographed copy in Museum of the Plains Indian.)

comrades in every major theater of the war. They flew bombing missions over Germany, they helped man destroyers and battle-wagons, they fought with our ground forces in North Africa and on the European continent, and they took part in amphibious operations in the Pacific. They learned many new skills and found they could perform them as well as their non-Indian buddies could.

At the same time, hundreds of other Blackfoot Indians went to work in aircraft plants and shipyards on the West Coast. Their manual skills equaled and in many cases surpassed those of their non-Indian fellow war workers.

Not only did the Blackfoot Indians contribute substantially to our war effort, but in the process some of them developed talents and skills for which there was little demand on the reservation but which helped them to make a good living elsewhere. Since the war the number of Blackfeet living away from the reservation has increased. By 1950 they numbered more than one-third of the tribal population. Among them were skilled workers in manufacturing plants and in the building trades, office workers, salesmen, teachers, and nurses. There is no logical reason why the Blackfoot Indian's selection of a life's work need be limited to a choice between raising livestock or farming.

The educational level of the Blackfoot Indians has been rising in recent years. By 1950 some 125 of them possessed college degrees. One-quarter of the Blackfeet over eighteen years of age had graduated from high school. The 497 who were still unable to read or write and the 112 who could not speak English were nearly all older people of a high degree of Indian blood who were a negligible factor in the working population.[14]

In the period of national prosperity following World War II, the average family income among the Blackfoot Indians continued to rise. By 1950 it stood at $2,639, a figure exceeded among few other Indian tribes in the United States.[15] However, this

[14] *Compilation of Material Relating to the Indians of the United States and Alaska,* U. S. House of Representatives, Serial No. 30, 1950, 736.
[15] *Ibid.,* 736.

index fails to point out the number of Indians who had virtually no earned income, or the number of successful Indians whose earnings from livestock operations or wages far exceeded the family average.

It is difficult to generalize on the subject of Blackfoot Indian economic progress during the first half of the twentieth century. Certainly the rapid progress toward self-support which their white friends prophesied for these Indians at the turn of the century did not materialize. One of the causes for this failure was surely the lack of any consistent government policy for these people. The vacillating policy of alternately encouraging the Indians to farm, then to raise livestock, was confusing to the Indians who participated in these programs. It was not surprising that many of them lost enthusiasm for government-sponsored programs presented as panaceas for their economic ills.

Indians, like other people, vary in individual ability, initiative, and diligence. Some became discouraged as a result of early failures, and lost heart. Others profited from those experiences and tried to work all the harder. So economic success or failure has been more of an individual than a tribal matter. Before the middle of the century, many of the Blackfoot Indians did "learn to walk alone." Many others are no better off economically than were their fathers or grandfathers half a century ago.

The most remarkable trend in the history of these Indians during the first half of this century has been the rapid growth in the mixed-blood element of the population. As recently as 1910, fullbloods comprised a majority of the tribal membership. In the next two decades the numbers of the mixed-bloods nearly doubled, while the full-blood population decreased by more than 15 per cent. By 1930 the mixed-bloods comprised two-thirds of the Indian population of the reservation and nearly three-quarters of the most vigorous portion of that population—those under forty years of age.[16] By mid-century the mixed-bloods numbered 85 per cent of the tribal membership of nearly six

[16] *The Indian Population of the United States and Alaska, 1930*, U. S. Bureau of Census, 73, 76.

thousand souls.[17] Their numbers were increasing at a rate several times higher than that of the national population as a whole. Meanwhile, the full-blood population continued to decline. They numbered 903 in 1950, less than 80 per cent of their total forty years earlier.

This rapid rise of the racially marginal mixed-bloods greatly accelerated the processes of acculturation among the majority of members of the tribe. Many of them were brought up in homes in which the English language was spoken and where the father could read and write. When they went to school, they were prepared to take advantage of their educational opportunities. Their experience with white men's values both at home and in school caused them to think and act more like whites than Indians. Traditional Indian customs held little appeal for many of them.

Better housed, better fed on a more adequate and more varied diet, better observers of the fundamental rules of sanitation, the mixed-bloods have been physically stronger than the fullbloods and better able to resist disease.

Better educated, the mixed-bloods have been better prepared to accept a greater variety of employment requiring specialized skills, understanding of written instructions, and legal contracts. Neither by name nor by physical features do many of these people reveal their Indian ancestry. They have not encountered the anti-Indian prejudice that has handicapped fullbloods in obtaining and holding permanent jobs in predominantly white off-reservation communities.

It is not surprising that members of this more progressive, acculturated mixed-blood majority have dominated the Tribal Council on the Blackfeet Reservation. Nor is it surprising that the fullbloods should feel that their interests have not been adequately represented in the council of their tribe.

The fullbloods, particularly the middle-aged and older members of this faction, have fallen farther and farther behind the

[17] *Compilation of Material Relating to the Indians of the United States and Alaska*, U. S. House of Representatives, Serial No. 30, 1950, 736.

ambitious, aggressive mixed-bloods. Reared in conservative homes where both parents spoke little or no English, many of them had difficulty in comprehending their white school teachers. They were embarrassed by their slow progress in comparison with their mixed-blood classmates and dropped out of school at an early age, qualified for no employment other than that of unskilled laborers. Most of the fullbloods were poorly housed, poorly fed on a limited diet of meat, bread, and coffee, and knew little of the basic rules of sanitation. Tuberculosis was so prevalent among the fullbloods in 1905 that the agency physician feared it might lead to their extinction.[18] Deaths from this disease have declined, but tuberculosis still takes a heavy toll of the lives of the fullbloods and others with a high degree of Indian blood. Many of these people have been handicapped by trachoma and plagued by ill health. Yet they have preferred to entrust their lives to the traditional medicine man rather than to call upon the agency doctor.

Among the fullbloods and those of a high degree of Indian blood who have been raised in conservative homes are found the skilled workers in traditional crafts, the owners of medicine bundles, and the participants and leaders in the sun dance. Many of them may be readily recognized by their moccasined feet, their long, braided hair, and their red-painted faces. Although the ranks of these true conservatives have been diminishing, their number has been augmented by adult fullbloods who have tried to follow the white man's way but have lost heart as they approached or reached middle age.

These fullbloods, who have become a small minority among their own people, are fiercely proud of their race. They regard themselves as the *real* Blackfoot Indians—the true descendants of the great warriors and wise leaders of old and the preservers of all that is left of Blackfoot Indian culture.

[18] Reports of the Commissioner of Indian Affairs, 1905, 237.

Bibliography

1. UNPUBLISHED MATERIALS

Agricultural Extension Agents' Reports, 1932–1943. (Typescript copies on file at the Blackfeet Agency, Browning, Montana.)

Ashby, S. C. Reminiscences on the Indian Trade of the 1860's. (Manuscript in Montana Historical Society Library, Helena, Montana.)

Bent, George. Letters to George E. Hyde on Cheyenne Indian History. (In the possession of George E. Hyde, Omaha, Nebraska.)

The Blackfeet Agency Archives. (Agents' Letter-books and miscellaneous papers from the old files of the Blackfeet Agency, in the Museum of the Plains Indian, Browning, Montana.)

Bradley, James H. (The Bradley Manuscript in Montana Historical Society Library, Helena, Montana. Published in part in Montana Historical Society *Contributions,* Vols. II, III, VIII, IX.)

Ewers, John C. Piegan and Blood Field Notes, 1941–44, 1947, 1951.

Hatch, E. A. C. Diary, June 7–October 15, 1856. (Typescript copy in Montana Historical Society Library, Helena, Montana.)

Lewis, H. P. Bison Kills of Montana. (Typescript copy in Missouri River Basin Archaeological Survey Offices, Lincoln, Nebraska.)

McBride, Freal H. Ten-year Program for the Blackfeet Indian Agency. 1944. Ed. by John C. Ewers. (Mimeographed copy in Museum of the Plains Indian, Browning, Montana.)

Mackay, James. Indian Notes. (Manuscript in Missouri Historical Society Library, St. Louis, Mo.)

United States Office of Indian Affairs Records. The National Archives, Washington, D. C. (Manuscripts include reports and correspondence of Blackfoot Indian agents with the Commissioner of Indian Affairs since 1855; proceedings of Treaty and Land Agreement Councils; copies of the unratified Blackfoot Treaties and of the Land Agreements; and miscellaneous papers bearing upon official relations with the Blackfeet.)

2. FEDERAL DOCUMENTS

Annual Reports of the Board of Indian Commissioners, 1870–1926.

Annual Reports of the Commissioner of Indian Affairs, 1854–1912.

Congressional Globe, March 10, 1870.

Congressional Record, January 6, 1885.

Kappler, Charles J. (ed.). *Indian Affairs, Laws and Treaties,* 57 Cong., 1 sess., *Senate Document 452.* 3 vols. Washington, 1903.

Pacific Railroad Report of Explorations and Surveys to Ascertain the Most Practicable and Economical Route from a Railroad from the Mississippi River to the Pacific Ocean, 1853–1855. 12 vols. Washington, 1860.

Twining, W. J. "Report of Capt. W. J. Twining, Chief Astronomer and Surveyor," in *Reports Upon the Survey of the Boundary between the United States and the Possessions of Great Britain from the Lake of the Woods to the Summit of the Rocky Mountains.* Washington, 1878.

U. S. Bureau of the Census. *Report of Indians Taxed and Not Taxed. Eleventh Census Report.* Washington, 1894.

———. *Indian Population in the United States and Alaska, 1910. Thirteenth Census Report.* Washington, 1915.

———. *Indian Population of the United States and Alaska, 1930. Fifteenth Census Report.* Washington, 1937.

U. S. House of Representatives. *Compilation of Material Relating to the Indians of the United States and the Territory of Alaska, Including Certain Laws and Treaties Affecting Such Indians.* Subcommittee on Indian Affairs. Serial No. 30. Washington, 1950.

———. *Piegan Indians.* 41 Cong., 2 sess., *Executive Document 269,* Serial 1426. Washington, 1870.

U. S. Senate. *Report of the Subcommittee of the Special Committee of the United States Senate Appointed to Visit the Indian Tribes of Northern Montana.* 48 Cong., 1 sess., *Senate Report No. 283.* Washington, 1883.

———. *Survey of Conditions of Indians in the United States.* Hearings

Before a Subcommittee of the Committee of Indian Affairs. 70 Cong., 2 sess., *Senate Resolution 79*, Part 23. Washington, 1933.

3. NEWSPAPERS

Helena Daily Herald, June 15, 1870; January 1, 1880.
Helena Daily Independent, May 22, 1874.
The Montana Post (Virginia City), December 9, 1865; June 9, 1866.
Saskatchewan Herald (Regina), November 3, 1879.
Weekly Independent (Deer Lodge), February 14, 1874.

4. BOOKS AND ARTICLES

Audubon, Maria R. (ed.). *Audubon and his Journals.* 2 vols. New York, 1897.
Bell, Charles N. "The Journal of Henry Kelsey (1691–1692)," The Historical and Scientific Society of Manitoba *Transactions,* No. 4. Winnipeg, 1928.
Bischoff, William N. *The Jesuits in Old Oregon.* Caldwell, Idaho, 1945.
Boller, Henry A. *Among the Indians: Eight Years in the Far West, 1858–1866.* Philadelphia, 1868.
Bradley, James H. "The Bradley Manuscript," Montana Historical Society *Contributions,* Vols. II, III, VIII, IX. Helena, 1896, 1900, 1917, 1923.
Brummitt, Stella W. *Brother Van.* New York, 1919.
Burlingame, Merrill G. *The Montana Frontier.* Helena, 1942.
Butler, Sir William F. *The Great Lone Land.* London, 1907.
Carnegie, James (Earl of Southesk). *Saskatchewan and the Rocky Mountains.* Toronto, 1875.
Catlin, George. *Letters and Notes on the Manners, Customs, and Conditions of the North American Indians.* 2 vols. London, 1841.
Chardon, François A. *Chardon's Journal of Fort Clark, 1834–39.* Ed. by Annie Heloise Abel. Pierre, South Dakota, 1932.
Chittenden, Hiram M. *The American Fur Trade of the Far West.* 2nd edition. 2 vols. New York, 1935.
Cocking, Mathew. *An Adventurer from Hudson Bay. Journal of Mathew Cocking from York Factory to the Blackfeet Country, 1772–1773.* Ed. by L. J. Burpee. *Transactions* of the Royal Society of Canada, Series 3, Vol. II. 1908.

Culin, Stewart. *Games of the North American Indians*. Bureau of American Ethnology *Twenty-fourth Annual Report* (1902–1903). Washington, 1907.

Dale, H. C. (ed.). *The Ashley-Smith Explorations and the Discovery of a Central Route to the Pacific, 1822–1829*. Cleveland, 1918.

Dempsey, Hugh A. "The Amazing Death of Calf Shirt," *The Montana Magazine of History*, Vol. III, No. 1 (January, 1953).

———. *Historic Sites of the Province of Alberta*. Edmonton, 1952.

Denig, Edwin T. *Indian Tribes of the Upper Missouri*. Ed. by J. N. B. Hewitt. Bureau of American Ethnology *Forty-sixth Annual Report* (1928–1929). Washington, 1930.

———. "Of the Crow Nation," Bureau of American Ethnology *Anthropological Paper No. 33, Bulletin 151*. Ed. by John C. Ewers. Washington, 1953.

Denny, Sir Cecil. *The Law Marches West*. Toronto, 1939.

De Smet, Pierre Jean. *Life, Letters, and Travels of Father Pierre Jean De Smet*. Ed. by H. M. Chittenden and A. T. Richardson. 4 vols. New York, 1905.

Dixon, Joseph K. *The Vanishing Race*. New York, 1913.

Dodge, Col. Henry. *Journal of a March of a Detachment of Dragoons under the Command of Colonel Dodge, in the Summer of 1835*. 24 Cong., 1 sess., *House Document 181*. Washington, 1836.

Ewers, John C. *Blackfeet Crafts*. U. S. Indian Service. *Indian Handicrafts Series No. 9*. Lawrence, Kansas, 1944.

———. "The Blackfoot War Lodge: Its Construction and Use," *American Anthropologist*, Vol. XLVI. No. 2 (1944).

———. "The Case for Blackfoot Pottery," *American Anthropologist*, Vol. XLVII, No. 2 (1945).

———. *Gustavus Sohon's Portraits of Flathead and Pend d'Oreille Indians, 1854*. Smithsonian Institution *Miscellaneous Collections*, Vol. CX, No. 7 (1948).

———. "The Horse in Blackfoot Indian Culture, with Comparative Material from Other Western Tribes," Bureau of American Ethnology *Bulletin 159*. Washington, 1955.

———. "Identification and History of the Small Robes Band of the Piegan Indians," *Journal* of the Washington Academy of Sciences, Vol. XXXVI, No. 12 (1946).

———. "The Indian Trade of the Upper Missouri before Lewis and

Clark: An Interpretation," *Missouri Historical Society Bulletin,* Vol. X, No. 4 (1954).

———. "The Last Bison Drives of the Blackfoot Indians," *Journal* of the Washington Academy of Sciences, Vol. XXXIX, No. 11 (1949).

———. "The North West Trade Gun," *Alberta Historical Review,* Vol. IV, No. 2 (1956).

———. *Plains Indian Painting.* Palo Alto, Calif., 1939.

———. "Self-torture in the Blood Indian Sun Dance," *Journal* of the Washington Academy of Sciences, Vol. XXXVIII, No. 5 (1948).

———. "Some Winter Sports of Blackfoot Indian Children," *The Masterkey* (The Southwest Museum, Los Angeles), Vol. XVIII, No. 6 (1944).

Ferris, W. A. Life in the Rocky Mountains. Ed. by Paul C. Phillips. Denver, 1940.

"Five-year Program on the Blackfoot Indian Reservation," *The Indian Leader,* Vol. XXVI, No. 25 (1923).

Flannery, Regina. *The Gros Ventres of Montana: Part I. Social Life.* The Catholic University of America Anthropological Series No. 15. Washington, 1953.

Garraghan, Gilbert J. *Chapters in Frontier History.* Milwaukee, 1934.

Grinnell, George Bird. *Blackfoot Lodge Tales.* New York, 1892.

———. *The Story of the Indian.* New York, 1895.

Hamilton, William T. "The Council at Fort Benton," *Forest and Stream,* Vol. LXVIII, No. 17 (1907).

———. "A Trading Expedition Among the Indians in 1858," Montana Historical Society Contributions, Vol. III (1905).

Hendry, Anthony. *York Factory to the Blackfeet Country. The Journal of Anthony Hendry, 1754–55.* Ed. by L. J. Burpee. *Transactions* of the Royal Society of Canada, Series 3, Vol. I (1907).

Henry, Alexander, and David Thompson. *New Light on the Early History of the Great Northwest.* Ed. by Elliott Coues. 3 vols. New York, 1897.

Hind, Henry Youle. *Narrative of the Canadian Red River Exploring Expedition of 1857 and the Assiniboine and Saskatchewan Exploring Expedition of 1858.* 2 vols. London, 1860.

Hodge, Frederick Webb (ed.). *Handbook of American Indians North of Mexico.* Bureau of American Ethnology *Bulletin No. 30.* 2 vols. Washington, 1912.

Hughes, Katherine. *Father Lacombe, the Black-robe Voyager.* New York, 1911.

Indian Rights Association. *The Action of Congress in Regard to the Piegan Indians of Montana.* N.p., 1885.

———. *Second Annual Report for the Year ending December, 1884.* Philadelphia, 1885.

Isham, James. *James Isham's Observations on Hudson's Bay: 1743.* Ed. by E. E. Rich. Toronto, 1949.

Kane, Paul. *Wanderings of an Artist Among the Indians of North America.* Toronto, 1925.

Kelsey, Henry. *The Kelsey Papers.* Ed. by A. G. Doughty and Chester Martin. Public Archives of Canada. Ottawa, 1929.

Klett, Guy S. *Missionary Endeavors of the Presbyterian Church Among the Blackfeet Indians in the 1850's.* Presbyterian Historical Society, 1941.

Larocque, François. *Journal of Larocque from the Assiniboine to the Yellowstone.* Canadian Archives *Publication No. 3.* Ottawa, 1910.

Larpenteur, Charles. *Forty Years a Fur Trader on the Upper Missouri. The Personal Narrative of Charles Larpenteur.* Ed. by Elliott Coues. 2 vols. New York, 1898.

La Verendrye, Pierre G. V. *Journals and Letters of Pierre Gaultier de Varennes de la Verendrye and His Sons.* Ed. by L. J. Burpee. Toronto, 1927.

Lewis, Meriwether, and William Clark. *Original Journals of the Lewis and Clark Expedition, 1804–1806.* Ed. by Reuben Gold Thwaites. 8 vols. New York, 1904–1905.

McClintock, Walter. *The Old North Trail.* London, 1910.

———. "The Tragedy of the Blackfoot," *Southwest Museum Paper No. 3.* Los Angeles, 1930.

McDonnell, Anne (ed.). "The Fort Benton Journal, 1854–1856, and the Fort Sarpy Journal, 1855–1856," Montana Historical Society *Contributions,* Vol. X (1940).

McDougall, John. *On Western Trails in the Early Seventies: Frontier Life in the Canadian North-West.* Toronto, 1911.

M'Gillivray, Duncan. *The Journal of Duncan M'Gillivray of the Northwest Company at Fort George on the Saskatchewan, 1794–1795.* Ed. by Arthur S. Morton. Toronto, 1929.

MacGregor, James G. *Behold the Shining Mountains.* Edmonton, 1955.

MacInnes, Charles M. *In the Shadow of the Rockies.* London, 1930.

Maximilian, Alexander Philip (Prince of Wied Neuwied). *Travels in the Interior of North America.* Vols. XXII–XXIV in Thwaites' *Early Western Travels* (*q.v.*).

Mengarini, Gregory. *Mengarini's Narrative of the Rockies.* Ed. by Albert J. Partoll. Montana State University, *Sources of Northwest History No. 25.* Missoula, 1938.

Miller, Alfred Jacob. *The West of Alfred Jacob Miller.* Ed. by Marvin C. Ross. Norman, 1951.

Morris, Alexander. *The Treaties of Canada with the Indians of Manitoba and the North-West Territories.* Toronto, n. d.

Partoll, Albert J. (ed.). *Blackfoot Indian Peace Council.* Montana State University, *Sources of Northwest History No. 3.* Missoula, 1937.

Point, Nicholas. "A Journey on a Barge on the Missouri River from the Fort of the Blackfeet [Lewis] to that of the Assiniboine [Union], 1847," *Mid-America,* Vol. XIII (1931).

Schultz, James Willard. *My Life as an Indian,* Boston, 1907.

Sharp, Paul F. *Whoop-Up Country.* Minneapolis, 1955.

Stanley, John Mix. "Report of Mr. J. M. Stanley's Visit to the Piegan Camp at the Cypress Mountain," in *Pacific Railroad Report of Explorations and Surveys* (*q.v.*), I.

Stevens, Hazard. *The Life of Isaac Ingalls Stevens.* 2 vols. Boston, 1900.

Stevens, Isaac I. "Isaac I. Stevens' Narrative of 1853–1855," in *Pacific Railroad Report of Explorations and Surveys* (*q.v.*), XII.

Stuart, James. "Adventure on the Upper Missouri," Montana Historical Society *Contributions,* Vol. I (1876).

Stuart, Robert. *On the Oregon Trail: Robert Stuart's Journey of Discovery (1812–1813).* Ed. by Kenneth A. Spaulding. Norman, 1953.

Thompson, David. *David Thompson's Narrative of his Explorations in Western America, 1784–1812.* Ed. by J. B. Tyrrell. Toronto, 1916.

Thwaites, Reuben Gold (ed.). *Early Western Travels, 1784–1897.* 32 vols. Cleveland, 1904–1907.

Tims, Rev. J. W. *Grammar and Dictionary of the Blackfoot Language in the Dominion of Canada.* London, 1889.

Turner, John Peter. *The North-West Mounted Police.* 2 vols. Ottawa, 1950.

Umfreville, Edward. *Present State of Hudson's Bay, Containing a Full Description of that Settlement and the Adjacent Country; and Likewise of the Fur Trade.* London, 1790.

Voegelin, Carl F. and E. W. "Linguistic Considerations of Northeastern North America," in Frederick Johnson (ed.), *Man in Northeastern North America.* Andover, Mass., 1946.

Wheeler, Olin D. *The Trail of Lewis and Clark, 1804–1904.* 2 vols. New York, 1904.

Wheeler, William F. "The Piegan War of 1870," in *Helena Daily Herald,* Jan. 1, 1880.

Wissler, Clark. "Ceremonial Bundles of the Blackfoot Indians," American Museum of Natural History *Anthropological Papers,* Vol. VII, Part 2 (1912).

———. *Indians of the United States.* New York, 1940.

———. "The Material Culture of the Blackfoot Indians," American Museum of Natural History *Anthropological Papers,* Vol. V, Part 1 (1910).

———. *Population Changes Among the Northern Plains Indians.* Yale University Publications in Anthropology, No. 1. New Haven, 1936.

———. "The Social Life of the Blackfoot Indians," American Museum of Natural History *Anthropological Papers,* Vol. VII, Part 1 (1911).

———. "Societies and Dance Associations of the Blackfoot Indians, American Museum of Natural History *Anthropological Papers,* Vol. XI, Part 4 (1913).

———. "The Sun Dance of the Blackfoot Indians," American Museum of Natural History *Anthropological Papers,* Vol. XVI, Part 3 (1918).

———, and D. C. Duvall. "Mythology of the Blackfoot Indians," American Museum of Natural History *Anthropological Papers,* Vol. II, Part 1 (1908).

Woehlke, Walter V. "Hope for the Blackfeet," *Sunset Magazine,* December, 1923.

Index